Rob Nash's *Moving the Equator* offers a bold, creative, substantive, and generous rethinking of Christian mission in a pluralistic, multifaith world. This work is, simultaneously, a significant and in-depth project in biblical interpretation, theological method, and missiology. It pulls no punches in challenging the "Euro-tribal" Anglo church and in offering an interpretation of what has gone wrong with our self-understanding and missionary engagement. I consider this a very significant book for our current moment.

—David P. Gushee
Distinguished University Professor of Christian Ethics
Director, Center for Theology & Public Life
Mercer University

Professor Robert Nash knows the Christian mission movement well, both by research and experience. In this superb study, Nash surveys the ideas and actions that sparked the church's vision of its global mission while challenging twenty-first-century Christians to renew that commitment by re-forming mission strategy, praxis, and yes, theology. His wise counsel should not be ignored.

—Bill J. Leonard
Emeritus Professor of Church History and Baptist Studies
Wake Forest University

With fresh perspectives on familiar Biblical texts and vivid anecdotes from the pastorate and seminary classroom, Rob Nash—professor of missions and world religions, pastor, and global citizen—challenges the Christian community to reimagine mission not as an errand into some godless wilderness, but as a journey to discover the divine presence already at work in the world's peoples and cultures. Sly, subversive, and Southern, Rob Nash soulfully channels the tones of wisdom and prophecy to call the Church to a radical act of *metanoia*, of conversion and repentance, for the gospel's sake.

—Gregory Mobley
Professor of Hebrew Bible and Congregational Studies
Andover Newton Seminary at Yale Divinity School

In this lucid and well-documented book, Robert Nash, Jr. has placed in our hands a comprehensive guide to understanding Christian mission in the modern era. Informed and informing, *Moving the Equator* is a groundbreaking volume about the fabric of God's mission in the world with threads and diversity of colors from many cultures. This book is a compelling argument that the Bible remains God's most reliable blueprint for transformation. As the biblical narratives continue to unlock God's grand vision for all creatures, and as believers in every land respond to God's mission, both the mission and the life of the church and participating communities of faith worldwide will never remain the same.

—Caleb O. Oladipo
Snellings Chair of Christian Mission and Evangelism
Campbell University Divinity School
Senior fellow of Baptist Scholars International Roundtable

MOVING THE EQUATOR

Smyth & Helwys Publishing, Inc.
6316 Peake Road
Macon, Georgia 31210-3960
1-800-747-3016

Library of Congress Cataloging-in-Publication Data

Names: Nash, Robert N., author.
Title: Moving the equator : the families of the earth and the mission of
  the church / by Robert N. Nash, Jr.
Description: Macon, GA : Smyth & Helwys Publishing, 2020. | Includes
  bibliographical references.
Identifiers: LCCN 2020007017 (print) | LCCN 2020007018 (ebook) | ISBN
  9781641732437 (paperback) | ISBN 9781641732444 (ebook)
Subjects: LCSH: Missions--Biblical teaching. | Church renewal. |
  Multiculturalism--Religious aspects--Christianity. | Christianity and
  other religions.
Classification: LCC BV2073 .N37 2020 (print) | LCC BV2073 (ebook) | DDC
  266--dc23
LC record available at https://lccn.loc.gov/2020007017
LC ebook record available at https://lccn.loc.gov/2020007018

Moving *the* Equator

THE FAMILIES OF THE EARTH
AND THE MISSION OF THE CHURCH

Robert N. Nash, Jr.

Also by Robert N. Nash, Jr.

An 8-Track Church in a CD World:
The Modern Church in a Postmodern World

The Bible in English Translation: An Essential Guide
(with Steven M. Sheeley)

Choosing a Bible that Fits
(with Steven M. Sheeley)

To Bill J. Leonard,
Teacher, Mentor, Friend

Acknowledgments

The origins of this book can be traced to a single day in 1967 when, as a nine-year-old, I walked with my missionary father into the shop of a Muslim merchant in Cotabato City on the island of Mindanao in the Philippines. Dad intended to purchase a copy of the Holy Qur'an, though I have always been unclear about his motivations. He couldn't read Arabic, so the simple possession of the text would not have helped him to understand Islam. Perhaps he wanted to show some respect to the majority religious faith on the island by displaying the book in a prominent place in our home.

Despite Dad's best efforts, the merchant refused to sell the sacred text to him, telling my father that, in his shop, only Muslims could purchase it. Both men were determined to convince the other—the merchant that Dad should not purchase the Qur'an and Dad that he should be able to buy it and carry it home. Deeply embedded in their conversation was a profound respect for the God that they both worshiped and a concern for the spiritual state of the other. I knew enough of Dad's theology to know of his burden for the eternal salvation of the Muslim merchant, and I could sense from the merchant a deep conviction that, because Dad was not a Muslim, he could not be trusted with the sacred words of the Holy Qur'an. We left without the book, and I began a lifelong study of religion and faith that would help me to resolve the religious and cultural differences that were obvious in the encounter.

I began writing this book on that day. It is the result of fifty years of reflection about God, life, faith, and religion, certainly through the lens of Christianity but not limited by that single perspective. For this reason, it is an enormous challenge to acknowledge all of those who have contributed to it. My parents, raised in northeast Georgia, possessed enough faith to launch themselves on a boat across the Pacific Ocean in 1964 with their two young sons, teaching us in the process to respect the beliefs of others while allowing those beliefs to deepen our Christian faith rather than to replace it. The relationships they cultivated with Muslim and Hindu friends in the Philippines allowed us to experience those religions in their purest forms as represented in the love and deep respect those friends showed to our family and to our understanding of God.

I also must acknowledge the contributions of a number of teachers over my twenty-five years of formal education, the first of whom was my own mother, who believed enough in herself to homeschool her sons through most of elementary school. She taught us the basics—from art to reading to English to math to science to music—as well as skills much more difficult to quantify—like hospitality, manners, and love.

Drs. Sarah Gordon and Tom Armstrong at Georgia College in Milledgeville, Georgia, modeled for me the highest standards of academic excellence and openness to perspectives far different from my own. They opened my eyes to the power of literature, poetry, and history to critically engage my own cultural space and transform my worldview and perspective.

Dr. Bill J. Leonard, my "Doktorvater," supervised my doctoral work at The Southern Baptist Theological Seminary in Louisville, Kentucky. My debt to him is beyond repayment. As he delivered his lecture in church history class on the first day of my seminary career, an angel whispered in my ear, "This is what God wants you to do." He taught me most everything I know about how to resurrect the histories of religions in general and of the Christian faith in particular in ways that transform. He also models for me and for many others a deeply personal commitment to racial reconciliation that moves through friendships to solidarity and action.

I am deeply grateful to the students whom I have had the privilege to teach—first at Judson College in Alabama and then at Shorter College and the McAfee School of Theology at Mercer University in Georgia. I have learned at least as much as I have taught. The religion majors at Shorter College and students in my missional theology and global perspectives classes at McAfee shaped the thesis and the content of this book. I especially thank the students in my global perspectives class at McAfee in the fall semester of 2019, who were the first class to read it and critically engage its contents.

In 2018, Heritage Fellowship Church in Canton, Georgia, took a risk and called me as its part-time pastor. Most of what they read here will sound familiar. They have heard it preached from the pulpit and taught on Sunday afternoons and Wednesday nights. In some ways, it is my only sermon, preached in various forms and from different directions. They have received it with open hearts and minds and have yet to complain about the repetition.

I thank Mercer University, the James and Carolyn McAfee School of Theology, and Dean Greg DeLoach for the sabbatical leave granted to me in the spring semester of 2019 to finish the manuscript. I wrote much of it at Independent Grounds Café in Kennesaw, Georgia, a coffee shop that employs adults with intellectual and developmental disabilities, and I am grateful for their mission and for the gift of a place to sit, think, read, and write. Special thanks also to Dr. Nancy Penton, who edited the final manuscript.

My children, Lindsay and Douglas, have been among my best teachers about how to embrace otherness and difference. Raised in a small town in northwest Georgia, they nurtured friendships with people of all races, religions, socioeconomic levels, and sexual orientations. They had the guts and determination to move out of their cultural space when it came to universities and careers and to seek their own paths in life. I am enormously proud of both of them.

Finally, I thank my wife, Guyeth, who has made this lifelong journey with me. Her great gift to me has been the space to be myself. She has pushed me, loved me, challenged me, encouraged me, and stretched me. She has risked much for our life together. Without her, there simply wouldn't be a book.

Atlanta, Georgia
Advent 2019

Contents

Chapter 1

Lifting the Equator

One of the most prominent examples of a cartographical pinpoint straying from the truth is the Middle of the World monument in Ecuador, visited by hundreds of thousands each year who want to straddle the Equator . . . . However, all is not as it seems. The genuine meeting of the two hemispheres is actually 800 feet to the north.

—Hugh Morris, *The Guardian*, August 9, 2017

The women missed it because they were the ones cleaning up the kitchen after the huge Sunday dinner at my grandfather's farmhouse in Athens, Georgia. Perhaps we Nash men should have known better, but it was the seventies after all, though late in the decade, and bad habits are hard to break. So, instead of helping out, we were rocking on the front porch and talking about the weather, specifically about how it was warmer in the winter than it used to be and colder in the summer. I suppose the weather was so hot that we could not imagine the winter bringing any relief.

Suddenly, from one end of the porch, a great-uncle opined, "I know why that is!"

Now, whenever this particular relative spoke, we were all ears—because you were never sure what might come out of the man's mouth.

No one spoke. He took this as an encouraging sign.

"I read about it the other day," he continued. "They've gone and moved the equator." He employed a qualifier before the word "equator" that I have omitted in this retelling.

My grandfather challenged this assertion. "They can't do that," he argued.

"Sure they can," his brother insisted. "I read about it in the *National Enquirer*. They picked that thing up and they put it down somewhere else. So it's hot where it used to be cold and it's cold where it used to be hot."

Having offered this convincing evidence, he reached down for his coffee cup with the napkin rolled up in the bottom and spat out a brown stream of Red Man tobacco juice, half of which made it into the cup.

At the other end of the porch, my brother and I struggled to retain our composure, trying not to roll straight through the screens and out onto the front yard. We had grown up in the Philippines as the sons of missionary parents and had sailed or flown over the equator on numerous occasions. We knew how hard it would be to move the thing.

My father, who always had an uncanny ability to keep a straight face in the midst of such family conversations, encouraged his uncle along.

"Well, that's very interesting," he said. "Who'd they say moved it?"

I thought for the briefest second that Dad had stumped my uncle.

Not to worry.

After a brief pause, he responded, "The United Nations moved it! They're always going and doing fool things like that."

It was not the first time he had blamed the United Nations for a global disaster.

Fortunately, the conversation had moved to a different topic by the time the women came out onto the porch from the kitchen. Had they been privy to the conversation, they would have been impressed by the fact that we Nash men were struggling to explain global warming even though nobody much talked about it at the time.

We soon discovered that we had experienced a "moment" in family history that would become part of the "Story," the family canon rolled out at Thanksgiving and Christmas. Inevitably, somebody will push their chair back from the dinner table and say, "Do you remember the time that Uncle So-and-So said they'd gone and moved the equator?" Then, even though we've heard it all before and we know how it starts and how it ends, we all listen and we laugh and we remember this story even as the number of us who were there for it shrinks.

I also remember the moment when it ceased to be quite as funny as it once was, and I remember where I was when I stopped laughing. I was sitting in my easy chair at home at some point in the mid-1990s. I do not remember what precipitated the moment. Maybe it was a news story on television or the fact that email and the internet were brand-new phenomena to which we were all growing accustomed. Maybe my computer had just issued the pleasant announcement, "You've got mail!" causing me to contemplate the revolution in communication that was rocking my world.

Whatever the source, a profound thought struck me, causing me to grab both arms of my easy chair:

"They've gone and moved the equator!"

I even added the qualifier.

Then the second insight came: "It's hot where it used to be cold and it's cold where it used to be hot!"

I suppose that somewhere up in the Great Beyond, that uncle was now laughing at me. He and the *National Enquirer* had been right all along. Without a doubt, the equator had moved. Somebody picked the thing up and put it down somewhere else. My thoughts raced. I reflected on my own life and the enormous change that had marked my relatively short thirty-five years. I recalled that, in 1964, as a five-year-old, I had sailed under the Oakland Bay Bridge on the *President Cleveland*, a trans-Pacific Ocean liner, on a twenty-one-day voyage across the Pacific to Manila. I also recalled that, in 1968, I had repeated the same trip in the opposite direction in twenty-one hours—nonstop—on an airplane. It had never occurred to me before that I had a front-row seat for the shrinking of the globe.

I also remembered that, back in those days, it took us two weeks to get mail in the Philippines from the United States and that we rarely had a phone conversation with relatives back home. Generally, we spoke only once a year to my grandparents in Georgia, and then only for five minutes. We had to go down to the Philippine Long-Distance Telephone Company in Manila to make the call. An operator in Manila, speaking English with a pronounced accent, would engage in a cross-cultural conversation with an operator in Atlanta, who responded in a heavy Southern twang. Barely able to understand each other, the two would eventually manage to connect us to that farmhouse in Athens. We never imagined that one day we would type messages on a keyboard in the United States that would be received instantly on the other side of the world, much less that we would be able to see each other on the screens of mobile phones that we carried in our pockets. Such science fiction was the stuff of Star Trek and Space Family Robinson.

Sitting in my lazy chair, I reflected on the fact that the missionary experiences of my family in the 1960s and 1970s in the Philippines had more in common with the experiences of missionaries in the late eighteenth and nineteenth centuries than the experiences of missionaries in the late twentieth century. In the early 1960s, we still traveled by boat. We rarely called home. The primary sources of our experience were handwritten letters and journals that now resided in my grandparents' attic.

Somebody moved the equator. It was hot where it used to be cold and it was cold where it used to be hot. A follow-up question also came to me, the one my father asked my uncle in an effort to stump him. Who moved it? Who possessed enough gall to pick the thing up and plop it down somewhere else? Here my blood kin and I do part ways. I am confident that it was not the United Nations. They have struggled with far simpler challenges than the relocation of the equator and with mixed results. I am convinced that the "mover" was either God or us, but I have yet to come down firmly on one side or the other. If God moved it, then God has been slow in letting the rest of us know what to do about it. If we human beings moved it, then those of us who profess to follow Jesus Christ must not have been in on it, at least not those of us who belong to what Alan Roxburgh has called "Euro-tribal churches."[1] We failed to do much advanced planning, assuming that our elevated role as the chief interpreters of Christian theology and practice was impregnable.

I suppose the truth rests somewhere in the middle, in that powerful interaction between God and humanity in which God works in the midst of various cultures and ages to bring to light new truths about God, about us, and about the world itself. Cultures shift and change. New realities emerge out of the interaction between peoples around the globe. New inventions create different patterns of interaction and community and new possibilities for the present and the future.

I have been telling this family story for some twenty years or more in congregations and seminars across the country as a way of helping the followers of Jesus Christ in the United States to grasp the enormity of the challenge that these transitions represent. My pattern is to begin a session by asking participants to "Raise your right hand and repeat after me, 'I will not repeat this story anywhere near Athens, Georgia.'" Obviously, I'm worried that one of my living relatives might be offended.

As far as I know, everyone has taken the oath. The only near exception to this occurred at Maranatha Baptist Church in Plains, Georgia, when former president Jimmy Carter sat in the congregation. Everyone looked toward him when I asked for the show of hands. He cocked his head to the side and only feebly raised a right hand, after which everyone else followed suit. It occurred to me later that I had asked a former president of the United States to "raise his right hand and repeat after me."

Hey, I said the equator had moved.

These are challenging times to which all of us who profess faith in Jesus Christ must respond, even former presidents—and President Carter has done better than most of us, by the way. The twenty-first century is fraught with challenge and opportunity for the Christian faith. The challenges are enormous. Seismic shifts rock our world, the result on the one hand of violence, war, poverty, disease, and environmental destruction and on the other hand of advances in technology, transportation, communication, and healthcare. Anxiety and fear overwhelm us even as we enjoy the benefits of these advances.

The migration of peoples is perhaps the most significant global shift that has occurred in the last few decades. I recently devoted an entire seminary course to exploring its ramifications. Samuel Escobar points out the missiological implications for the Christian faith that emerge in its wake as the gospel moves "from everywhere to everyone."[2] Latino Catholics fill what were once empty church pews in the United States and bring new spiritual energy to these congregations. Korean Christians, motivated by a desire to share the gospel of Jesus Christ in both word and deed, build hospitals in places like Ethiopia and Kazakhstan. Filipino believers, particularly domestic workers, share their faith in powerful ways in the Middle East. Carrying only a backpack and a Bible, Brazilian students move into the world to share the gospel.

American Christians are part of this grand global migration. We have elected to take our faith to the world through short-term mission engagements all over the globe. In 1988, only about 125,000 North American Christians engaged in such trips beyond the borders of the United States. In 2014, best estimates place the number of Americans who participated in short-term mission experiences at as many as four million.[3] The numbers are difficult to determine, but the evidence suggests a significant increase over the last five years. Now hundreds of churches regularly send members into the world. The relative wealth of US churches and enormous revolutions in transportation and communications enable us to move ourselves around and to ship medical supplies and food relief to those who need it. Such direct engagement both helps and hinders the lives of millions of people who live with the daily challenges of poverty, homelessness, and disease.

This global approach to mission and ministry has absolutely transformed the nature of the American missionary enterprise, again for both good and ill. In the latter part of the eighteenth century, churches in England and the United States created denominational sending bodies for sharing the gospel of Jesus Christ. Eventually these denominational missions organizations appointed thousands of missionaries. Because of their efforts, Christianity became one of the largest religions. Much more than just religious conversion occurred. Robert Woodberry has recently documented the ways in which the work of Protestant missionaries resulted in the establishment of democratic governments in other countries, largely because of the evangelical focus on individual rights, the defense of religious liberty, and the emphasis on education for the purpose of understanding Scripture.[4]

Like any effort by the church of Jesus Christ, mixed results emerged from this global engagement. Missionaries were as much the bearers of culture as they were the bearers of the gospel of Jesus Christ. In far too many instances, they carried with them an assumption of cultural superiority that compromised the basic tenets of the Christian faith. Yet they possessed a zeal and confidence in the gospel that they preached to such an extent that the Christian faith spread far beyond its former boundaries and into virtually every corner of the world.

Because of the increased mobility made possible by cheap transportation, local congregations have now become the center of the North American global mission engagement, replacing the denominational sending agencies that have led the movement to this point. Today, congregations expend enormous sums of money on direct mission efforts, including the funding of short-term mission teams and the direct support of missionaries and global ministries. Sometimes they direct their efforts at a particular ministry and partnership in long-term investment with another congregation or ministry partner. At other points, congregations simply seek out a place to spend a week in ministry and mission with little or no intention of engaging in a long-term commitment to that place. Huge sums of money that were once directed toward denominational agencies for the purpose of providing salaries and project funds for long-term missionaries are now being shifted toward these direct mission efforts and toward the direct support of missionaries, local ministries, and short-term teams that are generally composed of church members. Denominational agencies are struggling to determine how to support long-term missionaries and ministries in light of such a shift.

There is a much darker side to global migration. The United Nations, which my great-uncle blamed for moving the equator, recently reported the displacement of fifty million people worldwide, the highest displacement recorded since World War II. Counted among this group are refugees, asylum seekers, and internally displaced people who are refugees within their own countries. The highest source countries for displacement are Afghanistan (2.5 million people), Syria (2.5 million), Somalia (1.1 million), the Sudan (0.6 million), the Democratic Republic of Congo (0.5 million), Myanmar (0.5 million), Iraq (0.4 million), Colombia (0.4 million), Vietnam (0.3 million), and Eritrea (0.3 million). Surprisingly perhaps, the countries hosting the greatest number of refugees include Pakistan, Iran, and Lebanon. Among host countries, the United States ranked a distant ninth behind such nations as China, Kenya, Ethiopia, Chad, Jordan, and Turkey. In 2018, the US reduced the number of refugees it would accept to 30,000 per year, the lowest figure in decades. António Guterres, UN High Commissioner for Refugees, blames the global community for the displacement, pointing out that "the world has shown a limited capacity to prevent conflicts and to find a timely solution for them."[5]

In all too many instances, religion is either the source of the conflicts or the justification for them. The Christian and the Islamic worldviews function quite well within their own orbits when no challengers exist to threaten them, but either one can suddenly be the source of intense violence when they come into conflict in places like Sub-Saharan Africa, Southeast Asia, or the United States as a direct result of the increase in global migration. Tension emerges within Christianity or Islam as well as, for example, in the conflict between Protestants and Catholics in Northern Ireland several years ago or in the current Shiite-Sunni conflict in the Middle East.

Religion is hardly the sole source of the tension. Economic disparity continues to increase. Fully 80 percent of the world's population lives on ten dollars per day or less. Half the world's population lives on less than three dollars per day. One billion of the 2.2 billion children in the world live in poverty. This economic disparity creates a host of other challenges, including disease, lack of access to water, and illiteracy. Three million people die from HIV/AIDS infections each year while 40 million people live with the virus. One million people die of malaria, with African children accounting for 80 percent of its victims. Almost 2 million children die of diarrhea each year.

Perhaps the greatest global challenge is the lack of easy access to clean water. One billion people have inadequate access to this resource. To put it in perspective, the average person in the United States consumes 600 liters of water per day compared to the 20 liters per person consumed by 1.8 billion people in developing countries. Fully 72 million children of primary school age who should have been in school in 2005 were not able to attend, and, perhaps even more stunning, as recently as the year 2000, 1 billion people in the world were illiterate and unable to sign their own names.[6]

I recently witnessed the effects of poverty on the lives of people in a visit to Mumbai, India. As we walked through a densely populated, poor section of the city, a local pastor kept pointing to sandbags that prevented water from entering certain areas. I was intrigued and assumed that this was in preparation for the coming monsoon season that generally hits India in June and July.

"So, these sandbags are here to divert the rainwater that will come in the rainy season?" I asked.

My host looked at me quizzically. Then the light dawned. "Ah, no," he responded. "They are here to divert the water from the ocean that comes twice each day with the rising tide."

Twice a day, people in this area of Mumbai have to either climb up above the seawater to their upper-level rooms or vacate the neighborhood until the water recedes. Since this is the only way they can find shelter, they have no other choice.

Huge global patterns of immigration add to the tension, creating enormous cultural transformation in many parts of the United States and Western Europe and also around the world. Governments and other institutions must respond to the influx. Debates rage over such matters as immigration quotas, border fences, and the education of immigrant children.

Several huge concerns related to migration currently dominate the news. The first, of course, has to do with the migration of peoples of Central America and Mexico into the United States. Donald Trump promised that, if elected, he would construct a border wall to prevent this migration and that Mexico would pay for it. Violence in nations like Honduras and Guatemala has continued unabated, so, while immigration from Mexico has decreased, immigrants from Central America continue to make their way to the US–Mexico border in huge numbers, traveling in caravans for protection. They have little choice given the violence that threatens their families and livelihoods. US immigration policy has resulted in the separation of children from families and a huge crisis with no clear resolution. In similar fashion, displaced people from wars in Syria and Iraq have fled into Jordan and Lebanon and have migrated as far as Western Europe and the United States. Conflicts in Africa have resulted in an immigration road that stretches from Sub-Saharan Africa all the way up into Spain, France, Belgium, and the United Kingdom.

These patterns of migration have created a backlash as nationalist movements in Europe and the United States have revived isolationist sentiments and created a crisis over the increasing diversity that threatens "traditional ways of life." Nationalist politicians in the United States, Germany, Poland, the United Kingdom, the Czech Republic, Austria, and other parts of Europe have gained considerable power elicited by the fear of otherness and difference that has emerged within a significant portion of each nation's population. Much of this nationalist sentiment is born out of the fear of loss of place, prestige, and power for the dominant culture in each nation. Violence has erupted in the United States as mass shootings by White nationalists, motivated by hatred and prejudice, have resulted in the deaths of hundreds of innocent people.

Local congregations often find themselves on the front lines of the immigration debate because of the influx of immigrants into US towns and cities and because of their desire to treat immigrants with respect, love, and care. Churches assist with immigrant relocation. New congregations of Guatemalans, Hondurans, Chileans, Ghanaians, and Ethiopians emerge in the fellowship halls of Baptist, Methodist, and Presbyterian churches. Today, the largest churches in the United Kingdom are composed of African immigrants, a pattern that is likely to repeat in the United States. Already in the U.S., the annual gatherings of immigrants of various denominations are far outpacing in size the gatherings of the parent and predominately White or Black denominations.

These patterns of migration, whether forced or unforced, create enormous global challenges that have either never existed before or have now been magnified, including issues of just war, food distribution, access to clean water, global healthcare, and rising nationalism and anti-immigration tensions. Huge missiological challenges emerge as well. Despite our best intentions, US churches often fail to engage in sustainable ministries and thus render the people whom we seek to serve dependent on us and not on themselves for such basic needs.

Such failure is the partial result of a raging debate over the missionary priority of Christianity. Some followers of Jesus warn that our urgent concern should be to share the gospel of Jesus Christ with non-Christians out of fear that their lack of faith in Jesus Christ will lead to their eternal damnation. They insist on taking Christ to the least "evangelized" people of the world. Their priority is the conversion of the world to the Christian faith. Social engagement becomes little more than thinly veiled evangelism.

On the other side of this great divide, many followers of Jesus insist that our priority should be meeting the needs of the most marginalized peoples in the world and that we should direct our efforts toward alleviating poverty and disease. Some among this group view conversion to Christianity as a secondary concern at best. Their motivation is much the same as the motivation of any government or nongovernment organization seeking to engage in community development and transformation. In the process, they lose the powerful spiritual motivations that have long served as the foundation for such engagement. This divide is the legacy of a modern world that eschewed a holistic and integrated understanding of what it meant to follow in the footsteps of Jesus and that offered instead a categorization of the Christian life into such components as evangelism and social justice.

Someone has moved the equator. It is hot where it used to be cold and it is cold where it used to be hot. Suddenly, the Southern and Eastern hemispheres are centers of Christian faith in the world, and the Northern and Western hemispheres are experiencing revitalization, not from within but rather from without, as immigrants from the South and East move into the North and the West and as the missionary impulse of the South and East becomes the dominant global mission expression.

A couple of years ago, I returned to Manila and spent my first night at the grand Manila Hotel on Manila Bay. General Douglas MacArthur lived at the Manila Hotel during his command of US forces in the Philippines just prior to World War II. You can imagine my excitement when I saw on the hotel marquee that Faith Academy, my high school alma mater, was holding its junior-senior prom in the hotel that very evening. For the briefest moment, I forgot that the equator had moved. I imagined a junior-senior prom much like the one I attended in 1977, a gathering of US missionary kids, largely White, happily enjoying dinner and each other's company (dancing is not allowed at Faith Academy).

At the appointed time, I made my way down to the Grand Ballroom of the hotel, hoping to see one of my old high school teachers. Imagine my surprise to walk into a ballroom full of South Korean missionary kids, hardly a White face in the room. The majority of the students were the children of missionaries who now serve across Southeast Asia, having taken the place of those US missionaries who once composed the majority of missionaries in the region. Korean teachers had mostly replaced my old teachers from the United States.

A couple of days later, I would stop briefly in Angeles City on my way north to the mountain resort of Baguio. My family served in Angeles in the early 1970s when I was a sophomore in high school. I attended the tenth grade at Clark Air Force Base there while my father served as pastor of the Clark Field Baptist Church. All of this occurred at the height of the Vietnam War. Missionaries and US military personnel were everywhere in the area.

On this visit, though, few Americans were in sight. The US handed Clark Air Force Base over to the Philippine government in the late 1980s. A Korean missionary hosted me. He lived only about three or four blocks from the house my family had occupied in 1975. The equator had moved. It was as if God had called a "time-out," determined that the team on the field was not up to the challenge, and replaced it with a new set of starting players. As a member of the old squad, I was struggling with this new reality. I was getting the strong impression that the new team on the field might be there for a while.

Andrew Walls and Philip Jenkins have pointed to this shift in the center of the Christian faith, documenting its movement from the North and the West to the South and the East.[7] By South and East, they are not referring to Atlanta and Nashville; rather, they mean Seoul, Beijing, Nairobi, and Mumbai. Sociologists of religion now predict that in a few short years, the most Christian nation in the world (in sheer numbers) will be the People's Republic of China. This essentially means that we followers of Jesus Christ in the North and the West are living in the backwaters of Christianity and must look to immigrants from the South and the East for spiritual revitalization.

There is much to celebrate about the reality that the global church is taking its place at the table of theological and missiological reflection. No longer are Western European and North American missionary-sending agencies dictating the direction of the global mission engagement. The leaders of such Western institutions have become increasingly quiet. I was privy to global conversations among leaders of missionary-sending entities all over the world in my role as the leader of one such US-based and Baptist institution. To be perfectly honest, we Western mission leaders had very little to offer.

The fact that the equator has moved is eliciting much hand-wringing among Euro-tribal churches and denominations, the primary heirs of a Protestant theology that insisted that the church was the place where "the Word was rightly preached and the Sacraments rightly administered."[8] This assumption of theological and spiritual primacy for the church stood it in good stead for some 500 years. Then, suddenly, the equator moved and no one is sure exactly where to place the blame for this loss of ecclesiastical place.

Some castigate the church for its lack of accommodation to and separation from the wider culture, while others decry its captivity to the very same culture. Some blame the baby boomers or the millennial generation (or both), who seem perfectly content to pursue faith apart from the church or not to pursue it at all. David Kinnaman is of the opinion that, unlike previous generations of young people, the millennials will not come back home. They have rejected the church altogether (Prodigals), or they have integrated other forms of religion and spirituality into it (Nomads), or they are determined to create something Christian and new that has nothing to do with it (Exiles).[9] Others blame the Boomer generation for its lack of commitment to institutions like church and marriage, or the Builder generation for its enslavement to old forms.

Some blame mainline denominations that have been the center of American religious life throughout the twentieth century but that suddenly find themselves on the margins and in far greater distress than even local congregations, who deem them irrelevant in a world in which a church is perfectly capable of locating its own resources and sending its own missionaries. The charge is that denominations focused too much attention on their own survival and ignored their responsibility to assist churches toward the work of God's mission in the world. Spiritual vitality gave way to programmatic institutionalization and a loss of vision. Certainly, some of the blame is directed at the wider culture and at the prevailing scientific worldview that moved God from the center of life to the margins, along with miracles and angels and resurrection and all the rest.

So what are we to do? In 1997, I wrote a little book titled *An 8-track Church in a CD World: The Modern Church in the Postmodern World.*[10] While many people appreciated help identifying the challenges the church was facing, others took me to task for not spelling out exactly what the church ought to do about the context in which it found itself, how it should respond, and what it should become. I remember one particular conversation in which a conference attendee asked the following question: "So you tell us what the problem is, but what are we supposed to do about it?"

I responded, "I can tell you what you need to do, but I can also tell you that you aren't going to do it."

I went on to suggest that a church ought to declare that its rolls were empty; essentially, it had no members. Then it should undertake a yearlong focus to renew its perspective about what it meant to be the church and for its members to be followers of Jesus Christ in the world. At the end of that year, the church should announce to its former membership what would be required to be part of the church in the future and to invite people to join with the church as members if they agreed with its new direction. My assumption was that such a church would more clearly define itself and its mission through such a process. After my explanation, the conference attendee did not miss a beat: "You're right!" he said. "We're not going to do that."

Indeed, most of us are not—or at least we are not going to do it in that way. We are, however, going to do it. The reality is that God is at work in our midst, both inside the church and outside the church, renewing our hearts and minds to such an extent that we become the people and communities that God desires us to be in the twenty-first century. This process of renewal has happened repeatedly in the history of the church. What followers of Jesus have been in one age they cease to be in the next age, or at least they transform themselves into something different. In the best of circumstances, we build on what we have received from our spiritual forebears in order to conform ourselves more closely to Christ. In the worst of circumstances, we reject what we have received from our spiritual forebears because they absolutely missed the boat. Most of the time, though, we do our best to take their best and to reject their worst in order to fashion a new and more committed people and church, and we also acknowledge the reality that our own efforts will both add and detract from the values of God's community on earth.

This book is about what the church ought to look like in the twenty-first century as it seeks to participate together with God in transforming the world. It is at once a book about the church and a book about the mission of God in the world. This book takes seriously the truth of the gospel that we have received from our spiritual forebears, but it also recognizes that the culture to which the gospel speaks shapes that gospel. It celebrates the reality that God has created human beings as intentionally diverse and with our various cultural perspectives in order to bring about a deeper understanding of God shaped by each one of those perspectives. To put it another way, it recognizes that Scripture and the tradition of the church are sacred but also affirms that our various cultural realities are sacred and designed by God to contribute to our common understanding of the nature of salvation, of church, of the Holy Spirit, and of God's mission in the world.

I recognize that such a perspective on culture has not been the traditional understanding that has shaped the Christian faith across its history. We prefer to think of the church as a community of "resident aliens" who inhabit life in this world but whose allegiance is to a kingdom that is not of this world.[11] We view cultural difference as a necessary part of human experience that will one day fade away in a new heaven and a new earth in which everyone will speak the same language and worship the same way. We have tended to privilege the past, and particularly the early church of the first century, as the closest approximation to God's intention and purpose for the church. We celebrate the experience of the first Christians in the book of Acts as our vision of what the church should be:

> All who believed were together and had all things in common; they would sell their possessions and goods and distribute the proceeds to all, as any had need. Day by day, as they spent much time together in the temple, they broke bread at home and ate their food with glad and generous hearts, praising God and having the goodwill of all the people. And day by day the Lord added to their number those who were being saved. (Acts 2:43-47)[12]

Yet this church was itself the product of a particular cultural moment in the history of the faith. Acts 2 records the experience of a group of Jewish followers of Jesus who viewed Jesus' death and resurrection as a powerful manifestation of what God would accomplish for Israel. They lived in a day of revolution in which there was deep hope for the appearance of the Messiah. They listened as Peter "let the entire house of Israel know with certainty that God has made him [Jesus] both Lord and Messiah" (Acts 2:36). Their Jewish hope for a Messiah fueled their desire to sell their possessions and hold everything in common as much as did any other reality. This was a first-century Jewish context in which a group of Jewish people from all over the known world came together to place their hopes for Israel on the resurrected Jesus of Nazareth.

Though this is certainly a contextual moment that shaped the history of the church, it is not a picture of what the church should look like or be like throughout its history. It would be impossible for us to replicate this church. This is a church that emerged in the immediate aftermath of the resurrection appearances of Jesus, a church with a particular cultural context that shapes all understandings of the church that follow simply because it is the first evidence of the followers of Jesus gathering themselves into a community. Every subsequent expression of church, however, will also be rooted in a context and in a culture from which it will emerge. The unique combination of the expression of the faith that it has received and its own cultural context will add new depth to our common understanding of God, the creation, and the church.

We also tend to privilege the understanding of church that emerged early in our own particular era of the history of the Christian faith. For many of us, this understanding emerged out of the Protestant Reformation and the great revivals of the American frontier. When we say "church," we mean our particular experience of church. We certainly do not mean the church of the Middle Ages or even of the second century. We mean the Baptist, Methodist, Presbyterian, Congregational, Episcopal, and other churches that shaped American culture and that were shaped by it. We also mean the denominations that emerged across the nineteenth and early twentieth centuries that served as the foundation for a powerful national religious identity. This notion of church will eventually give way to other perspectives and understandings. New institutional forms will emerge that will be much different.

Perhaps the most difficult challenge for us is to realize that human cultures are themselves divine gifts in much the same way that Scripture, the church, and the Christian tradition are divine gifts. The Holy Spirit works in the context of our various cultures and perspectives to bring about deeper understandings of God, humanity, and the universe. This under-standing of culture demands that we who follow in the footsteps of Jesus be able to read the cultural tea leaves to discern the movement of God in the world and to rediscover in the context of our own theological and missio-logical traditions the foundational realities that can shape us for ministry and mission in this new day.

There is no single way to be church in the world any more than there is any single way to be a follower of Jesus in the world. This is good news for a church that suddenly finds itself, after some thousand years of a commonly held Judeo-Christian perspective on reality, in a context in which no over-arching worldview or meta-narrative exists. It is as if we have moved from the cathedral with its huge and vaulted ceiling and all of its little chapels and altars and have suddenly found ourselves at the fair, where there is no commonly held worldview or cathedral ceiling to hold reality together.

Many years ago, I took my family to visit a monastery in the mountains of northwest Georgia. I had read about it in the Atlanta newspaper and had assumed that it was a Catholic monastery. They offered horse-back-riding lessons, and I thought we might combine a nice family outing with the opportunity to learn a bit about the Catholic monastic tradition. We made our way up into the mountains and soon discovered a crudely lettered sign that read "Swan Center Monastery." I suddenly doubted that this monastery was the kind that I was seeking.

Our arrival at the top of the mountain confirmed my suspicions. We came upon some stables and could discern the faint odor of horse manure and hay. I parked the car and we all headed toward the stables. A young man saw us coming and made his way toward us. Sticking out my hand in greeting, I said, "Hi! We're here to ride horses and, if possible, we'd love to see your monastery church."

Without missing a beat, the young man waved his arms up toward the heavens and declared, "Ah, the sky is our ceiling!" Then, sweeping his hand down toward the ground, he added, "And the dirt is our floor!"

I suddenly felt a bit like Dorothy when she found herself in Oz. I thought to myself, "Toto, I don't know where we are, but I know how they talk in the mountains of northwest Georgia, and it isn't like this!"

"The sky is our ceiling and the dirt is our floor." This new reality challenges the Christian faith in the twenty-first century. It calls us as followers of Jesus and as the church to discern what God is doing in the world and to participate in it. No overarching worldview shapes our cultural context except that most every worldview and perspective gain some sort of hearing. No commonly accepted authority such as Scripture or church tradition exists to which everyone ascribes.

We walk a tightrope in such a moment. We must fight the tendency to hold more tightly to the theological and missiological traditions that have shaped us in the past. To do so is to fail to recognize what God is saying to us out of our own cultural context. We also must fight the tendency to sacrifice these traditions and convictions on the altar of cultural accom-modation. In the process, we might fail to offer a prophetic word to our culture. We face a great challenge that is terribly complicated by the break-down of the institutional forms that have shaped us through much of the twentieth century, including denominations and our larger traditions such as mainline Protestantism, Catholicism, and Evangelicalism, and yet that is also helped along by our freedom from such forms. Our challenge is to read the Scriptures and the tradition of the church through the lens of our own context and, in the process, to create new theologies, institutional forms, and perspectives adequate to this day.

The reality is that the church has never been capable of negotiating such moments of historical and cultural shift under its own power and within its own institutional frameworks. Generally, a completely new understanding of what it means to be Christian and to be the church of Jesus Christ in the world revolutionizes our foundational assumptions about the Christian faith itself, and often such revolution comes from outside the institutions of the church and not from within them.

As a case in point, consider three historical movements in the life of the church—monasticism, revivalism, and the world missionary movement. None emerged out of the institutional church. Spiritual energy from beyond the church served as their fuel. The monks took to the desert in the fourth and fifth centuries in a radical expression of the nature and reality of Christian discipleship and the renunciation of worldliness. Revivalism in its British and American expressions emerged in the eighteenth century beyond the walls of the church as preachers and evangelists like John Wesley and George Whitefield took to open pastures, cemeteries, and green spaces and as the faithful flocked out of local churches to experience a spiritual vitality that their own congregations did not offer. As for mission, in the late eighteenth and early nineteenth centuries, George Liele, William Carey, Ann and Adoniram Judson, Luther Rice, and Lott Carey gathered in haystack prayer meetings and preached at associational gatherings in order to galvanize churches toward world mission.[13] Eventually the institutional church came to the table to celebrate all three movements, but only after the spiritual energies created by them had seeped into the church from outside.

Therefore, we should not be surprised in a context as disruptive and challenging as that which we face in the early twenty-first century that the institutional church and its denominations are not the source of the transformation that God is going to bring to them. We have learned at least this much from the history of God's interaction in the world. The church as an institution enables the force and energy of spiritual revolution to carry itself across history, but it is not the source of such force and energy. The source is generally external to the church, something out there beyond us that works its way into us and that eventually transforms us.

The best we can do as the church in such moments is to make ourselves ready, to cultivate within ourselves openness to whatever God is going to bring. We know that something is coming. Someone or something has moved the equator. Reality has shifted. Books and sermons have documented this movement. Conference after conference and retreat after retreat have described this new reality. We only need to look around to see the manifestations of it in every area of human culture and interaction.

This book is about that process of making ready; it is about how to make sense of what God is doing in the world and to build on it in ways that help and do not hinder that mission. It is at once a book about what has been and about what can be. Grounded in Scripture itself as the source of the Story of God's interaction in the world and of the history of God's mission in the world, it posits a reframing of these foundations in ways that will be both challenging and terrifying. By going back and identifying the divine patterns of the past, we free our imaginations to interpret the movement of God afresh. Our own cultural context contains within it a sacred impulse, one that adds new perspectives and dimensions to our understanding of the gospel. At the same time, the diversity of cultures and movements of peoples in our own day offer a depth of interpretation for the church that has never before been accessible.

This book emerges from my own social location as defined by my gender, race, social class, age, ability, religion, sexual orientation, and geographic location. I am of predominately Anglo-European descent (White)[14] and a heterosexual male, cisgender, sixty-year-old North American Christian Protestant third-culture child[15] raised in an Asian country, the Philippines, by missionary parents who were US citizens. The dominant religious and social culture of my childhood was that of the American South, though I spent my formative years in Southeast Asia. I have benefited significantly from both my Whiteness and my maleness. Within my own historic White Baptist tradition in the South, I am as privileged as I can possibly be. Despite this social location, I do not write only to others who share this same location. Certainly, such people are a primary audience for the book. But this is a book for Christian people of various social locations who, in a diverse and multicultural world, are trying to make room for each other, overcome their differences, and move into God's future vision for the creation. I believe that most of us have missed something deeply embedded in the pages of Scripture that is only now coming to full light as a result of the gospel's movement "from everywhere to everyone."

Let me state my thesis plainly. God's purpose and intention from the beginning has been a diverse world that shapes our understanding of God from multiple perspectives. For this reason, God commanded humanity at several points in the book of Genesis "to be fruitful and multiply and fill the earth" (Gen 1:22, 28; 8:17; 9:1, 7). Humanity has constantly frustrated this purpose as families, nations, and ethnicities focused on their particular blessing and uniqueness and forgot or ignored God's intention that the families of the earth should bless each other. Israel, for example, chosen by God as an exemplar of divine blessing, fixed upon the Law as the source of its own election and purity. Jesus, the Gospel writers, and Paul issued clarion calls to Israel to check its privileged status at the door and to remember and embrace the Abrahamic covenant that promised mutual blessing to all the families of the earth.

The church, in all of its varied ethnic expressions, has fixed upon various legalistic interpretations of the gospel to legitimate its own election and purity. Like Israel, its calling is to embrace the Abrahamic covenant, reflecting diversity within its own body and overcoming the walls that so often divide it. In this way, it celebrates the blessing of every human family by rising above tribe, nation, and culture and becoming a community of otherness and difference that demonstrates the power of God's original intention to bless every human family.

God dispersed the families of the earth into various languages, ethnicities, religions, and cultures at the Tower of Babel with the full realization and hope that, one day, human families would come together again as a New Humanity that understood God more fully because of these various perspectives. The path to the full knowledge of God is not a singular cultural or religious path. No ethnicity, tribe, nation, or religion possesses the full truth about God. The church must commit itself to the engagement of otherness and difference in its own space as well as in public spaces for mutual blessing and deeper understanding of God's mission in the world.

To this end, this book calls for the church to reimagine three markers that have always determined our self-understanding as followers of Jesus Christ and as the church. First, we must fully understand the *culture* or worldview that we now inhabit and what God is saying to us in the context of it, embracing the gift of diversity that it offers. Second, we must allow the new cultural reality to change our perspective on *the biblical text*, understanding it differently because of the realization that it celebrates and affirms the very diversity that we are now experiencing. Finally, we must nurture *communities* of Christ's followers that are open to the possibilities and gift of this diverse age, *churches* that are prepared to move beyond their fear of otherness and difference and that are not preoccupied and captive to the singular perspective on truth championed by an era that has faded. Only by being open to such possibility can the church of this age fully participate in the mission that God has been on from the very beginning, a divine vision for a diverse and multicultural world marked not by hatred and enmity but by love, unity, and the humble acknowledgment of the blessings that come to us from other families of the earth.

Notes

1. See Alan J. Roxburgh, *Structured for Mission: Renewing the Culture of the Church* (Downers Grove, IL: InterVarsity Press Books, 2015), 13–14. By "Euro-tribal," Roxburgh means "those Protestant churches that are the inheritors of the European reformations of the sixteenth century and European migrations that followed." Composed primarily of descendants of the tribes of northern Europe, particularly Anglo-Saxons, Celts, and others, they include people whose ancestors migrated from Germany, Austria, England, Scotland, Ireland, Wales, the Scandinavian countries, and elsewhere in Europe and into the United States. These congregations are mainly White and of various denominations of both mainline Protestantism and Evangelicalism. Over time, the boundaries of inclusivity for the descendants of the Anglo-Saxons have expanded for racially charged reasons to include most anyone of European descent. I explore these reasons later in the book.

2. See Samuel Escobar, *The New Global Mission: The Gospel from Everywhere to Everyone* (Downers Grove, IL: InterVarsity Press, 2003), 14–15. Escobar notes that this global gospel "is marked by a culture of poverty, an oral liturgy, narrative preaching, uninhibited emotionalism, maximum participation in prayer and worship, dreams and visions, faith healing, and an intense search for community and belonging" and points out its challenge to "Evangelical leaders who have long emphasized the clear and correct intellectual expression of biblical truth and the rationality of the Christian faith."

3. Kurt Alan Ver Beek, "The Impact of Short-term Missions," in *Missiology: An International Review* 34/4 (October 2006): 478.

4. See Robert Woodberry, "The Missionary Roots of Liberal Democracy," *American Political Science Review* 106/2 (May 2012): 244–74.

5. Quoted in Barbara Surk and John Heilprin, "UN: 50M displaced worldwide," *The Atlanta Journal-Constitution*, June 21, 2014, p. A5.

6. Anup Shah, "Poverty Facts and Stats," *Global Issues: Social, Political, Economic and Environmental Issues that Affect Us All,* updated January 7, 2013, http://www.globalissues.org/article/26/poverty-facts-and-stats.

7. See Andrew F. Walls, *The Missionary Movement in Christian History: Studies in the Transmission of Faith* (Maryknoll, NY: Orbis Books, 1996), 24, and Philip Jenkins, *The Next Christendom: The Coming of Global Christianity* (New York: Oxford University Press, 2011), 1–2.

8. Timothy George, *Theology of the Reformers* (Nashville: Broadman Press, 1988), 90.

9. See David Kinnaman, *You Lost Me: Why Young Christians Are Leaving Church and Rethinking Faith* (Grand Rapids, MI: Baker Books, 2011), 25.

10. Robert N. Nash, Jr., *An 8-track Church in a CD World: The Modern Church in the Postmodern World* (Macon, GA: Smyth & Helwys Publishing, 1997). Note that my title itself illustrates the point of the rapid shift and change that we are experiencing. It encouraged the church to embrace the postmodern world while using a technological image (the CD) that was immediately passé.

11. See Stanley Hauerwas and William H. Willimon, *Resident Aliens: Life in the Christian Colony* (Nashville: Abingdon Press, 2014).

12. All Scripture quotations are taken from the New Revised Standard Version of the Bible.

13. For additional reading in the areas of monasticism, revivalism, and the world missionary movement that grounds the roots of these movements outside the boundaries of the institutional church, see Jeffrey Burton Russell, *A History of Medieval Christianity: Prophecy and Order* (Arlington Heights, IL: AHM Publishing, 1968); G. M. Ditchfield, *The Evangelical Revival* (London, UK: UCL Press, 1998); Frank Lambert, *Inventing the "Great Awakening"* (Princeton: Princeton University Press, 1999); and Andrew F. Walls, ed., *The Missionary Movement in Christian History: Studies in the Transmission of Faith* (Maryknoll, NY: Orbis Publishing, 1996).

14. In her book, *Why Are All the Black Kids Sitting Together in the Cafeteria and Other Conversations about Race* (New York: Basic Books, 2017), Beverly Daniel Tatum uses the term "White" "to refer to Americans of European descent" and "Black" to "refer to people of acknowledged African descent" (95). Tatum capitalizes these terms in the same way that

similar terms such as African American or Anglo-American are capitalized. I have elected to capitalize the terms for slightly different reasons. My conviction is that White persons need to be confronted with the realities of White privilege and with the social construct of Whiteness that groups of color must face daily. Only by acknowledging the systemic reality of Whiteness together with the privilege it affords solely on the basis of color and the pernicious effects that it has on other families of the earth can White persons acknowledge realities that we would rather ignore. The capitalization of the words "White" as well as "Black" helps to remind us of those realities and helps us toward full acknowledgment of them.

15. A third-culture child is a person raised in one country by parents who hold passports and/or citizenship in another country. The parents of such children include refugees and displaced people, missionaries, international business people, military personnel, diplomats, and those who are engaged in other occupations that require families to move from one nation to another in order to meet the obligations of their chosen career paths or for their own safety or financial security.

Chapter 2

Context—Moving the Equator

It is not strange if . . . the church has failed to keep pace with a movement so rapid. But neither is it strange if humanity, amid the pressure of such new problems, fails to be stirred and guided by statements of truth . . . adequate to obsolete conditions.
—Walter Rauschenbusch, "The New Evangelism," 1904

Let us be honest. Despite the fact that Christianity proclaims a compelling and transformative vision of love and unity for individuals and communities, it often fails to live up to this vision or to attract people toward it. I read Brian McLaren's book, *Everything Must Change: Jesus, Global Crises, and a Revolution of Hope* several years ago and was disturbed by a series of questions he raised:

> *Why hasn't the Christian religion made a difference commensurate with its message, size, and resources? What would need to happen for followers of Jesus to become a greater force for good in relation to the world's top problems? How could we make a positive difference?*[1]

Many people are quick to brand the particular expressions of the Christian faith that they see today in many congregations and denominations in the United States as inadequate to the world's problems and to the challenge of bringing meaning and purpose to people's lives and experiences. Younger Americans are abandoning the church in record numbers. Attendance is waning. Various emerging religions are at least as adept as the Christian faith at offering meaning and purpose and motivating people to make a difference in the world.

This is a perplexing problem for the church. We know as followers of Jesus Christ that our faith is capable of such transformation. We have witnessed it in the biblical story, observed it in the history of the church, and often experienced it in our own lives. We also know that only rarely does our impact and influence as Christian people rise above the impact and influence of other people and organizations that have no connection to the Christian faith. We believe and assert that we hold the answers for the challenges that the world is facing, yet no one who could benefit from what we have to offer seems willing to listen to our Story. The equator has moved, and we, who once basked in the adoration of the masses, now find ourselves often ignored.

Such a reality is not a new one for the church; we have been here any number of times in the course of our history as a faith. Each time, there have been people of God who sensed the shift that was occurring and managed to lift the church up out of the ruts in which it had become mired and toward a renewed vision for itself and for the world. Interestingly enough, the source of the church's transformation, its salvation if you will, was to be found at least as much if not more in the context that was emerging around it as it was to be found in a return to its biblical and theological foundations.

God does not speak and work only through the Christian faith in its institutionalized expression as the church. Such a truth seems obvious. It is a truth, however, that the church rarely acknowledges or accepts. Walter Rauschenbusch, one of the founders of the Social Gospel movement in the United States and professor of church history at Rochester Seminary in the early twentieth century, served as a herald of this preoccupation with building up the church as an institution at the expense of God's mission in the world. Building on the work of Albrecht Ritschl, Rauschenbusch insisted that the church had abandoned the idea of the kingdom of God as a force for moral renewal as early as the second century in order to position itself at the center of power and authority on earth, even as it marginalized concern for this world and for communities and societies beyond itself.[2] He pointed to three major substitutions that the church had made in order to legitimate itself. These three substitutions carried the church down a path from which it has never fully recovered.

First, Rauschenbusch argued that the church had substituted heaven for earth in its perspective on the kingdom, pointing out that "the kingdom of the heavens has become the kingdom which is in heaven. Our hope is that we may go hence to the kingdom, and not that the kingdom may come upon earth."[3] Second, he insisted that an unchecked individualism had replaced the communal reality of the kingdom and twisted and perverted

God's intentions. Here he affirmed the Apostle Paul, insisting that "we have lost the corporate ideal. Paul's profound doctrine of the sin of the race in the first Adam floats upon the mill-pond of our systematic theology like the bowsprit of a sunken ocean vessel. It has become a joke to many because they understand nothing but individualism." Finally, citing Augustine's *City of God*, he argued that "the idea of the kingdom has been swallowed up in the idea of the church."[4]

Here is how Augustine understood that City:

> In regard to mankind I have made a division. On the one side are those who live according to man; on the other, those who live according to God. And I have said that, in a deeper sense, we may speak of two cities or two human societies, the destiny of the one being an eternal kingdom under God while the doom of the other is eternal punishment along with the Devil.[5]

Augustine never equated the kingdom of God with the institutional church. Many of his successors did, however, and the result was a simple substitution of the church for the City of God. Phyllis Tickle observed that "one of the most potentially destructive things that can happen to a faith is for it to become the accepted and established religion of the political, cultural, and social unit in which its adherents live."[6] Indeed, as the church amassed power and wealth, whether in Rome or in other earthly cities, it was quite easy for the church to maintain the illusion that divine legitimation should be placed on the work it did in the world as opposed to the work accomplished by other human beings and their communities and institutions. In the process, it sacrificed much of its spiritual legitimacy. Luther and other reformers held on to this understanding of the power and authority of the church as evidenced in their assertion that the church is the place "where the Word is rightly preached and the Sacraments rightly administered."[7] No "right preaching" or "right administration" can occur outside the church.

Rauschenbusch insisted that heaven, the individual, and the church were all "good and indispensable" elements of the kingdom but that none of them, even taken together, encompassed the kingdom of God. The substitution of heaven for the kingdom had resulted in a defensive attitude dominated by an ascetic separatism. Because of this substitution, the church could direct most of its focus to otherworldly concerns like personal salvation and corporate worship and leave such matters as the challenges of urbanization and poverty in the hands of government and nonprofit institutions. The substitution of the individual for the kingdom led to the crippling of the missionary focus of the church. The church's primary focus became the conversion of souls for the next life rather than the transformation of communities in this life. By the time the church started to recover from this preoccupation, it was too late. Other institutions were fully engaged in community development and transformation, and the church appeared to be the last institution to come to the table.

Perhaps of primary concern, the substitution of the church for the kingdom "left the bulk of human life unsanctified even in theory."[8] The very act of legitimating its own prestige and authority in the wider culture caused the church to advance the notion that the world beyond the church was profane and that it was only through the church itself that God engaged in mission in the world. In this act, the church sealed its own fate. It became increasingly clear through the course of the twentieth century that much good existed in the world quite apart from the church. Yet the church continued to insist that it was only through the church that God accomplished God's purposes in the world. The result was the marginalization of the church instead of the marginalization of the world beyond the church. People left the church because there appeared to be little substantive difference between what the church did in the world and what other institutions accomplished.

For Rauschenbusch, the only means by which such paralysis could disappear was through the recovery of the powerful idea of the kingdom that was intended to transform the lives of individuals, of the church, and of society itself.[9] Reformation is not only about a return to the past; it is also about an embrace of the present and of the future. And generally, each time that the church re-formed itself for a new day, it recovered a spiritual truth that it had forgotten over time—i.e., that it was to be a conduit for God's blessing of the world rather than the goal and end of that blessing. Each time, the church confused its own election with the mission with which God had entrusted it. It forgot that God operated in the world quite apart from the church and that true reformation of the church only happened when God spoke to it from outside its own Scriptures and tradition. It then was compelled to understand its own Scriptures and traditions through the transformative lens of its own cultural reality.

Put differently, the church had to come to the realization that it was so disconnected from its cultural context that it was no longer offering to the world the blessing that God intended for it to offer. Its only recourse was to look around to see what God was doing in the world, discern where God was working, and then reshape its tradition and its understanding of the biblical story to fit that new reality and compel it toward that new vision.

I study religion and culture by utilizing an approach known as *phenomenology*. Based on the belief that, to understand a religion or culture, one must begin with the lived experience of those who practice it, phenomenology advocates observation of the practitioners of religions and the cultures they inhabit and then seeks to understand those cultures, belief systems, and rituals from the standpoint of that observation. Phenomenology encourages immersion in another religion or culture in order to make sense of it.

My hope in using the phenomenological approach is that students will come to see that religion at its core is simply the way in which human beings make sense of life in the context of their own cultural realities and then answer the basic questions of human existence. Why are we here? Why do we suffer? Why should we behave? What happens to us when we die? Is anybody "up there"? In fact, the word "religion" comes from the Latin word "religare," meaning "to bind together." A religion then is the way in which a particular group binds its experiences together to create a unified system that is sufficient for the challenges that its followers will face in the course of life and in the context of their own cultural reality. Over time, this system creates a set of beliefs and rituals grounded in a compelling Story that its followers embrace.

The phenomenological approach removes many barriers to religious and cultural understanding because it allows students to study religion and culture on the level of shared experience. It tends to make the unfamiliar familiar and the familiar unfamiliar because students begin to see the connection between ritual and meaning. In the process, their own faith and culture become a bit more strange to them, and another religion or culture becomes a bit more familiar. They observe a Hindu person pausing in front of the image of Ganesh to remove mental obstacles that inhibit worship, and they realize that this Hindu person is engaging in the same act that a Christian performs during the organ prelude at the point designated in the worship order as "Preparation for Worship."

Most people do not study other religions and cultures in this way. The standard approach is to read about them, learn their histories, talk with experts who understand them, and then, only in the end, visit and experience the culture itself and its sacred spaces and sacred texts. In the process, we are often surprised that what we observe fails to square with the objective knowledge that we thought we possessed.

I would suggest that the first step in creating an understanding of the Christian faith that is sufficient to the challenges and possibilities of the twenty-first century is to approach our understanding of our own culture and context in a phenomenological way, to begin with the actual experience of people among whom we live and work. To start here is to ask the question, "What is reality like?" That is, what are people experiencing deep within their own minds and souls? What questions are they seeking to answer? What gives meaning and purpose to their lives? What real-life demands are causing them anxiety? Where do they find hope?

This is not where we usually start as the church. We generally begin with the faith that we have received and with the understanding of that faith that has sustained the church and its people to this point in our history. We look to the past first. We carry with us a huge trunk, and in that trunk we keep the basic tenets of our faith, the "body of truth" that is the product of all the challenges we have faced and the opportunities we have seized in the past. That trunk is our equator. It is the thing that grounds us and upon which we stand. Armed then with the objective understanding of truth that is in that trunk, we engage our own time and space. We apply the truth we know to the context and culture in which we live.

Generally, such an approach works, and when it works it tends to work over a long period—several hundred years at least and perhaps a thousand years or more. It usually quits working, however, at the point of a powerful revolution in one key area of human interaction, namely the migration of peoples. Whenever patterns in human migration undergo a significant shift, a seismic earthquake occurs that necessitates a new hermeneutical framework or interpretive grid that is sufficient to the revolution that has occurred. The equator shifts, and at such moments all religious and intellectual systems that seek to give meaning and purpose to people's lives must be pulled up out of their trunks and repacked in different trunks.

Think for a moment about those periods in the history of the church when such reformation occurred or when the dissonance between the life of the church and its surrounding culture became so pronounced that an entirely new hermeneutic or interpretive grid had to emerge. In every instance, a shift in migration patterns or an increase in those patterns is evident. The church faced such a moment at the point of the invasion of the Roman Empire by Germanic tribes in the fifth century. This migration forced the church to embrace new understandings of conversion as it sought to evangelize the "barbarians."[10] A similar re-formulation occurred as Islam made its way across North Africa and eventually into Spain in the eighth century. The interaction between Islam and Christianity challenged the Christian faith so powerfully that, by the thirteenth century, it had reinterpreted its entire theological and sacramental system along the lines of the Aristotelian philosophy that it inherited or at least rediscovered from Islam. Finally, the age of exploration and discovery beginning in the sixteenth century eventually led to the world missionary movement, chiefly the product of the churches of Western Europe and the United States, and to the creation of the institutions and theological framework that carried the Christian faith for almost 500 years until the midpoint of the twentieth century.

We live in the context of such a profound shift. It started slowly with the invention of the airplane in the early twentieth century. In 1914, passenger aircraft began to operate. By the early 1960s, passengers were hopping their way across the United States from Atlanta to Dallas to San Francisco. The inaugural nonstop flight by Delta Airlines to the West Coast happened only in the latter part of that decade. To put it in perspective, US airlines carried some 62 million passengers in 1960 compared to 720 million in 2010.[11] In that same decade, jets began carrying people across the Atlantic and Pacific oceans. Estimates are that more than 3 billion people now fly around the world on commercial airlines each year.[12] The implications of these statistics are profound. A huge revolution in patterns of migration has occurred and, based on the history of the Christian faith, we can expect that this revolution will demand the reimagination of what it means to be the people of God in the world. It always has.

The experience of enslaved Africans in the United States is one example of how such reimagination can occur even in the context of the forced migration of a community by its oppressors. How is it possible that the religion of slaveholders in the early history of the United States could also be the religion that sustained many of the people whom they enslaved? The answer rests in the conviction of those who had been enslaved that the God of Jesus Christ did speak to them in the context of their bondage and that this God offered to them hope, courage, and grace even in the worst of circumstances. Identifying with the experience of the Hebrew slaves in Egypt, they read the biblical story through that lens, discovering in the process a more powerful and liberating gospel than the one preached by their oppressors—one that could sustain them in their distress.

This realization, coupled with the pernicious system of White domination and supremacy that continues to infuse our current cultural context, propelled the Black church in the United States toward a transformative vision that freed it from many different forms of intellectual and spiritual bondage. Our refusal to admit that our context is determining our interpretation of the text is the very thing that traps us in inadequate interpretations. Despite what we might learn or teach in seminary or in the church, context and text are both dictating our interpretations, and it might be best if we simply confessed that it is difficult for us to know which one is superseding the other. The only means whereby we can somehow hear God speak is to pay equal attention to both, at least as nearly as we can do so.

This is much more difficult than it would first seem. It is almost impossible for us to recognize our own captivity to a particular worldview or culture. Our worldview or culture is the reality that surrounds and embraces us to such an extent that we hardly know it exists at all until we are able to step outside of it in the encounter with a person who possesses another worldview or perspective.

Let me use the example of a particularly frustrating meeting I attended in Seoul, Korea. A group of churches there had banded together to form a global mission-sending organization and asked if my own organization might take them under our wing and appoint and send their missionaries. I was opposed to the idea because it made little sense to me for a U.S.-based mission-sending agency to be appointing and sending Korean missionaries. Unfortunately, my organization had signed an agreement just prior to my appointment that said that this was exactly what we would do.

It was up to me then to travel to Korea and share with my Korean brothers and sisters that we could not do what we had promised them we would do. They were quite frustrated with me and for good reason. Our deliberations went back and forth about what we could do together and what we could not do. At one point very late in the evening, just as we had reached some consensus and it appeared that we would finally be able to sign another agreement, the lead pastor said something to the entire room in the Korean language that my translator elected not to translate. Everyone laughed at the joke but me, since I did not speak the language.

I turned to my translator and asked, "Could you please tell me what the pastor just said?"

Embarrassed, the translator smiled at me and patted my arm. "Oh, it is not important."

"No," I insisted. "I think whatever he said might be very important and helpful to me."

With reluctance, the translator answered my question. "The pastor said that it is sometimes very hard to understand the White mind!"

I absolutely agree! It is very hard to understand the White mind, and it is particularly difficult to understand the White mind when you are the one who possesses that mind and therefore have absolutely no idea that such a thing exists. On one level, no one lacks a full understanding of my cultural worldview and perspective more than I do. I constantly fail to see myself for who I really am because I exist in a cultural context shaped and framed by others who are just like me. Together we assume that our cultural understanding is the one that makes the most sense in the grand scheme of reality. Everyone else has a cultural bias and perspective. I live in the real world.

Several years ago, I was traveling in Thailand with a group of college students for the purpose of experiencing Buddhist meditation practices and studying the Buddhist worldview. I had arranged a conversation or "monk chat" with the monks at a monastery in the city of Chiang Mai, where we were fortunate to have a session with the abbot. His insights and wit were mesmerizing, and we listened as he talked at length about Buddhism and its monastic practices. After a time, he paused and asked if we had any questions.

I was foolish enough to raise my hand and ask if the abbot could explain the Buddhist notion of "nirvana" to us. Nirvana is, of course, the ultimate goal or state for a Buddhist person in which they experience liberation from the process of birth and rebirth. The nature of the state of nirvana is difficult to grasp, much more difficult than our own Christian notion of heaven. Without missing a beat, the abbot told me that my question reminded him of the story of the fish and the turtle, and he went on to explain that the two creatures were once swimming together in the ocean. They swam for quite some time, enjoying each other's company. After a few hours, the turtle left the fish and decided to go up on the dry land and take a nap. When he woke up, he went back into the water and looked for his friend the fish.

When the fish saw the turtle, he asked the turtle a simple question: "Where have you been?"

At this point, the abbot paused and peered over his glasses at me. "Dr. Nash," he asked, "how would the turtle answer?" Then he sat back in his chair to wait for whatever insight I might have to offer. Of course, I simply stared back, a puzzled expression on my face.

Indeed, how would the turtle answer? How do you explain a completely new reality to a fish who has never known anything except the ocean? How do you talk about a tropical breeze or the way the sun warms you while you are sleeping on the sand? The task is impossible. It turns out that this is just the point. The abbot would never be able to offer to me an understanding of "nirvana" that would satisfy me. I swim in an entirely different reality, one that makes it virtually impossible for me to understand this difficult Buddhist concept. I think the abbot would say that no human being can understand nirvana until they attain it.

The same challenge exists with any effort to divorce the biblical text from the context in which we interpret it. We swim in an ocean that is invisible to us. We cannot fully grasp the extent to which that ocean dictates our interpretation of the text. The best we can do is to view our context for what it truly is, an encounter between the human and the divine that expresses new realities and truths about both. Armed with this new understanding of context, we can then seek out those points of intersection between context and text that lead to the transformation of our perspective on God, humanity, and the rest of the creation.

The only way then to "hear" the text is to realize that we are "hearing" it contextually. This is hardly an earth-shaking realization! Here is an earth-shaking realization, however, one that if properly understood represents the movement of the equator from one place to another: the equator does shift for us when we realize and affirm that our context itself is a creation of God and therefore a powerful source of divine revelation. Our context is a sacrament, meaning that it is a means by which God's grace expresses itself in history. To understand context in this way is to affirm that God's work of creation has continued into our own space and time to such an extent that the interrelationship between God, humanity, and creation in our own day (our context) is leading to new truths that have never before been accessible to us. They do not exist in the biblical text. They are separate and possible apart from the text. They would exist whether we possessed the biblical text or not.

I would argue that this reality of context as the source of divine truth cannot simply be explained away as general revelation. The truths that emerge in this intersection of God, humanity, and the world are specific to a particular group of people who share a particular worldview or a particular ethnicity or who inhabit a particular historical moment. Only after this group of people has received this truth or truths and appropriated it into their experience can they share it with others who are not privy to it.

David Bosch, in his profound work *Transforming Mission*, points to five eras in the history of the church in which the people of God have wrestled with particular contexts, listened to God in the midst of those contexts, and somehow managed to grasp new divine truths that emerged from both context and text. It is his conviction that the contexts themselves gave rise to significant truths about God that shape the church's theological and missiological perspectives on the nature of God, humanity, and the world.[13] These five eras include the apostolic age, the Hellenistic-Roman age, the Middle Ages, the age of the Reformation, and the modern missionary age. In each era, new perspectives and understandings emerged because of the intersection between context and text. Bosch challenges us to uncover the new truths that are emerging at the point of the intersection of text and context in our own day.

His understanding creates a flexibility of interpretation that is far more fluid than most. Yet this understanding emerges out of a theological reality that is foundational to both Judaism and Christianity. God created the world and immediately thereafter declared that it was good . . . all of it. Light was good. The earth and the seas were good. The vegetation was good. The sun, moon, and stars were good. The creatures of the sea and the birds of the air were good. The living creatures on the earth were good. Human beings, male and female, were good. I suppose we might call this moment of creation the first "context." The word stems from the Latin fusion of the two words "con" or "to join with" and "texere" or "to plait or weave." It literally means "to join by weaving." Here, at the point of creation, God wove humanity and the creation into relationship with each other and with God, each playing a particular part in the grand divine drama. Context has thus always preceded text. We experience the divine and then we relate the Story of that experience—i.e., what happened to us because of it.

The Genesis story of creation sets the stage within the Judeo-Christian worldview for all of the intersections between God, humanity, and the creation that follow. All subsequent stories exist beneath this first one. All subsequent contexts that emerge as God, humanity, and the creation continue their relationship with each other must integrate it. God creates repeatedly, renewing humanity and renewing the creation. New contexts emerge at every moment with the births and deaths of human beings, of animals, and of vegetation. Civilizations come and civilizations go. Nations are born and nations die. Cultures emerge and then shift and change as the generations pass.

In this first Story, God observes that all of creation is good. This foundational divine perspective sets the pattern for all future encounters between God, humanity, and the world. In the midst of these interactions, God expresses goodness and grace. New truth and understanding about the interrelationship of the three partners in this divine dance emerge out of the interplay between them. For this reason, each human culture, each age is the source of some new perspective on God that had not existed prior to it.

Three basic realities then occur in the context of each age. First, the church in that age discovers new understandings about God and the creation that emerge out of the new context itself and apart from the tradition that it has received. Second, the church in that age takes the core understandings of God, humanity, and the creation that it has received from previous ages and reapplies these new understandings to that new context. Finally, a new consensus emerges that represents the blending of the new truths that the church has uncovered with the tradition it has received. It then tests this new consensus against the biblical text itself, reformulates its understanding of the text and of the context, and moves forward with a new perspective on reality that has never been possible before.

The church in the Hellenistic age, for example, received from the apostolic church certain fixed understandings that had been honed in an era in which the church was emerging from its close connection to the Jewish faith and toward a context in which it had been a minority mystery religion of Rome. The creed of the church in this early era was the simple assertion that "Jesus is Lord," but it quickly became apparent that this assertion would constantly demand clarification. Where did the authority reside to make such determinations? Church leaders like Clement of Rome and Ignatius of Antioch insisted that church authority resided in the office of bishop, and they identified Scripture as the source of this authority.

The church in the Hellenistic-Roman era embraced this assertion. It carried forward what it had received. It recognized and affirmed that some limits had to be placed on the theological and practical formulations of the church. Some authority had to be invested in the office of bishop and in the pronouncements of church leaders gathered in councils to resolve theological and practical conflicts. In this way, the church in a Hellenistic context managed to determine what orthodoxy was and what heresy was, at least for its own day. Discordant voices like those of Marcion, who branded the God of the Hebrew Bible to be an evil god, and of Montanus, who proclaimed himself a spokesperson for the Holy Spirit, challenged the church to specify its canon and to determine the role of the Holy Spirit in the life of the faith. The church embraced what it had received from its spiritual forebears and insisted on certain boundaries of interpretation generally represented in the pronouncements of recognized church authorities.

Tertullian of Carthage is one church father who represents this fidelity to the traditions received from a previous era. Greatly influenced by the persecution that Christians experienced, he wrote out of a defensive posture intended to combat this terrible treatment. He argued for the Christian worldview from within the tradition itself, to legitimate it based on its own internal truth and merits. For this reason, he focused on the biblical text and the early affirmations of the church. He raged against the unwillingness of Christians to face martyrdom courageously and without compromise. He believed that the church was far too quick to forgive the lapsed when they recanted the faith in the midst of persecution. His was one voice insisting that the church cling to the truth it had received from the early church and eschew any form of compromise either in theology or in practice. He denounced all compromise: "Away with all attempts to produce a mottled Christianity of Stoic, Platonic, and dialectic composition! We want no curious disputation after possessing Christ Jesus, no inquisition after enjoying the gospel!"[14]

A different sort of response also emerged in the Hellenistic age of the church as represented in a number of Christian theologians who embraced Hellenistic philosophical perspectives as divinely ordained truth. Unlike Tertullian, these theologians were not content to simply sit back and insist on the Christian understanding of reality received in Scripture and tradition as the sole source of divine revelation. Rather, they insisted that the Greek philosophers had uncovered divine truth in their own intellectual pursuits and quite apart from any influence of Christian or Jewish thinkers. Origen, following the example of his spiritual father, Clement of Alexandria, legitimated the Christian faith in the eyes of its philosophical detractors by "baptizing" the Greek philosophers themselves into the faith. Along with other theologians of his day, he identified some of them as being Christian before there were Christians because of their contributions to the emerging Christian understanding of reality.

Origen's embrace of the worldview of Hellenistic philosophy occurred out of his own sense that the theological perspective received from the early church was inadequate for the third century of the church's existence. It was not simply that Origen was appealing to that Greco-Roman worldview in an effort to make the faith relevant to Greco-Romans; rather Origen sensed a level of dissonance and inadequacy within the Christian theology and biblical interpretation that demanded reevaluation. The challenges of the day were such that the interpretations of Scripture and the body of doctrine that had guided the church to this point in history were no longer adequate interpretations. The Hellenistic cultural context demanded an interpretation of Scripture and doctrine through the lens of the context rather than that the reverse approach should hold sway.

Robert J. Daly has argued that Origen did far more than simply accept the Christian faith handed on by the apostles to him and to the church of his day:

> From his constant research, from his incessant questioning and speculating, and from his own personal and spiritual experience, he was continually bringing in new insight and understanding to the church's understanding both of the bible and of its own rule of faith. His was not only the vision and insight to broaden and deepen, not only the courage to admonish and correct, but also the boldness and adventuresomeness to question and speculate.[15]

It is for this reason that the church sometimes deems Origen to have been a heretic on any number of points related to historic Christian doctrine. He was absolutely out on the edge, ahead of the church, beckoning it toward the reevaluation of its most foundational assumptions about God, Jesus, the Holy Spirit, and the world. He erred on the side of context as the most important element in the engagement between the emerging texts of the Bible and the prevailing worldview. Fortunately for him, the canon of Scripture was still undefined, and he was able to function without the official limits that such a canon would have necessitated.

In time, the church would test the orthodoxy of Origen and other Christian philosophers against the weight of the biblical text and the historical tradition of the church, but even as it tested this orthodoxy, it would be doing so through the lens of that culture and context at least as much as it was doing it through Scripture and the previous theological formulations of the church. The theological and philosophical formulations of Clement of Alexandria, Origen, Irenaeus of Lyons, and others would become the chief body of doctrine that would serve as the foundation for the Western church.

Then, as this orthodox interpretation of Scripture and Christian doctrine that was honed in the Greco-Roman world moved across the ages, it became increasingly more rigid and weighty. It was, after all, interpreted and reinterpreted in light of a successive number of challenges to which it responded. Obviously, each time it rose to the occasion because each time it survived the challenge, reimagined itself for a new day, and reached a consensus that enabled it to merge with the prevailing worldview. A new consensus emerged out of the dynamic engagement between the new cultural understandings of the divine never previously imagined and the faith received from the previous era. In every age of the church, the previous consensus proved insufficient, the foundations shook, and the reimagination of text and theology in light of new divine revelation in the context emerged.

We can see this pattern play out across the history of the church and through the various ages that Bosch has identified. Origen had it far easier in his day than did Augustine in the fifth century, St. Francis of Assisi in the thirteenth century, Martin Luther in the sixteenth, John Wesley in the eighteenth, Sojourner Truth in the nineteenth, or Martin Luther King, Jr. in the twentieth. It became increasingly difficult to challenge the authority of the various compromises that text and context had made in the previous history of the church, especially the consensus forged in the Hellenistic world. There was far more complexity and ideology that now had to be challenged in order to fashion a new consensus for the next era.

Certainly, the synthesis forged by the Christian philosophers and theologians of the Greco-Roman age is the most powerful synthesis that has occurred across the history of the church. For most of Christian history, the Western theological tradition has held the primary place as the interpretive framework for biblical interpretation. The assumption through most of the twentieth century was that a proper understanding of the Christian faith was possible only through a Western lens. The church swam in this sea. The assumption was that this lens was the only truly unbiased lens that allowed for a proper understanding of Christian doctrine and that offered a truly biblical perspective on human history and thought. In time, the Western church forgot the contextual realities of the Greco-Roman age that were shaping its perspective on theology and Scripture. That perspective became the "fixed" theology of the church.

This assumption was the inevitable result of the historic movement of the Christian faith from the East to the West rather than in the opposite direction, a reality dictated by the rapid growth of Islam in the seventh century CE that essentially turned Europe into an island that was separated from its former centers in the Eastern Roman empire and in North Africa. If it had not been for the Battle of Tours in 732 CE in southern France, most Westerners today would be repeating the basic creed of the Islamic faith that "There is no God but Allah, and Muhammad is his prophet!" Instead, Charles Martel, the Frankish general, defeated the Islamic forces and the stage was set for the consolidation of Christian Europe.

Building on the theological legacy inherited from its embrace of Hellenistic philosophy and after its victory at Tours, Christianity retreated into itself for some four or five centuries as it evangelized the Germanic tribes that had invaded the old Roman Empire and the relatively small part of the world that it could now call its own. By 1054, its internal struggles were so pronounced that it split into two different camps, namely an Eastern Orthodoxy weakened by the challenge of Islam and by its own theological struggles and a burgeoning Western Catholicism in Europe. Thomas Aquinas and other philosophers of the Western church built on the good work of Islamic scholars who had rediscovered Aristotle and the Greek philosophers, fashioning a second renaissance of the Greek philosophical tradition within Christianity. A consensus emerged that created a powerful Church of the Middle Ages and legitimated the authority of the Bishop of Rome as the head of the church.

This theological consensus lasted for about three hundred years until the Reformation forced various schisms in the church, primarily as reactions against the excesses of church power and authority over the lives of common people and the inevitable corruption that went along with this unchecked power. The entire system of the Church of the Middle Ages was built on a synthesis of Scripture and Aristotelian thought that held that what happened here on earth by virtue of the authority of the church also happened in the heavenly realm. On the positive side, this reality meant that a physical substance here on earth could be transformed into a heavenly substance, and so bread itself could change in its substance into the very body of Christ and wine could be transformed into the blood of Christ. Tangible indulgences granted here on earth freed the faithful from having to pay for their sins in purgatory. The confession of one's sins here on earth to a priest of the church resulted in forgiveness in heaven.

Martin Luther, John Calvin, and Ulrich Zwingli championed reform in the sixteenth century, but even their efforts at reform were conditioned as much by the context in which they lived as they were by the biblical understanding of truth that they championed. Protestantism, of course, proclaimed its fidelity to the biblical foundations of the faith and championed the central role of the individual human person in determining their relationship to God. But Renaissance notions that placed humanity at the center of history and early Enlightenment perspectives on individualism influenced the theology behind such concepts as priesthood of the believer and justification by faith. Once again, context served as the lens for biblical interpretation, opening up new theological perspectives that would not have been possible apart from it.

The more things changed, the more they stayed the same. Schisms quickly emerged within Protestantism as Zwingli and Luther disagreed over the nature of the Eucharist and as the radical reformers, including Anabaptists, Baptists, Mennonites, and others, insisted on a regenerate church membership. Interestingly, Zwingli insisted that the bread and the wine in Communion remained simply that, bread and wine, and that there was no such thing as a Eucharistic miracle that transformed the substance of the elements. His perspective and the resulting conflict with Luther marked a return to the age-old debate between Aristotelians and Platonists over the nature of reality itself. Was the Supper merely a memorial that celebrated something God had accomplished in the heavenly realm with the death and resurrection of Jesus Christ, or was it an earthly thing as well that legitimated the fact that God had created the material world and called it "good"? In addition, were the radical reformers correct that baptism of infants into the arms of the church accomplished absolutely nothing in terms of their salvation in the heavenly realm? These discussions were as much philosophical debates, rooted in Hellenistic philosophy, as they were biblical arguments grounded in Scripture and tradition.

By the late seventeenth century, the Enlightenment or Age of Reason emerged as an intellectual movement in Europe. It challenged ideas of tradition and faith and championed the sort of knowledge gained through the scientific method. Its major proponents and thinkers were philosophers such as René Descartes, John Locke, Voltaire, and David Hume. Following along in their wake, we now mistakenly assume that we can understand the original meaning of the biblical text by virtue of Enlightenment tools like the historical-critical method and objectively apply that meaning to our lives or, as ministers, to the lives of our parishioners.

Evangelicals, mainline Protestants, and Catholics made such assumptions in equal measure. George Marsden, Mark Noll, and others have helped us to see that Fundamentalism and Protestant Liberalism were two sides of the same Enlightenment coin in the nineteenth and twentieth centuries.[16] Both movements were highly rationalistic efforts to render the Christian faith intellectually defensible in the context of the triumph of the scientific worldview, despite the constant protestations of both movements that they were faithfully interpreting the text. Fundamentalism defended the Bible by insisting that it was internally consistent and that, ultimately, its assertions would be scientifically provable. Liberalism or modernism, on the other hand, simply ripped the supernatural heart out of the Bible by explaining away its miracles, healings, and exorcisms. For both sides, context was far more important than the text itself except that neither side was willing to admit its own captivity to the prevailing modern worldview and to the fact that it was subsuming Scripture to that perspective. The context dictated our interpretation of the text. We were reading Scripture through the lens of our particular scientific and rationalistic worldview instead of the other way around.

John Parratt in his *Introduction to Third World Theologies* points out that such theologies have generally rejected the theological agenda of the West by calling for a renewed focus on the context from which theology emerges. It is his conviction that "while no theology can help being in one way or another contextual, making *explicit* the centrality of contextual issues does represent a departure from the current Western mainstream." Most "third world theologies" prefer to begin with context and then move to such traditional sources as Scripture and tradition. He concludes that "context has therefore become primary for the theological task."[17]

For this reason, moments of upheaval in the wider culture demand that the church practice what might best be called "theological play," a willingness to open up its own theological formulations to the challenges of a new context so that God can reveal deeper and perhaps even new truth to it that has never been possible before. Generally, doctrine plays a powerful and conservative role in the Christian faith, one that offers a stable perspective on the divine and is the product of all that has come before it. This is not the only responsibility of theology. It must also be open to the realities of the limits of the previous contexts that have produced this theological consensus.

Juan Luis Segundo points out that, following in the best traditions of
its heritage, Western traditional theology tends to view its task as one of
applying "the Divine Word to present day reality." This approach assumes
that the truth that has been discovered in the past as a result of the interplay
between scripture and context can be applied in the present "inside some
antiseptic laboratory."[18] The consensus that has been fashioned in previous
ages becomes the truth that must be believed, carrying with it a weight and
authority that are essentially unquestioned. The church formulates its basic
doctrines under the umbrella of the new consensus. Our understanding of
God, of Jesus Christ, of the nature of the church, and of its mission in the
world is subsumed under that umbrella.

Here we might use our own age as an example. For most of us, our
notions about church are the product of a particular contextual and textual
consensus that was worked out in the age of the Enlightenment, the
Industrial Revolution, Protestant revivalism, and the context of space and
religious freedom that emerged with the birth and growth of the United
States. Revolutions in transportation, communication, science, manu-
facturing, and agriculture created enormous anxiety and dissonance that
called into question the theological consensus that had been received from
previous eras, even one as recent as the Protestant Reformation. Our experience forced us toward a reinterpretation, indeed, a reimagination, of the
biblical text itself and the transformation of Christian doctrine to conform
to the new reality

A number of challenges emerged to the old prevailing order, and eventually that old order crumbled. State churches lost their political authority
and power under the weight of the Enlightenment focus on the centrality
of the individual human mind and the rights of individual liberty. Denom-
inationalism emerged when no single church or tradition could gain the
upper hand in the new context. Voluntarism in matters of religious affiliation became the means by which citizens determined the denomination
and particular church to which they would belong. The scientific worldview and perspective emerged as the dominant worldview, the sea in which
everyone in the wider culture swam and to which all religious traditions
had to conform. The pragmatic expression of faith, both individually and
personally, came to be the order of the day in much the same way that effi-
ciency and order came to characterize the industrial world.

A new reality emerged that compelled us to seek consensus between
text or theology and the new context in which we found ourselves. God
was indeed doing something new or at least bringing to the attention of
the faith divine truth that had always existed but that it had never noticed
before. Such new truths included a focus on individual liberties and human

rights, the evils of slavery, the realities of human oppression, and the benefits of democracy. The notion of individual liberty squared nicely with
the evangelical and revivalist notions of the conversion of the individual
human soul. The successive waves of revivals that ripped across England
and its American colonies introduced a process for individual conversion to
Christ. Suddenly, particular Scriptures seemed to legitimate such a process
even though nothing much like it had ever existed before. As the age of
exploration opened up new possibilities for the extension of the Christian faith around the world, a new missionary activism emerged that called
for the conversion of the entire world utilizing modern methodologies for
bringing people to salvation.

Once the state church had been dethroned, local churches multiplied
in huge numbers—Methodists, Baptists, Presbyterians, Church of Christ,
and any number of other denominations began to compete for members.
Every town in the nation had at least three or four churches at its center, and
these eventually split or more churches came along to such an extent that
the United States became a nation of churches. Membership rolls became
a means of determining which citizens belonged to which church, and a
careful process was put in place to ensure that members could carry their
membership from one church to another. This was an essential step in a
context with no state church. Training unions and Sunday schools emerged
as the means by which the faithful could be educated in both Scripture and
in Christian tradition. Each church identified with a particular denomination and looked to that denomination for the sending of missionaries, the
creation of educational materials, and various other services.

In short, a new consensus was born that was able to offer biblical and
theological justification that squared nicely with the challenges of the day.
The anxieties that had existed prior to the creation of the new order gave
way to a sense that all was once again right with the world. The assumption
was that this new reality was the final reality that would stand the church in
good stead for the rest of its history. The age was so confident in its perspective that it could not imagine that the day would come when its hard-earned
consensus of text/theology and context would be challenged. Its approach
to mission is best summarized in the following statement: "Our purpose is
to bring as many people to Christ as possible in as short a time as possible
and to encourage those new Christians to form as many new churches
as possible as quickly as possible."[19] It certainly found adequate biblical
and theological justification for such a perspective, and it also existed in a
culture and context that could understand these values as legitimate ones.

Like all of the ages of the church before us, our particular age assumed
that its perspective on the Christian faith, its consensus of text and context,

represented the pinnacle of that faith. We had finally gotten it right. Because of our ability to grasp the fullness of truth, we could share that truth with the entire world in ways that the world could grasp and comprehend. Perhaps this perspective and attitude is best represented in the 1910 Edinburgh World Missionary Conference, largely a gathering of the Western church, at which most delegates assumed that the conversion of the entire world by the end of the twentieth century was a real possibility. Stephen Bevans describes the missionary perspective at the moment of the Edinburgh Conference as "an exercise of power—the power of Christendom aimed at 'heathendom,' the power of the West to the 'rest.'"[20] It took place at just the moment that the Western church was about to embark upon a massive global effort to extend the Christian gospel to the ends of the earth.

Indeed, the missionary movement of the twentieth century was, by most standards, a huge success. By taking advantage of advancements in transportation, mission agencies dispatched thousands of missionaries from the Western world to "the ends of the earth." Again, revolutions in patterns of migration made all the difference. This rapid advancement resulted in the establishment of churches and denominations all across the globe and appeared to herald the final triumph of the Christian faith against the other religions of the world. One could hardly blame its missionaries and leaders for assuming that the faith had achieved its highest expression.

Even as the churches of the Western world celebrated this missionary expansion, the foundations that rendered it so powerful were crumbling. World Wars I and II challenged the heady optimism in human progress and scientific achievement that undergirded the movement. The Great Depression undermined the financial stability of the global mission endeavor. The Vietnam War, the civil rights movement, Watergate, and a host of other challenging events called into question the moral authority of the Western world and the validity of the faith that it espoused.

Segundo points out that at certain points in the history of the faith, so much dissonance and anxiety emerges in the context that the superstructure that has carried the faith to that point ceases to function effectively. Such anxiety forces the church to the deepest levels of reflection. It questions most everything, including the theological and biblical foundations that it once accepted without question. At such moments, the church reexamines its most basic assumptions about what it means to follow Jesus Christ and to be the church. It opens itself up to theological speculation and reconceptualization because of the challenges of its cultural context. In such moments, the context rises to the same level as the biblical text, forcing the church to read and understand the biblical text in new ways and through different lenses.

Segundo points out four steps that occur in this process that he calls "the hermeneutical circle: our life experience creates ideological and theological suspicion; we apply that suspicion to the superstructure of our worldview; we realize that our prevailing interpretations of Scripture are inadequate; and we arrive at new interpretations adequate for the day.[21] First, our contextual experience leads us into fear and ideological and theological suspicion. The old ways are no longer functioning adequately. We begin to question such basic doctrines as the nature of God, Christology, and the church and to challenge accepted notions about Christian morality and ethics. Issues once considered beyond question or taboo suddenly become matters for intense conversation and speculation. Is Jesus the only way to God? Why should I join a church? Should the definition of marriage in the church be redefined to include same-sex unions? Can I be both a Buddhist and a Christian?

In some sense, this hermeneutical circle occurs constantly. We always question our sources of authority and the viability of our particular worldviews. Young people challenge the validity of the belief systems of their parents. Life experiences cause us to reject some particular understanding of God or truth. At certain moments in history, however, the anxiety and fear are so deep and so profound that the entire system is challenged— the interpretation of the sacred texts, the theological presuppositions, the ethical framework, indeed the entire foundation of the civilization itself.

We live in such a moment. The reason for our anxiety and fear is not just that others beyond the boundaries of the church challenge or threaten our religion or our culture. The reason for our anxiety is that we ourselves are questioning our religion and our cultural assumptions. We are questioning the entirety of our own worldview and perspective, including our philosophical foundations, our Judeo-Christian heritage and worldview, our Enlightenment notions about individual rights and religious liberty, and our basic assumptions about reality. We assumed that all of these things were unassailable. Now that others and we are questioning them, we experience the deep trauma of personal and cultural anxiety and fear. We are suddenly asking questions that our own superstructure, civilization, and religion seem incapable of answering.

We might protest that this is not what is going on. We might insist that we are clinging more tightly to the truths and worldview that we have received. We also might ask why we are sensing the need to cling more tightly to that truth if not because we perceive that it is under threat and in danger of extinction. The louder our insistence upon our own worldview and religious faith, the more likely it is that we ourselves are questioning their legitimacy. The Christian faith is at its strongest when it has no need to enact laws to guard its primacy and when it has no need to force others to convert to its beliefs. It is at its strongest when other religions do not threaten it but rather it can coexist easily with them. It is at its weakest when it loudly insists upon its own primacy, enacts laws to ensure that primacy, and does its best to prohibit the free exercise of religion by people of other faiths.

It makes sense that our confidence in our own faith and in our own particular worldview should be waning. The products and inventions of our civilization are proving to be the source of our undoing. Revolutions in transportation and communication have created new patterns of inter-action and engagement with the world. Millions of people embrace new realities, religions, and worldviews around the world. Our assumption had been that, once the world received our particular understanding of God and truth, it would eagerly embrace it, but the opposite has happened. Christianity, the faith of Western civilization, has failed to experience much growth at all in the context of these revolutions and remains about the same percentage size of the world's population in 2019 that it was in 1900 (about 32 percent). In the meantime, other faiths, including Islam and Buddhism, have rapidly increased in proportion to Christianity, particularly in our own context in the United States.

At the same time, we have faced the challenge of conflicts in Iraq and Afghanistan brought on by Saddam Hussein's invasion of Kuwait in 1990 and by the terrible events of September 11, 2001. In both instances, we entered the conflicts convinced that victory would occur easily given our military superiority and that we would be welcomed as liberators. Once again, the very opposite happened. The peoples of Afghanistan and Iraq resented our presence and often refused to support us in our efforts. Our own media quickly hopped on the patriotic bandwagon of support for war, at least until such time as they discovered that the political justifications for war had little basis in reality. Our allies in Western Europe were only reluc-tant participants in the conflicts, hardly moved by our protestations that Saddam Hussein and the Taliban were threats to freedom. In the aftermath of these wars, we are dealing with far worse enemies than we faced in the beginning, enemies like ISIS, al-Qaeda, and White nationalist terrorists within our own borders. The result is a profound anxiety about our own abilities and about our vision for ourselves, for our nation, and for the world.

The anxiety and fear have moved on to the individual level as well. Because of technological advances, we live in a world in which we are constantly threatened as individuals and as families. One person with a smartphone at the supermarket can quickly discover all sorts of private information about the person standing next to them in line. Identities are stolen. Credit card accounts are easily hacked. The public shaming of individuals is becoming a daily occurrence, something we have not faced in American culture since the colonial era of the whipping post and the stocks. A recent story in the *New York Times Magazine* documented the terrible experiences of several people who had posted comments on their Facebook pages or who had sent tweets that, out of context, appeared to be thoughtless, racist, or sexist and whose lives, as a result, have been destroyed.[22]

Revolutions in communications and transportation create as many challenges as they resolve. As recently as the 1970s, only three or four television networks were available to us, and most of us received the news from the same sources. This reality created a shared perspective on what was happening around the world. With the advent of the internet and the rapid growth in cable and satellite television, however, we have access to thousands of perspectives on reality. Rather than enabling a better-informed public, these advances sometimes cause us to silo ourselves within whatever worldviews or perspectives we choose to embrace. As a result, we are often far more hostile toward perspectives that are different from our own than we used to be because we choose to hear only the ones that support our prejudices and that legitimate our fears.

We turn our anger and fear upon our own institutions, both political and religious. Our political system becomes increasingly polarized. Our churches either grow empty as a result of apathy and hostility toward the Christian faith and its inability to speak to the challenges of the day, or they fill up with people who are convinced that the answers to their fears and anxieties can be found in a prescribed religious faith that considers these same anxieties and fears to be legitimate in a day in which the Christian faith itself is threatened.

Anxiety and fear pervade. This is the first step in Segundo's hermeneutical circle. Our experience leads us toward ideological and theological suspicion. Why is it that others do not accept our perspective on truth? Why is it that they cannot see the benefits of the perspective we offer and embrace? When the superstructure of a civilization holds, then the obvious answer to this question is that there is something wrong with "them." This answer has been the particular answer of Western civilization since at least the period of the Renaissance and the Reformation, the last time such anxiety and fear were pervasive enough to produce a new consensus. When the superstructure itself is under suspicion even from its own adherents, questions are directed at the superstructure by those who previously embraced its formulations.

For many of us, this superstructure is the well-reasoned faith of the twentieth century that affirmed the legitimacy of the scientific world-view and championed a pragmatic and institutionalized approach to faith represented in the great denominations and in a commonsense approach to faith. This superstructure, at least for most American Protestants, was the product of a revivalist understanding of salvation and faith that was concretized in the Baptist, Methodist, Presbyterian, and Congregationalist churches of America's town square. It was marked by a conviction that the best sort of faith was a reasonable faith that could be accepted by most human beings because of its sensible expression.

We then take the second step in Segundo's hermeneutical circle. The superstructure must account for its inadequacy. The challenges stem from a number of contextual realities that suddenly rise up to demand answers. Religions like Buddhism, Hinduism, and Islam emerge in the American context and challenge the legitimacy of the Judeo-Christian understanding of reality. People suddenly determine that there is no need for any religious affiliation whatsoever, and the culture is forced to create a category for such persons by describing them as the "nones," something hardly conceivable just forty years ago. No one feels guilty about not attending church, and churchgoing people seem to be the ones who are engaging in countercul-tural behavior. Words like "Christian" and "church" carry baggage that cause even Christians and churchgoing people to struggle to find new ways of defining themselves and the communities to which they belong.

At this point, Segundo's third step occurs when we arrive at "a new way of experiencing theological reality that leads us to exegetical suspicion, that is, to the suspicion that the prevailing interpretation of the Bible has not taken important pieces of data into account."[23] This is a profound moment and the very moment that we now inhabit. We have convinced ourselves that the prevailing assumptions of the previous era in Christian history, the one lasting for the last five hundred years, were the best and highest expres-sions of Christian faith and that these particular expressions would offer the foundation on which the next era would build. Nothing could be further from the truth, though this suspicion of the previous era in no way contra-dicts the assertion that its basic assumptions were adequate for its own day and perhaps that some of its assertions were even divinely sanctioned.

The previous era did its work remarkably well and should be congrat-ulated for its accomplishments and critiqued for its failures. Across five centuries or more, it too moved through this same hermeneutical circle. It questioned the prevailing assumptions of the previous era, beginning perhaps as early as the late fourteenth century with John Wycliffe and the Avignon Papacy and ending in the early seventeenth century as the

Protestant Reformation became institutionalized and a new consensus emerged within Lutheranism, the Reformed Church, the Church of England, and the various dissenting groups that emerged from these traditions, including Baptists, Quakers, and Methodists. Its ability to frame and shape a new superstructure is evident in the emergence of denominations and of the world missionary era that is its legacy. Because of the new consensus that it framed, Christianity emerged after the age of exploration and discovery as one of the major living world religions. This is the greatest evidence of the success of the previous era in building an understanding of the Christian faith adequate to some of the challenges of its time, keeping in mind that all of its accomplishments were tainted by the evils of colonialism, slavery, and White domination.

The emergence of a new superstructure is the final stage in Segundo's hermeneutical circle, the creation of a new framework by which we make sense of our experience in a way that is biblically sound and theologically consistent with our context instead of with the context that preceded us.[24] Such a perspective seems quite perplexing at first. Why would we attempt to leap over the conclusions and various consensuses of previous eras? Shouldn't these inform our own understanding? Haven't these other eras also offered a new perspective on God, the creation, and humanity on which we can build our own superstructure? The obvious answer is that, yes, they have managed to form new superstructures, but the challenges of our own day are challenges that the Christian faith has never confronted before. A new creation has occurred in our context, and that new creation demands that its first test should come up against the original contextual story of the faith rather than up against the contexts that succeeded that first one.

Therefore, at the point of such profound and deep fear and anxiety, we begin first with our own context and then we move back to the biblical story itself and read our context through the lens of the biblical story. This approach flies in the face of everything that we have been taught. We are moving the equator of context itself. We have been taught to start not with context but with Scripture and then to move to the tradition of the church and eventually to return to our own context to read it through these other lenses. I am suggesting that we begin first with our own context and that we then look back to Scripture as a means of relocating ourselves in the text before we move on to see what truths we might glean from other eras of the history of the faith. Again, this is what the Christian faith has always done at such moments. It is what Clement and Origen did. It is what Augustine and Aquinas did. It is what John Wesley and William Carey did. It is what Sojourner Truth and Martin Luther King, Jr. did. We must do the same—we must shape and frame a superstructure that is adequate for our own time and that enables the faith to speak to the deepest needs of humanity now.

Perhaps the first official herald of this shift in our own age was offered in the pronouncements of the Second Vatican Council called by Pope John XXIII in 1962. In its conclusions in *Dei Verbum* or *The Word of God*, the council issued the following statement:

> There is a growth in the understanding of the realities and the words which have been handed down. This happens through the contemplation and study made by believers . . . through the intimate understanding of spiritual things they experience . . . . As the centuries succeed one another, the Church constantly moves forward toward the fullness of divine truth until the words of God reach their complete fulfillment in her.[25]

Enzo Bianchi, in his theological analysis of the pronouncements of the council, points out that "if revelation is historical in the full sense of the term, then theology too must be historical . . . it must positively recognize history as a hermeneutical locus for discerning, proclaiming, and narrating the presence of God."[26]

Such an understanding of the work of God in human history represents a seismic shift in our approach to Scripture and to theology. If the church fully understands the way that God works in history, then it ceases to be a fortress protecting the truth that it has received and becomes an interpreter of the mysterious engagement between God and history that leads to new revelations about God's nature and mission in the world. If such a statement can be made about God, then it can certainly be made about Scripture. The church is not called to protect Scripture from erroneous interpretation as much as it is called to faithfully engage in a reading of Scripture through the lens of its culture and context and vice versa.

Certain moments of upheaval in human history like our own demand that we err for a brief time on the side of the former, allowing the age or context to transform our interpretation of the sacred text itself. Perhaps what we are doing in such a moment is simply being honest about what the church has always done at such moments, in much the same way that Augustine allowed his context to dictate his response to cultural upheaval in *The City of God* and Luther allowed it to dictate his response in his *Commentary on Romans*. We are not so much recovering a biblical truth that has been lost to us in the past as we are appropriating a new truth that never would have been available to us without the context that elicits it.

We have now emerged on the other side of the Enlightenment context and the great period of denominational and missionary expansion without a full understanding of the extent to which the Enlightenment context has dictated our boundaries and theological formulations. We embraced the various critical methodologies applied in other areas of study in order to legitimate our own worldview. In the process, we rendered ourselves captive to a practical, enlightened, and wooden interpretation that is inadequate to the context of a post-rational and post-Enlightenment age. It is now up to us to read the Scriptures again through the lens of our new cultural context and to be honest about what we are doing to such an extent that we are able to actualize those Scriptures into becoming the living word of God for us again.

To put it another way, we have yet to complete Segundo's "hermeneutical circle." Our disorientation and dissonance come at the point of the realization of the inadequacy of the superstructure. We know that the prevailing hermeneutical framework is inadequate, but we have failed to this point to achieve a new theological consensus that is adequate to the reality we are experiencing. What we failed to do is to actualize the Scriptures alongside the context in such a way that a new foundation for being Christian and being church in the world can emerge.

The only way this can happen is through a new interpretive framework for our understanding of Scripture "which is dictated by the continuing changes in our present day reality, both individual and social."[27] Old things must pass away and all things must become new. Scripture must be read in light of the context and not vice versa. This must occur for a time and for a season until new meaning emerges that is adequate to the challenges of the day.

It ought to bring some comfort that we have done this repeatedly throughout the history of the church. We Protestants are quite content to talk about how wrong the church was in its interpretation of Scripture prior to the Reformation. We do not feel any need to somehow bring resolution to the theological direction of the church in the Middle Ages. We rail against the power and authority of the papacy in that day. We are quite content to leap over at least one thousand years of church history and the pronouncements of church councils and the writings of church fathers and brand these pronouncements and writings as erroneous. My own tradition, which is that of the Baptists, is even content to reject most of the rest of the history of the church and to justify ourselves as the only true church. We are not alone in this regard—our Church of Christ and Pentecostal siblings are quick to join us in a similar appeal to purity and truth.

The challenge for our day is that we must be as open and creative in our attention to what God is saying to us in our context as Origen was to what God was saying to him in his. We live in a powerful moment that demands the best of creative reflection on the part of the people of God to understand what God is saying in the midst of the cultural reality in which we swim and *outside* the biblical text itself and the inherited tradition of the church. The people of God have never inhabited this particular space in this moment and at this time. It is a space that challenges every doctrinal formulation and every previous contextual reading of Scripture. Reality has shifted for us in a way that is as profound as the reality shift that occurred with the church's appropriation of a Greek philosophical perspective on reality in the first three centuries of Christian history and that has continued to occur as the church has sought to offer a compelling vision across the last two thousand years.

So what is God saying to us in the context of our own culture? Where is God speaking? Where do we find God working in our own day? We cannot answer these questions adequately without first cultivating a spirit of humility within ourselves and the institutions of the church to which we belong. Such a step is not an easy one for a faith that prides itself on offering the answers to the needs and challenges that the world faces. The reality is that the church is often answering questions that the world is not asking. Its only course of action is to admit its failures, engage in the ancient practice of confession, seek God's forgiveness and restoration, listen once again to its context, and then move out into the world with a new vision for a new day.

I love Donald Miller's story in *Blue Like Jazz* about the booth that he and some friends set up during a festival at Reed College in Portland, Oregon.[28] They anticipated that students would engage in a long evening of partying that would include the consumption of all manner of intoxicating substances. Over the door of their booth, they put up a sign that read, "Confessional Booth," and then they sat and waited for anyone who might stop by. The reality of a college party is that people have any number of regrets through the course of the evening, and so, sure enough, one by one students appeared at the door to offer their confessions. Miller and his friends stunned them when they asked if the students would listen to Miller and friends as they confessed the sins of the church. Their long list of such sins included racism, sexism, slavery, violence, and other forms of oppression.

I once shared this story in a sermon at a church that I served as interim pastor. During a luncheon right after the morning worship service, a woman made her way over to my table, her husband trailing along behind her.

Her face was red with fury and she wasted no time getting straight to the point.

"What do you mean by 'the sins of the church'?" she demanded.

I swallowed hard and said, "I mean the racism, sexism, and other forms of hatred that so many churches have engaged in over the centuries."

I thought it might help if I brought some other churches into the mix.

She turned around and around in circles, looking first at her husband and then turning to look back at me. He had nothing to offer except a small shrug of the shoulders.

Finally, with deep frustration, she looked at both of us again and said, "Well, I never!"

Then off she went, her husband again tagging meekly along behind.

Her response reminded me of the response of most churches to such a challenge. We tend to turn around in circles. Confession is never easy for the church in any age.

What is it that we have to confess? First, we must confess our own enslavement to ways of being church and being followers of Jesus Christ that are inadequate to the challenges of our own day. Of course, I don't mean that we have failed completely. In many instances, churches and Christian people have risen to the challenge. We have managed to point beyond ourselves to the world around us. But we have also failed to do so. Our greatest sin has been to view the church itself as the focus of God's mission in the world rather than to understand the church as one primary means of God's accomplishment of that mission and purpose.

Second, we must confess to our failure as the church to pay attention to what God is doing in the world apart from the church and its institutions. We have often not been good partners with civic, governmental, and non-governmental institutions in seeking to transform our communities. Each semester, I send groups of my students into communities and neighborhoods in the metropolitan Atlanta area with a charge to pay attention to what they see God doing in those places. Without exception, the groups return with stories of community gardens and neighborhood associations and fire stations and coffee shops that are accomplishing good in those neighborhoods. Included in that number are some churches, though the number of churches having a direct impact and influence on the neighborhood is generally quite small. The majority of the churches are focused on their own growth as institutions and not on the development or transformation of the neighborhoods in which they reside. Churches rarely partner with each other in such work, much less with nonreligious organizations. The present and future demand partnerships with institutions beyond the church.

Finally, we must confess that, as the church, we often reflect the culture that we inhabit far more than we transform it. The Christian faith should never simply reflect the highest aspirations of its culture; instead, it should call its followers beyond the highest aspirations of its context and toward the attainment of a vision that is superior to anything it could create apart from the selfless love and all-consuming grace that rest at the heart of the gospel of Jesus Christ. To be "good" in the Christian sense of the word is not to be "good" in the cultural sense of the word. To be good in the context of a twenty-first-century world is to utilize the resources and possibilities of that world to transform the entire human community, to bless the families of the earth, and not just to legitimate our own power and authority as the church. It is to rise above nationalism and church-centrism in order to affect the good of the entire creation.

So what is that "good"? Where is God working in the world? How do we as the church of Jesus Christ join God in that good work? How do we partner with others beyond the church to accomplish it? These questions are the primary questions that the church should be asking in the twenty-first century. Moreover, God is working in a number of ways in our communities and in the world, bringing about the transformation of the creation to conform to God's purpose and vision.

First, it is becoming painfully obvious to all of us, including the church, that no single system, whether governmental, religious, or philosophical, can resolve all of the world's challenges because no system is capable of overcoming its own self-interests and inadequacies. This includes even the Christian faith that is composed of sinful human beings who, despite our best efforts, cannot overcome the fact that we "see through a glass darkly" and thus cannot fully comprehend God's intentions and purpose for the world. We can take our best stab at it. We can insist that the Way of Jesus is the best way for the world. But we can never fully grasp that Way, nor can we ever fully embrace it. Always, our human limitations will frustrate our ability to follow Christ's path.

I do not think we have been able to comprehend the extent of this limitation until this moment in history. We have assumed that most people would, upon exposure to our faith, eagerly embrace it. We must now admit that our own inability to live it out according to the dictates of its founder will generally preclude many people in the world from embracing it. We must also admit that, despite our best efforts, we cannot ultimately know the mind and heart of God and thus we must be honest about our inadequacies and accept that other people and systems in the world might offer to us some perspective that will enable us to better understand ourselves and the world. This admission in no way detracts from the reality that the way of Jesus Christ offers hope and grace to all of humanity; it simply admits our own inability to fully grasp that way and to admit our reliance on others to help us toward it.

This admission leads to the second way in which God is working in the world. Despite what we might think, the religious tensions that exist today provide evidence that humanity continues to seek God and tries to make divine sense of its experience. Religions themselves have an opportunity to rise above their differences to celebrate this "hunger and thirst after righteousness." To this point, religions have largely failed to do so. The possibility exists, however, for people of deep religious faith to come together to transform themselves and the wider human family. The major religions of the world, including Christianity, Islam, Judaism, Buddhism, Hinduism, the Chinese philosophies and religions of Taoism and Confucianism, and a host of other religious systems possess at their core and without exception a deep passion for peace and wholeness in the world. It is possible for religions to work together toward the attainment of this vision. To this point, however, we have allowed our differences in theology and practice to circumvent our possibilities.

Patterns of migration have brought religions together in a variety of cultural contexts, including the United States. People of faith are now meeting each other within their communities and neighborhoods. Most of us simply want a good life for ourselves and our children. It is now possible to work across religious lines of division to accomplish this vision and to come to see each other not as objects but rather as people of faith with similar hopes and desires. The Christian faith can contribute to such a possibility by creating within its own fold what Miroslav Volf has called "catholic personalities," or people who are able to see from the perspective of the "other" and to learn to embrace rather than to exclude.[29] How might the church help to create such personalities in its midst?

Third, God is working in the context of the millennial generation who has grown up in a religiously and ethnically diverse world and who are passionate about global transformation. It has been my privilege as a professor for some twenty-five years to watch this generation grow up and to see, firsthand, its potential to achieve a powerful future. It is this generation, primarily, that is calling the church beyond its own walls and challenging its preoccupation with itself. My own children are part of this generation. They grew up in a small southern town in northwest Georgia that appeared at first to be quite monocultural. Yet, in that environment, they learned to celebrate diversity and to get along well with people who were other and different. Each year, we sent a note to school that gave our son permission to celebrate the end of the Ramadan month of fasting with his close friend, a Palestinian Muslim. Their celebration occurred at Chuck E. Cheese's in Atlanta, and it is safe to say that our son eagerly anticipated the event.

Finally, God is working in the midst of the transition from a hier-archical approach to change and transformation to a localized approach to such change and transformation. We are discovering that governments, even local ones, are not always going to have the best interests of a commu-nity at heart and that it is up to local citizens in such communities to be the locus and force for community development. We are learning to form partnerships with other entities in the community and beyond, both reli-gious and civic, to effect change. We are learning the power of advocacy and of such partnership to achieve results that would not otherwise be attainable. In other words, we are learning to work together as communities rather than as individuals and as separate organizations. In the process, we are learning not to reinvent the wheel but to partner in ways that take full advantage of our individual and organizational gifts and assets.

These are some of the ways in which our context is speaking to us and demanding that we reexamine our biblical and theological foundations in order to fashion a vision for the church and for the world that is adequate to sustain us in such a time and place. It is a world in which no single reli-gious, political, or social reality holds sway over all others. It is certainly a day in which the consensuses of the previous era of the Enlightenment and modernity with its assumptions of Western cultural and theological superi-ority are wholly inadequate. It is a day in which we must fashion a religious vision for hope and possibility that lifts us up beyond religious difference and toward the cultivation of "catholic personalities" within the human community. It is a day in which the millennial generation points us toward transformative possibilities. And finally, it is a day in which God is calling us toward new patterns of partnership that are localized and that move us toward the full use of the assets and gifts at our disposal.

The challenge now becomes one of learning to read the biblical text again with this divine action in mind and with a view toward discovering the foundations for a renewed expression of the Christian faith. Indeed, "they've gone and moved the equator." Within the pages of Scripture is a vision that enables the blessing of the families of the earth for our own day in the way that God has intended from the very beginning. We simply need to locate it, claim it for ourselves, and then determine how to embrace it.

Notes

1. Brian D. McLaren, *Everything Must Change: Jesus, Global Crises, and a Revolution of Hope* (Nashville: Thomas Nelson Publishing, 2007), 12.

2. Walter Rauschenbusch, "A Conquering Idea," *The Examiner*, July 31, 1892, reprinted in Winthrop Hudson, *Selected Writings of Walter Rauschenbusch* (Mahwah, NJ: Paulist Press, 1984), 71–72.

3. Rauschenbusch, "A Conquering Idea," in *Selected Writings*, 71–72.

4. Rauschenbusch, "A Conquering Idea," in *Selected Writings*, 72.

5. Saint Augustine, *City of God: An Abridged Version*, trans. Gerald G. Walsh, Demetrius B. Zema, Grace Monahan, and Daniel J. Honan (New York: Bantam Doubleday Dell Publishing, 1958), bk. 15, p. 233.

6. Phyllis Tickle, *The Great Emergence: How Christianity is Changing and Why* (Grand Rapids, MI: Baker Books, 2008), 161.

7. Quoted in Timothy George, *Theology of the Reformers* (Nashville: Broadman Press, 1988), 90.

8. Rauschenbusch, "A Conquering Idea," in *Selected Writings*, 73.

9. Rauschenbusch, "A Conquering Idea," in *Selected Writings*, 73.

10. E. Glenn Hinson, *The Evangelization of the Roman Empire: Identity and Adaptability* (Macon, GA: Mercer University Press, 1981), 283–89.

11. Katia Hetter, "The Golden Days of Air Travel: How Glorious Were They," *CNN Travel*, updated May 26, 2012, http://www.cnn.com/2012/05/25/travel/nostalgia-travel.

12. "New Year's Day 2014 Marks 100 Years of Commercial Aviation," *International Air Transport Association Bulletin*, December 31, 2013, http://www.iata.org/pressroom/pr/Pages/2013-12-30-01.aspx.

13. David Bosch, *Transforming Mission: Paradigm Shifts in Theology of Mission* (Maryknoll, NY: Orbis Books, 1991), 185–87.

14. Tertullian, *Prescription Against Heretics*, http://www.newadvent.org/fathers/0311.htm, chap. 7.

15. Robert J. Daly, S.J., *Origen, Spirit and Fire: A Thematic Anthology of His Writings*, ed. Hans Urs von Balthasar (Washington, DC: Catholic University of America Press, 1984), XVIII.

16. See George M. Marsden, *Fundamentalism and American Culture: The Shaping of Twentieth Century Evangelicalism, 1870–1925* (New York: Oxford University Press, 1980) and Mark A. Noll, *The Scandal of the Evangelical Mind* (Grand Rapids, MI: Eerdmans Publishing, 1984).

17. John Parratt, ed., *An Introduction to Third World Theologies* (Cambridge, UK: Cambridge University Press, 2004), 8.

18. Juan Luis Segundo, *The Liberation of Theology* (Maryknoll, NY: Orbis Books, 1976), 7.

19. This quotation was repeated by many missionaries of the Southern Baptist Convention during my childhood in the Philippines in the 1960s and 1970s as a way to describe their understanding of their primary calling as evangelical missionaries.

20. Stephen Bevans, "From Edinburgh to Edinburgh: Toward a Missiology for a World Church," in *Mission after Christendom: Emergent Themes in Contemporary Mission*, ed. Ogbu U. Kalu, Peter Vethanayagamony, and Edmund Kee-Fook Chia (Louisville, KY: Westminster John Knox Press, 2010), 7. Of the 1,215 delegates to the conference, only 19 came from outside North America, Europe, Australia, or New Zealand, and these 19 were all from Asia.

21. Segundo, *Liberation of Theology*, 9.

22. Jon Ronson, "How One Stupid Tweet Blew Up Justine Sacco's Life," *New York Times Magazine*, February 12, 2015.

23. Segundo, *Liberation of Theology*, 9.

24. Segundo, *Liberation of Theology*, 9.

25. See document *Dei Verbum*, Sec. 8 or p. 8 as quoted in Enzo Bianchi, "The Centrality of the Word of God," in *The Reception of Vatican II*, ed. Giuseppe Alberigo, Jean-Pierre Jossua, and Joseph A. Komonchak, trans. Matthew J. O'Connell (Washington, DC: The Catholic University of America Press, 1988), 124.

26. Bianchi, "The Centrality of the Word of God," 124–25.

27. Segundo, *Liberation of Theology*, 8.

28. Donald Miller, *Blue Like Jazz: Nonreligious Thoughts on Christian Spirituality* (Nashville, TN: Thomas Nelson, 2003), 116–18.

29. Miroslav Volf, *Exclusion and Embrace: A Theological Exploration of Identity, Otherness, and Reconciliation* (Nashville, TN: Abingdon Press, 1996), 30. The entire book is devoted to an exploration of the theological transition from "exclusion" toward the embrace of otherness and difference.

Chapter 3

Mission and the Hebrew Bible

"But the earth will be filled with the knowledge of the glory of the LORD,
as the waters cover the sea."
—The Prophet Habakkuk (2:14)

Like many parents, I dreaded my oldest child's fifteenth birthday and the visit to the local state patrol office to secure her driving permit. I knew it marked a significant transition in our relationship.

I waited nervously as she easily passed her driving test and then extended an open hand into which I dropped the car keys. In a few moments, she pulled out onto a major four-lane highway while I sat nervously in the passenger seat, weak-kneed and white-knuckled, palms sweating, one arm extended toward the dashboard and the other stretched out behind her, ostensibly to assure her of my presence but certainly to be able to grab the wheel if circumstances warranted.

Several miles down the road, I advised her that she needed to move into the right lane to make a turn.

I will never forget her response to my very clear directive.

"We're not going that way, Dad."

That was it. Simple. Direct. Her tone implied that there was little point in arguing. I was going home by a different route; or perhaps I was not going home at all. The equator of my world had shifted. She considered fifteen years of a well-traveled route and decided she might know a better way.

There is something in us that loves a routine—a route that carries us along familiar roads in order to reach our destination. I have already pointed to the routines that have marked the history of the church across the ages.

Those routines are the result of the sacred compromise between text and context that has shaped each age. The challenges and possibilities of a new era demand a shift in the Story, a new way home that makes sense in a different reality. At certain moments, we must embrace the ancient Story of the faith by allowing the cultural context that we inhabit to become the lens through which we read and hear it.

Take the great missionary and denominational age of the church that is just now ending. Sensing the missionary possibilities of the age of exploration, the church repeated a single text across some three centuries of history. Found in Matthew 28:16-20, we call it the Great Commission. Though Jesus certainly said it or something quite like it, he never called it "the Great Commission" and perhaps never intended that we should. Most any evangelical Christian can recite it from memory: "All authority has been given to me in heaven and on earth. Go, and make disciples of all the nations, baptizing them in the name of the Father and the Son and the Holy Spirit, and teaching them to observe all that I have commanded you. And, lo, I am with you always, even until the end of the age." The words leap from the page—Authority. Go. Make. Baptize. Teach.

For more than two centuries, this passage has served as the primary lens through which Euro-tribal churches read the Bible and from which they received their missionary calling. In 1792, a British missionary named William Carey took it as the text for a treatise titled *An Enquiry into the Obligations of Christians to Use Means for the Conversion of the Heathens*. He insisted that the church in his own day had ignored the Great Commission at its own peril and that, as a result, "multitudes sit at ease and give themselves no concern about the far greater part of their fellow sinners, who to this day, are lost in ignorance and idolatry."[1]

Carey went on to suggest a new approach to the evangelization of the world. No one previously had ever imagined the method that he would suggest. For many of us, it now shapes our definition of the mission of the church to such an extent that we have trouble envisioning anything different:

> Suppose a company of serious Christians, ministers and private persons, were to form themselves into a society, and make a number of rules respecting the regulation of the plan, and the persons who are to be employed as missionaries, the means of defraying the expense, &c. &c. This society must consist of persons whose hearts are in the work, men of serious religion, and possessing a spirit of perseverance; there must be a determination not to admit any person who is not of this description, or to retain him longer than he answers to it. From such a society a *committee* might be appointed, whose business it should be to procure

all the information they could upon the subject, to receive contributions, to enquire into the characters, tempers, abilities and religious views of the missionaries, and also to provide them with necessaries for their undertakings.[2]

Carey's approach would become the model for mission on the part of Euro-tribal churches for the next two hundred years. Its shaping influence would result in the creation of denominational mission boards and agencies that would send missionaries into the world to fulfill the Great Commission and to take the gospel of Jesus Christ to the ends of the earth.

The model was successful beyond anyone's imagination. Because of the Western missionary movement that it spawned, Carey's approach would fuel the growth of Protestant Christianity beyond Western Europe and the United States into Africa, Asia, and South and Central America. Protestant missionaries would join Roman Catholic missionaries in the work of global evangelization to the point that Christianity would become the world's largest religion. Robert T. Coote has tracked the growth of career (full-time) missionaries in the Protestant tradition across the twentieth century as the number grew from 1,200 missionaries serving in 1918 to 43,600 serving in 1996, quite possibly the high point of the board/agency approach to global missions that Carey inaugurated.[3]

Even by the mid-1960s, this model was in decline as evidenced by the fact that the number of missionaries serving around the world remained constant between 1965 (34,300) and 1980 (35,600).[4] The previous chapter traced some of the reasons for this stagnation, including the advent of jet travel, which, ironically, enabled congregations to engage more directly in mission in ways that relied less heavily on a constant professional missionary force. The growth of the global church was also a factor as the churches that missionaries had planted across two hundred years gained enough strength to create their own denominations and to train and send their own missionaries. Perhaps most significantly, the cultural entrapment of the Western church within its own prevailing worldview resulted in an overemphasis on human reason and the objectification of people in the process of evangelism. As a result, the moral and spiritual energy that had proven so powerful in the beginning was exhausted.

This exhaustion is nothing new. Every age of the church has experienced it. New realities force the church to reassess the old superstructure put in place at the point of a previous revolution. Once sufficient to the possibilities and challenges, the superstructure crumbles, toppled by foundations that have become worn and unstable. Marcus J. Borg has pointed to the need for a new set of lenses through which to read the Bible in order to bring new life to the stories and truths that it contains. He argues, "What is needed in our time is a way of seeing the Bible that takes seriously the important and legitimate ways in which we differ from our ancestors." He advocates a "way of being Christian that has very little to do with believing" and that emerges from "a relational and sacramental understanding of the Christian life" and a "deepening relationship with the God to whom the Bible points."[5]

This chapter builds on Borg's thesis, advocating a new interpretive and specifically missional lens, a lens that grounds our understanding of the Bible in the cultural context that the church inhabits now rather than the disappearing context of modernity that is sapping its spiritual energy and limiting its participation in God's mission in the world. Such a different reading begins with a critique of the missiological assumptions made under the old lens, namely,

1. that God created the world in order to bring all people to a common belief about God;

2. that God chose Israel as a "light to the nations" that would attract all people toward its particular understanding of God;

3. that Israel failed in this mission and so God sent Jesus Christ into the world to inaugurate the church as God's new "light to the nations";

4. that God now works primarily through the church to bring about God's purposes in the world; and

5. that God's intention is to bring about the individual salvation of human beings so that they can spend eternity with God and each other in heaven.

None of these assumptions is particularly helpful in the new context that has emerged. As the globe shrinks and the various religions and cultures of the world cohabit much of the same space, these assumptions are diametrically opposed to the new interpretive lens that is emerging. We can no longer look past each other. I sense the presence of God in my Muslim friend. I learn from my Korean Christian brother a deep appreciation for my own ancestors whose lives I have not been very good at celebrating. I contemplate in a Hindu temple the possibility that God is much bigger than my own peculiarly American and Western mindset can accept.

Where do these thoughts come from? How am I to make sense of them when the old route that the Christian faith took in the modern world is now fading? Where do I go in the biblical story to make sense of these new attitudes and perspectives? How do I integrate them into my own Christian experience? What have I missed that God is trying to tell me in the biblical story that I cannot see because of my own cultural reality?

The new day demands a robust spiritual energy that reaches back to God's intention and purpose for humanity as expressed in the creation itself and in God's original covenants with humanity found in Genesis 1–12.[6] The thesis of this chapter is that the Great Commission of Jesus in Matthew 28:16-20 was simply commentary on God's divine intentions as expressed in this primeval history, an effort to call the church toward something that had been lost, as much by Israel as by all of humanity. By grounding the new interpretive lens in Genesis 1–12, the chapter then seeks to make sense of the rest of the Hebrew Bible and, in later chapters, of the New Testament.

Both the Hebrew Bible and the New Testament represent particular understandings of the mission of God in the world. Before we consider the biblical text itself, we need to explore the meaning of the word *mission.* Perhaps no other theological word has been as compromised by the modern missionary period of the last two hundred years. We sometimes forget that it is not a biblical word; it first emerged as a diplomatic term referring to a group sent on behalf of a king, queen, or government for an official and particular purpose. Even today, it can refer to diplomatic or military missions or even to space exploration. We talk about the Apollo moon missions or the missions to the space station.

The Jesuits were the first to apply the Latin word *missio* to God's efforts in the world to extend the gospel to those who were not part of the church. Prior to the sixteenth century, Europeans baptized infants into the arms of the church, and so there was no reason to try to convert the unconverted. During the age of exploration, Catholic missions carried a European gospel to the Americas as well as to Africa and Asia, where it had already existed from the earliest centuries of church history. The Protestant missionary movement of the last three centuries only further restricted the word *mission* to the effort to evangelize the world beyond Europe and the United States.

The School of Theology at Mercer University where I serve as a faculty member recently participated in a strategic planning process.[7] We focused considerable time and effort on the difference between the word *mission* and the word *vision.* We reached the conclusion that the word *mission* described our current work as a school and that the word *vision* represented our dreams and aspirations for what we might become in the future. This distinction between *mission* and *vision* is a good place to start in describing God's mission in the world. God's mission is God's work now that moves humanity along toward the vision that God has for creation in the future. Christopher Wright puts it this way: "our mission . . . means our committed participation as God's people, at God's invitation and command, in God's own mission, within the history of God's world for the redemption of God's creation."[8] David Bosch defines *mission* more broadly as "that dimension of our faith that refuses to accept reality as it is and aims at changing it."[9] N. T. Wright goes so far as to connect every good act in the world that seeks to make the world a better place as a missionary act that nurtures God's community on earth.[10]

The book of Genesis offers the best starting point for understanding God's mission in the world now and in light of the challenges and possibilities of this particular moment in history. For centuries, the church has read Genesis 1–12 through a modern lens, one that addresses the goodness of creation, the reality of human sinfulness and divine forgiveness and grace, and the restoration of a covenant between God and humanity. Such a reading misses one of the main points of the primeval history. A single phrase repeats at the beginning and again toward the end of these opening chapters of Scripture, a phrase that has somehow been lost to modern interpreters and particularly to the church's understanding of its mission and calling in the world. The phrase, directed at both humans and animals, brackets the entire primeval history. We hear it first in Genesis 1:22 when God directs the creatures of the sea and the birds of the air to be "fruitful and multiply and fill the waters in the seas" and "multiply on the earth." Later in the same chapter, God commands humanity to do the same thing (Gen 1:28): "Be fruitful and multiply, and fill the earth and subdue it; and have dominion over the fish of the sea and over the birds of the air and over every living thing that moves upon the earth."

The phrase repeats again in Genesis 9:1 and 9:7 at the point of the story of Noah and the flood. Here God makes clear that the original command to be fruitful and multiply continues despite the destruction of all forms of life except for the creatures on the ark. It occurs in its final form in Genesis 11:9, when humanity has refused to disperse after the flood and God confounds the human effort to build the Tower of Babel by "confusing their language" so that they are forced to disperse. This phrase ties the entire primeval history together, connecting God's covenant with humanity at the point of the creation with God's covenant at its re-creation after the flood and with God's covenant with one specific family of the earth, dispersed with other families at the Tower of Babel.

Some commentators have traditionally understood the repetition of the phrase both early and late in this passage to refer to God's frustration with human efforts to be like God, knowing good from evil (in the case of Genesis 1) and arrogantly seeking to reach heaven (in the case of Genesis 11). The Tower of Babel story then becomes God's final punishment of the families of the earth for their disobedience, a story with considerable punishment but little grace.[11] What if an entirely different reading is possible, especially in a day in which humanity has filled the earth? What if the repetition of the phrase signals God's frustration with humanity's refusal to disperse? It then becomes a story of divine grace by which God drives human families away from each other to accomplish some greater good. It demonstrates that deeply embedded in God's mission in the world is a particular kind of blessing that emerges out of the diversity of human cultures as those cultures "bless" each other with their various perspectives and understandings of God, creation, humanity, and life. Such an interpretation seems valid in light of the fact that God issued the command in the very first creation story.

Nancy deClaisse-Walford argues for just such an interpretation, insisting that "Genesis 11 indicates that God does not want all of humankind to share the same life experiences, to speak the same language, to begin and end in the same place, to be mirror images of one another. If we do not, cannot, will not acknowledge our differences and live and work together in our diversity, then we commit the same sin of fear as the original 'tower-builders.'"[12] To put it differently, God's intention from the beginning has been exactly the sort of multicultural world that we now inhabit. Human families, tribes, and cultures that once had very little contact with each other are now colliding or colluding. Technological developments, especially in transportation and communication, have resulted in significant tension and conflict on the one hand and unbelievable possibility for human achievement on the other.

So is there a way to read the biblical text that offers purpose and meaning for this new world—or, to put it another way, to discover an understanding of the biblical story that can serve as the foundation for a new superstructure adequate to the challenges and opportunities of this new day? Consider the following as an interpretive lens that could empower God's people in a day in which the various families of the earth encounter each other constantly, bringing with them the various cultural perspectives and worldviews that God intends as sources of mutual blessing:

1. that God called humanity to be fruitful, multiply, and fill the earth because the diversity of human cultures, religions, languages, and perspectives was part of God's design from the creation;

2. that God blessed all families of the earth and intended for those families to become blessings to each other;

3. that humanity refused to fulfill this calling, clinging tightly together and maintaining a single perspective and worldview;

4. that God intended for Israel and later the church to help all families of the earth grasp the reality of their unique blessing, purpose, and perspective on God, creation, and humanity;

5. that the life and ministry of Jesus, including his death and resurrection, beckoned humanity toward the full embrace of otherness and difference through forgiveness and the healing of broken relationships; and

6. that each family now brings to the common table an understanding of God that would be impossible for other families to grasp without its particular presence at the table.

This new reading of the biblical story assumes that the admonition to "be fruitful, multiply, and fill the earth" is not simply a reference to procreation, to the distinction between animal and human life, to such inanimate objects as the sun, moon, and stars, or to God's desire to populate the earth. The command to "be fruitful, multiply, and fill the earth" is an interpretive lens or key that unlocks God's intention and purpose for all of humanity. Two stories, closely connected in Genesis 11 and 12, reveal the significance of the phrase when read in light of our current global and cultural context. The first story recounts the tale of the Tower of Babel. The second is the story of the call of Abram, the father of Israel and of a multitude of other families of the earth.

Genesis 11:1-9: The Tower of Babel

The Tower of Babel story in Genesis 11 begins with the assertion that "the whole earth had one language and the same words" (11:1). At first glance, this statement seems to contradict earlier statements in Genesis when, immediately after the flood, the descendants of Shem, Ham, and Japheth separated to various parts of the earth "by their families, their languages, their lands, and their nations" (10:5; 10:20; 10:31). Bill Arnold has suggested that Genesis 10 "seems more naturally to follow the Tower of Babel episode as effect follows cause." He concludes that the events are intentionally arranged non-sequentially in order to highlight a "spread of sin, spread of grace" theme throughout Genesis 1–11.[13]

Another explanation is also possible. After the flood, human beings follow only one part of God's command. They become fruitful and multiply, but they do not "fill the earth." Instead, they migrate together "with one language and the same words" (Gen 11:1). Journeying from the East, they happen upon the plain of Shinar, located in southern Mesopotamia, and decide to settle there and build themselves a city "and a tower with its top in the heavens" (11:4). The reference is clear to Jewish readers of the Genesis story who lived in exile in Babylon in the sixth century BCE at the point when the Torah or Law took its final written form. The city is Babylon and the tower is probably the Temple of Marduk.[14] This city and this temple had led the people of Israel and Judah to reflect differently upon the meaning of their own primeval history.

In the Tower of Babel story, human beings appear to have two motivations. First, they want to "make a name" for themselves, creating something like a single empire from which they will be able to rule the earth as a single entity or nation. The reference is most likely to the empire of Babylon and the expression of hope for judgment against it, but it is also a call for various families or nations of the earth to live peacefully apart from each other. Second, human beings appear fearful of separation from one another and being "scattered abroad upon the face of the whole earth" (11:4).

Such fear is understandable. Emergence mythologies of various tribal groups connect closely to a particular place. Such geographical features as a mountain and a river mark that space, and the space becomes the land or place of that particular people. To leave the center of that space is to journey into the unknown where danger lurks and the existence of a people is threatened. This scenario is exactly what occurred for Israel when Babylon carted it off into exile. Here the emergence mythology of humanity in the Jewish story contains within it the seeds of a similar fear. These early human families desire to stay together to protect themselves and to make their name great.

God has other plans for humanity. God is not happy that the group remains together after the flood. God comes down to see the city and the tower and concludes that since "they are one people, and they have all one language . . . nothing that they propose to do will now be impossible for them" (11:6). God has lost patience with the human propensity to hang together. This tendency obviously frustrates something inherent in God's vision for humanity. Human beings have refused to "fill the earth," so God flings them out from their shared space "over the face of the earth" by confusing their speech and driving them away from each other (11:7-8).

The focus on language in this passage offers some insight into God's intentions for humanity. The relationship between language and culture is fiercely debated. Franz Boas, a great American linguist, believed that culture shaped language.[15] Edward Sapir has argued for the very opposite, what he calls linguistic determinism, asserting that "human beings . . . are very much at the mercy of the particular language which has become the medium of expression for their society . . . the 'real world' is to a large extent unconsciously built up on the language habits of the group."[16] Intimately connected, language and culture influence one another, even if the relative weight of one upon the other is the subject of debate.

With this in mind, the dispersion of people to the various parts of the earth and the confusion of languages were essential steps for the emergence of human cultures. Apart from such dispersion and confusion, human culture would have remained monolithic, as would the emergence of a full understanding of God and God's purposes in the creation. A single human culture possesses only a limited understanding of the divine. That limited understanding is shaped and formed by the particular location of the culture—near the ocean, for example, where the experience of the divine is shaped by such nautical references as "safe harbor" or "raging seas," or in the desert where the references would be to "an oasis" or to a "deep thirst." The historical experiences of the group as oppressors of other cultures or as an oppressed people also shapes its understanding. The group's identity as hunters or gatherers, matriarchal or patriarchal, and a host of other shaping influences determines that group's culture. In other words, a Sub-Saharan perspective on God, humanity, or the creation received in the context of Nigerian history, dialects, and worldview is radically different from a Southeast Asian perspective shaped by Indonesian history, dialects, and worldview.

Is it such a leap to consider the possibility that cultural difference was God's intention from the very beginning? In other words, God created human beings and animals with the intention that they would "be fruitful and multiply and fill the earth" so that at some point in the distant future their various perspectives on the divine, the creation, and even humanity itself would have a shaping influence on each other. God knew that the only means by which human beings could understand God's highest purposes and intention for the creation would be through the lens of cultural diversity as various families of the earth shared their perspectives and learned from each other.

In what other way can we possibly interpret the existence of the repeated phrase, "be fruitful, multiply, and fill the earth"? God's intention cannot simply be human and animal reproduction. God had some deeper purpose in mind. God had encouraged human beings and animals from the beginning to fill the earth. God's creatures failed to obey the command, so finally God does the dispersing. God emerges as the source of the variety of human languages and dialects. God says, "Come, let us go down, and confuse their language there, so that they will not understand one another's speech" (11:7). This action by God reminds me of something my own mother used to say to my brother and me when we refused to heed her call to quit fighting with each other. From the top of the stairs we would hear her say, "Don't make me come down there and put the two of you in your separate corners." In the end, God has to come down and send humanity to its separate corners.

Genesis 11:10-26 comes immediately after the Babel story and contains the ancestry of Abram, the father of Israel, through the line of Noah's son, Shem. This text is a bridge between the primeval history of Genesis 1–11 and the history of Israel that will be the focus of the rest of the Hebrew Bible. It links both the past and the future. It links the story of Abram back to the creation and forward into the history of Israel. Jesus, Paul, and others will eventually connect the call of Abram and the history of Israel to the identity and nature of Jesus and the mission and calling of the church. This reality makes Genesis 11 and 12 the most significant passages in either the Hebrew Bible or the New Testament, particularly in an age of cultural diversity and the constant interaction between families of the earth. Genesis 11 describes God's ultimate accomplishment of God's original calling to humanity to "be fruitful, multiply, and fill the earth." Genesis 12 provides the first clue to how God intends to bless humanity in light of its recent dispersion.

Genesis 12:1-4: The Call of Abram

The call of Abram in Genesis 12 is a central story to the three great religions of Judaism, Christianity, and Islam, all of whom claim the calling of Abram as foundational to their own religious identity. Judaism understands Abraham to be the father of Israel and the source of God's covenant with Israel. Jesus and Paul view Abraham as the central figure in Jewish history through whom God would bless the nations of the world. Islam claims Abraham as the one who restored the worship of the one true God and who rebuilt the first place where Adam and Eve worshiped God after they left the garden of Eden.

For now, let us focus on the understanding of Abraham in the Jewish and Christian faiths. If we are to understand Jesus' particular purpose, then we have to understand his motivations as a Jewish person as opposed to the meaning of his life for Christianity and the church. The call of Abram in Genesis 12:1-4 served as Israel's justification for its own existence and mission in the world:

> Now the LORD said to Abram, "Go from your country and your kindred and your father's house to the land that I will show you. I will make of you a great nation, and I will bless you, and make your name great, so that you will be a blessing. I will bless those who bless you, and the one

who curses you I will curse; and in you all the families of the earth shall
be blessed."

If we are to fashion a superstructure that is adequate for the new challenges
that confront us today, then this new superstructure demands, indeed
requires, a robust spiritual energy that reaches back to this original covenant with Abram. Instead of viewing the Great Commission of Jesus in
Matthew 28:16-20 as the central mission of the church, perhaps we should
understand it as simple commentary on the call of Abram in Genesis 12
and a reminder to Israel and later to the church of God's original intention
to bless the families of the earth.

John Stott, the great twentieth-century missiologist, argued in his 1975
Chavasse Lectures in Wycliffe Hall at Oxford University that sometimes we
neglect Jesus' dependence on his Jewish spiritual heritage with our overemphasis on the Great Commission. Stott insisted that

> We should not regard this as the only instruction that Jesus left us. He
> also quoted Leviticus 19:18, "You shall love your neighbor as yourself"
> (Matthew 22:39), called it the second and great commandment (second
> in importance only to the supreme command to love God with all our
> being), and elaborated on it in the Sermon on the Mount. There he
> insisted that in God's vocabulary our neighbor includes our enemy and
> that to love means to "do good," that is, to give ourselves actively and
> constructively to serve our neighbor's welfare.[17]

The implication then is that the Jewish understanding of the mission of
Israel and of the love of God and neighbor grounds Jesus' perspective on
his own mission in the world. Jesus is offering Midrash or commentary
on the calling of Israel in the Hebrew Bible by citing the Law in Leviticus
that guided the people of Israel in their relationships with each other and
with strangers or foreigners. Rather than calling his followers to a different
religion or faith, he is calling them back to a renewed perspective on the
mission of Israel itself, something that has been lost that Jesus is determined
to expose. As David Bosch points out, "[Jesus] understands himself as being
sent to his own people. His call for repentance concerns this people . . . .
He devotes himself to Israel with unconditional devotion while declining
every other solicitation."[18]

Jesus expresses this understanding on at least two occasions in the
Gospels. In Matthew 10:5-7, Jesus sends the twelve disciples out with the
following instructions: "Go nowhere among the Gentiles, and enter no
town of the Samaritans, but go rather to the lost sheep of the house of
Israel. As you go, proclaim the good news, 'The kingdom of heaven has

come near.'" In Matthew 15 and Mark 7, a Canaanite woman approaches him and asks him to heal her daughter. In Matthew's account, the disciples tell him to send her away and he seems more than willing to heed their advice. He insists, perhaps to himself as much as to them, that he "was sent only to the lost sheep of the house of Israel" (Matt 15:24) and not to the Gentiles. In Mark's Gospel, he responds, "The children [implying the children of Israel] should be fed first, for it is not fair to take the children's food and throw it to the dogs" (Mark 7:27).

These passages make clear Jesus' own self-understanding. His purpose or mission in the world emerges directly from the mission of Israel. He is calling Israel back to its original purpose, much like the prophets of Israel and Judah. His work among the Gentiles seems much more in line with the calling of the Law and the prophets to love the stranger and the foreigner than it does with embracing the stranger and the foreigner into a new faith intended to supersede the faith of Israel.

The calling of Abram and his family by God certainly seems to elevate one particular family of the earth above all the other families and raises questions about God's intentions. The implication seems to be that what God started with Adam and Eve and then with Noah, God now will continue with a single man and his family who will become the seed of righteousness or yeast within all of humanity. Is it possible that Jesus is attempting to correct this particular interpretive understanding? Could he be calling Israel to a different perspective on its own history and calling?

Abram's family lived in Ur of the Chaldees, a Sumerian city-state near the mouth of the Euphrates River at the Persian Gulf. It was far south of Babylon but part of the Babylonian empire at the point of the Jewish exile there in the sixth century, so no Jewish reader of Genesis would miss the point that Abram and his family resided in what would eventually become part of that empire.

The genealogy of Abram in Genesis 11 says that Abram's father Terah determined that his son Abram and his grandson Lot, together with their families, should migrate from Ur to Canaan. Following the path of the Fertile Crescent and likely in search of adequate farmland, Terah and his son and grandson reached Haran in what is now southern Turkey, and there they settled for a time. In the context of the biblical story, we might read this migration as part of the Tower of Babel narrative. It is here that God called Abram in a unique and unexpected way. Thomas Cahill in *The Gift of the Jews* says that without the call of Abram and the history of the Jewish people, "we would see the world through different eyes, hear with different ears, even feel with different feelings . . . . The screen through which we view the world would be different."[19]

Cahill's perspective is that humanity viewed the world in a cyclical fashion before the Jewish people emerged on the scene. The idea that Abram would leave his father's place and the cycle of family and tribe resulted in an emerging linear view of human life and history. The phrase "so Abraham went" represents the emergence of a radically different understanding of the arena of God as a historical arena in which the intentions and purposes of the God of Israel somehow connected to all of humanity. God simply spoke to Abram and Abram did as God commanded: "Go from your country and your kindred and your father's house to the land that I will show you" (Gen 12:1). Abram left his place because of a universal calling and responsibility to all of humanity and not simply for the blessing of his own family and tribe. He became an example of God's grace to all families of the earth who, by virtue of his example, would recognize and affirm their own divine blessing. He represents God's blessing of all earthly families. God makes this clear in Genesis 17:3 when he clarifies his covenant lest Abram and Israel interpret it as a covenant with a single family of the earth: "You shall be the ancestor of *a multitude of nations*. I will make you exceedingly fruitful; and *I will make nations of you, and kings shall come from you*" (italics mine).

Abram's calling was then both a particular and a universal calling. He was to leave his particular country and his kindred and his father's house and go to the land that God would show to him. Walter Brueggemann points out that "Land is a central, if not *the central theme* of biblical faith. Biblical faith is a pursuit of historical belonging that includes a sense of destiny derived from such belonging."[20] God's promise was that God would make of Abram "a great nation, and I will bless you and make your name great, so that you will be a blessing" even as God promised to make Abram the ancestor of a "multitude of nations." God also assures Abram of God's protection, perhaps hoping to encourage Abram beyond the fear of dispersion that had plagued humanity at the tower: "I will bless those who bless you," he says. "And the one who curses you I will curse" (12:3).

God ends with a very unusual phrase, one that has challenged biblical translators for centuries: "And in you all the families of the earth shall be blessed" (12:4). Most biblical translators have translated the passage in this way, though this is not quite what the text says. The text is much more ambiguous and in ways that are quite significant. The word "blessing" in Genesis 12:3 comes from the Hebrew word *barak*, and it occurs here in its Niphal or passive form as it also does in Genesis 18:18 and 28:14, both times in reference to the promise to Abraham. It occurs nowhere else in Scripture in this passive form. This small sample makes it quite difficult to determine the exact meaning of the Niphal form. Elsewhere the Hithpael form of *barak* is used, and the meaning is much clearer.[21]

Two traditions of translations of Genesis 12:3 have emerged because of this textual ambiguity. The first is the traditional one: "in you all the families of the earth shall be blessed."[22] This translation carries with it the implication that the blessing begins with Abram and extends from him to all the families of the earth. Such a translation implies that Abram and his descendants are the source or conduit of the blessing of God to the families of the earth even though it does not say this explicitly. The second translation tradition conveys a different subtlety of meaning: "All the families of the earth shall bless themselves by you" or some variant of this particular phrasing.[23]

The difference between the two translations, though slight, is significant. In the traditional translation, Israel is the source of the blessing. Without Israel, the families of the earth appear to be without blessing and thus devoid of hope. In the second and more literal translation, the families of the earth are themselves the source of their own blessings, with Israel functioning as an example of what can happen as these families realize their own blessing and embrace it. Israel certainly plays a role in the blessing of the families of the earth, but the exact nature of the role is somewhat ambiguous and the participation of other families in their own blessing is elevated. James Okoye posits that the shift from the second and more literal understanding to the first and more traditional perspective occurred "with the growth of universalism after the exile."[24] In other words, Israel's perception on its role in God's mission in the world transitioned from a narrow and rigid nationalism that ensured self-preservation and toward a more universalistic understanding in the context of the exile.

I often ask students to talk about the differences between the two translations and to explore the nuances and subtleties that exist within each one. They interpret the traditional translation as one that empowers Israel. Israel is the conduit of God's blessing of the families of the earth, chosen because humanity in general was incapable of living righteously and so God needed a single family or tribe who could live righteously and who could then call others toward holiness and purity in the context of life. In the second translation, Israel is simply one among the families of the earth, all of whom have been blessed by God and all of whom have a calling to recognize and affirm that blessing and to respond to it in a divine covenant unique to them in which they "bless themselves" by Israel. Israel is an example of the blessing of God extended to all the families of the earth; but its blessing is not unique. All families of the earth are blessed.

How does the grand biblical story shift in light of this new reading? It means that God calls and blesses all families of the earth and not just Israel. No single family is elevated above any other family. Such a perspective is very much in line with the words of the prophet Amos in Amos 9:7: "Are you not like the Ethiopians to me, O people of Israel? says the LORD. Did I not bring Israel up from the land of Egypt, and the Philistines from Caphtor and the Arameans from Kir?" Israel is just one among the families of the earth, all of whom God has called and blessed and each of which possesses its own language and culture and a particular perspective on God and the world that is its unique blessing or gift.

So then why does Israel's call and blessing receive such a prominent place in the biblical story? Rather than viewing Israel as the source of God's blessing of the families of the earth, we should understand Israel as one family of the earth that God calls to live in covenant with God in the context of its own cultural reality. In this way, it becomes an example of what covenantal relationship with God means for other human families when they enter into their own covenant with God. God is not calling the families of the earth to become like Israel; rather, God is calling the families of the earth to enter into covenant with God out of the context of their own cultural perspectives and uniqueness.

This perspective on the text helps to connect God's admonition to "be fruitful and multiply and fill the earth" with God's decision to call and bless Israel through Abram. God's intention is not that all the families of the earth will become like Israel. This would violate God's admonition to humanity to spread itself out over the face of the earth by calling the families of the earth to enter into the same covenant with God as Israel has entered. Why would God call for such a dispersion if God's ultimate purpose is to make everyone the same? The point of the dispersion over the face of the earth is the opposite. God desires for all human families to find their own space in the world, nurture their own particular cultures, languages, and religions, and, eventually, enter into mutual blessing of each other. Israel simply serves as a microcosm of what God intends to do with every human family.

This is exactly what God does with Israel. During the period of the matriarchs and patriarchs, Israel inhabits the land that God has given to it, its own particular place. That land becomes sacred to the people of Israel by virtue of the experiences of their ancestors, Abraham and Sarah, Isaac and Rebekah, Jacob and Rachel and Leah. The sacred space is marked. The boundaries are set. Altars are built. The ancestors become examples of faithfulness to the covenant of God with Abraham or examples of disobedience to that covenant. The story of ancient Israel then is very much like the story of any human family. Space is a divine gift. The ancestors become the source of the family's culture and language. The land is a safe place for the tribe. To live in the land is to inhabit the happy space of comfort and security. To leave the land is to enter into strangeness, otherness, and difference where danger lurks and the people are no longer safe.

Ellen Davis makes the powerful point that "The Bible as we have it could not have been written beside the irrigation canals of Babylon, or the perennially flooding Nile, any more than it could have emerged from the vast fertile plains of the North American continent."[25] It is a localized story, grounded in the land variously known as Israel, Palestine, or Canaan. For this reason, it is rooted in a particular language, worldview, and location.

The Joseph narratives toward the end of Genesis document what happens when the people leave their space and, in the process, encounter the languages and worldviews of other families of the earth. Sold into slavery in Egypt, Joseph becomes a hero when he is able to provide for his family during a time of famine. His provision for them, however, results in their eventual enslavement in Egypt when a pharaoh comes along who "did not know Joseph" (Exod 1:8). What happens to Israel in Egypt is what happens to any family of the earth forced from its particular space, the space given to it (at least in a mythological fashion) when God dispersed human families to the ends of the earth. Powerless outside its own space, the Israelites become slaves of the Egyptians. Here Moses enters the picture as the savior of Israel who will lead his people back to the particular land that belongs to them.

The story of Moses and of the exodus of Israel from Egypt is a twofold story that documents a forty-year period of wandering in which the particular culture, worldview, and perspective of Israel is forged in the wilderness. After this, Israel enters once again into the land God had promised to it. In the wilderness, Moses receives the Law of the Jewish people that is to guide the people in their relationship with God and with each other. It is a uniquely Jewish Law, intended to enable the people of Israel to live in peace or shalom with one another and with other families of the earth.

The story of Israel is then an archetypal story. All families of the earth share similar stories about their emergence as a people, the land or space that they inhabit, and the challenges and obstacles that they have overcome. Embedded in these stories is the cultural grounding, purpose, and calling that gives meaning to each particular family. The challenge is to find the point of intersection between the story of the family as expressed in its mythological framework and the intentions and purposes of God in the world. The story of ancient Israel offers one powerful example of the way in which the mythological framework and the work of God in the world connect.

Israel's story was never intended to be a story for other families of the earth to embrace. When other peoples have embraced it, the result has been the usurpation of Israel's story and the aggrandizement of another family. The United States possesses a powerful mythology taken from the stories of ancient Israel. Early Puritan settlers in New England believed themselves to be "marked and chosen by the finger of God."[26] They viewed themselves as the New Israel with a mandate or divine errand to carry the gospel to the world. The twin mythologies of chosen people and the national errand eventually became justifications for the institutionalization of White and male privilege and for the creation of an empire that forced people into its own image rather than nurturing the kind of diversity that God intended. The history of the United States is a history of one people after another forcibly insisting on their right to be included among the Chosen People of the nation—first Jews, then Catholics, then women, then Black Americans . . . on and on the story goes. Chosen people do not willingly expand the boundaries of their own chosenness.

The usurpation of the story of the Jewish people to fashion a mythology for the American colonies and later for the United States was a brilliant strategy for a people who possessed no real claim to the land or a common tribal story that could give meaning and purpose to their claims or to their existence as a people.[27] Seizing upon the Jewish story, they laid claim to the North American continent and embraced the grand story of the conquest of Canaan to give legitimacy to their own aspirations. Devoid of a story, they seized upon the Jewish story and thus claimed divine blessing for themselves and their descendants.

One of the great missiological errors of Euro-tribal churches during the age of mission advance over the last two to three hundred years has been to assume that the story of Israel was the story that every human family needed to embrace over and beyond its own particular story. Embedded deeply in this assumption was the conviction that the story of Israel was the story of the Western or White church that had usurped Israel's place. To become a follower of Christ was to embrace the notion of White superiority or chosenness and to minimize one's own cultural story by substituting the Western or White story in its place.

Some of the most successful efforts to communicate the Christian faith beyond the West, however, have been efforts that connected not so much to the story of Israel as to the emergence mythologies and cosmologies of particular family and cultural groups. For example, in early 2019, I visited the Mae La refugee camp in central Thailand, located on the

Thai-Myanmar border. The camp has been the home of as many as 50,000 refugees from Myanmar since 1984 when it was established. Ninety percent of its population are Karen people, a tribal group in southern Burma who have generally refused to accept the authority of the Myanmar government and who are seeking self-rule. The Myanmar military responded with ethnic persecution, burning Karen villages repeatedly and engaging in the brutal destruction of homes and property. At first, Karen villagers fled their villages and attempted to wait out the persecution, but the need to provide education for their children and to sustain themselves eventually led many of them to flee into refugee camps in Thailand.

The Karen people are primarily Buddhists or animists, but about thirty percent of them are also Christian and Baptist. The evangelization of the tribe began in the late 1820s when US missionaries George and Sarah Boardman and Adoniram Judson settled in southern Burma near Moulmain and Savoy. Their evangelistic efforts proved quite effective, primarily because the first Karen convert, a man named Ko Thah-byu, recognized a connection between Karen tribal stories and the Christian faith, especially the story of the creation in Genesis. Here is the story of humanity recounted in the oral tradition of the Karen people:

> Y'wa formed the world originally,
> He appointed food and drink.
> He appointed the "fruit of trial."
> He gave detailed orders.
> Mu-kaw-lee deceived two persons.
> He caused them to eat the fruit of the tree of trial.
> They obeyed not; they believed not Y'wa.
> When they ate the fruit of trial,
> They became subject to sickness, aging, and death.[28]

The Karen people believed that the Karen language and many of their tribal stories had been lost when a younger brother, a White man, stole a golden book from the tribe. Karen legends said that, one day, the White brother would return with the lost book. Ko Thah-byu converted to the Christian faith because of his belief that either Boardman or Judson was that White younger brother and that the golden book was the Bible that would explain how the people could return to Y'wa and restore the tribe to its Creator. Because of Ko Thah-byu's realization and his work with Judson and Boardman in translating the Bible into the Karen language and evangelizing the tribe, thousands of Karen people embraced the Christian faith.

During my interviews with Karen teachers at the Kawthoolei-Karen Baptist Bible School and College, the power of this connection between the Karen people and the Christian faith was evident. Several recounted the harrowing stories of the destruction of their villages, their efforts to survive in the aftermath of that destruction, and their own commitment to pursuing graduate-level study in theology in Nagaland in India, an education that required a difficult two- to four-week journey back and forth across Burma. The Bible School now serves the purpose of educating Karen ministers for Karen congregations.

In 2006, some nine countries of the world agreed to take Karen refugees from Mae La and other camps in an effort to provide them with stable lives and a means by which to make a living for themselves and their families. Christians among the Karen viewed this resettlement as God's way of enabling them to fulfill the Great Commission of Jesus in Matthew 28:16-20. Since leaving Mae La and other camps, they have joined congregations in places like the United States with the firm conviction that their calling is to share the gospel with the world. In the process, they have reinvigorated US congregations by insisting on worshiping together with their host churches.

I share the story of the Karen here because it is a story with so many parallels to the story of the call of Abram. The Karen people are convinced that God will bless them and make of them a great nation in much the same way that God intended to bless ancient Israel. They also understand themselves to be one of the families of the earth dispersed by God at the point of the building of the Tower of Babel. Through Abram, they have "blessed themselves" by embracing their own tribal stories, discovering points of connection between their stories and the biblical stories, and seizing upon the opportunity to share the gospel beyond their own place and people. They too have experienced a period of forced exile or wandering in the wilderness. They too seek their own restoration to the land that they believe God provided for them in Burma. Their story is the same archetypal story as that of ancient Israel.

The story of the Karen people provides an example of one way in which a single family of the earth "blessed themselves" by Abram. In Israel they found legitimacy for their own emergence story, but it is significant that they did not replace their own story with the story of Israel. Instead, they embraced God because of the affinity between their own stories and the biblical story. In Abraham and Israel, they found a similar story of God's promises to another family of the earth, God's provision for that family over the course of its history, and the devastating results that occurred when that family broke covenant with God. Israel's story legitimates their own story but does not replace their story. Now they are blessing other families of the earth in a significant way because of their own global resettlement.

The history of Christian mission might be quite different if other families of the earth had discovered similar connections between their own stories and the biblical story and had received nurture and encouragement toward the integration of the two stories. While this certainly did happen on occasion, the traditional approach in Western or White missiology has been to make the story of Israel the substitute story for the cosmological stories of the various families of the earth. Israel becomes the source of blessing rather than the example of blessing. Its stories become the only legitimate stories of the creation of the universe, the emergence of humanity, the origins of evil, and the general cosmology that makes sense of the world. In this sense, it remains a foreign story and in the process fails to offer space for the stories of the other families of the earth to receive validation.

The only means by which all human families can be afforded a legitimate place of blessing within the Judeo-Christian tradition is for their stories to remain their stories, their worldviews and cultures to remain their worldviews and cultures, and their perspectives on God and ultimate reality to find some means of expression within the full human story. This process would enable all families of the earth to bless each other by virtue of their own unique perspectives on the divine.

This reading of the Genesis story and of the call of Abram and of Israel is possible only if Israel is understood to be a representative human family very much like any other human family whom God gifts in particular ways that will bless other families of the earth. Israel is not to be elevated above other families. Israel's story exists as a representative story that documents God's intentions for partnership and covenant with other human families. Israel's particular gifts to the rest of humanity include the gift of a linear perspective on history, a willingness to wrestle with God over God's intentions and purposes in the world, and the conviction that God has an ultimate purpose in mind for the creation. In addition, the idea of shalom or wholeness as a way of experiencing life together as a human family provides a model for other families of the earth. The relationship between God and Israel is a model, though not the only model, for how other human families might embrace the Creator of the universe and enter into covenant with God. The covenant of God with Israel is a model for covenant as opposed to the only possible covenant. For this reason, Abram is a representative father whose faith and response to God's call models the possibilities for all human families. In this way, he becomes the father of "a multitude of nations."

Israel is called to be a community of shalom where human relationships are just and whole and in which all members of the family can achieve their full human potential. The Law of Israel given by God through Moses guides Israel in its communal relationships to God, to each other, and to other families of the earth. The prophets of Israel and Judah reminded the people of their commitments even as they railed against the injustices that broke that covenant. Jesus stands in the prophetic tradition as one who reminds Israel of its own mission and purpose even as he looks beyond Israel to reveal to all human families God's original intention for the creation.

The story of the people of Israel in the Hebrew Bible serves as one example of the way in which a particular human family wrestled with its own history, culture, and worldview in order to understand God more fully. It is also the story of how God reminded Israel repeatedly of its obligation to bless other families of the earth and to receive the blessings offered to it by those families. In other words, God always intended for Israel to learn something about God from beyond its own history and experience and not to assume the priority of its own stories and perspective. For this reason, the Hebrew Bible contains a powerful subtext, one that documents the blessing that other families of the earth extended to Israel and the unique insights on God that Israel experienced because of those encounters.

Across the centuries, the church has often ignored the subtext, as a powerful Euro-tribal understanding of the role of Israel in God's plan for the families of the earth has been the chief interpretive lens. The primary focus has been on the role of Israel as God's chosen people and, later, on the role of the New Israel, a Euro-tribal church that usurped Israel's place to legitimize its own authority and elevated role in God's mission in the world. In the process, that Euro-tribal church ignored the subtext of God's blessing of Israel through other families of the earth. Now the greatest theological and missiological challenge for Euro-tribal churches is an inadequate theology of otherness and difference that prevents a full understanding of God's mission in the world because it often refuses to receive or acknowledge the blessings extended to it by families of other religions, worldviews, and cultures. Unfortunately, in its own mission methodologies over the last three centuries, it extended this inadequate theology of otherness and difference around the world. The first step toward a recovery of openness to other worldviews and perspectives is to read the Hebrew Bible in a way that allows the subtext of the engagement with otherness and difference to take center stage.

The Psalms

Any exploration of the relationship between Israel and other families of the earth would be incomplete without consideration of the book of Psalms, the songbook of ancient Israel. The Psalter offers one of the most powerful connections between the mission of God in the world, the mission of Israel, and the mission and blessing of the nations of the earth in relationship to the mission of God. Nancy deClaisse-Walford points to the role of the Psalter as one element that assisted Israel to survive in the postexilic period: "Israel found a way to shape its poetry and prose . . . into a meaningful story of identity. And, with that Story, the Israelites were (and are) able to remain the people of God in the midst of the changing world of which they found (and find) themselves a part."[29] In similar fashion, the Psalms have provided for the Christian faith an intrinsic link to the mission of God in the world and the responsibility of the church to the families of the earth under the banner of that mission.

Like Genesis 1–12, the Psalms offer a universal perspective on the nature of God's relationship with all people, a relationship that is not restricted only to Israel. In the Psalms, the God who called Abram and promised to make of Abram a great nation calls all nations into relationship with God. Psalm 22:27-28 establishes this reality clearly and without insisting on a particular role for Israel: "All the ends of the earth shall remember and turn to the LORD; and all the families of the nations shall worship before him. For dominion belongs to the LORD, and he rules over all the nations."

Repeatedly throughout Psalms, the reality of God's rule on earth encompasses not just Israel but all the nations. According to Mark J. Boda, several psalms document this reality, including Psalms 46, 47, 72, 82, 97, and 113.[30] Boda points to four ways in which God's rule over the earth is displayed in Psalms: God's defeat of nations in battle, God's work of justice in the world, God's handiwork revealed in the creation, and the rule of God's anointed one over all the earth.[31]

The tradition in Jewish and Christian interpretation of Psalms has been to associate God's anointed one who will rule over all the earth and the place of the anointed one's reign in Zion as inextricably linked to Israel. The anointed one "reigns from Zion." His kingship is associated with Israel and thus directly linked to this particular family of the earth as the family from which God's intentions and purposes for the world will emerge. What if God's anointed one, however, is identified with Israel simply because it is Israel who is telling the story of God's intentions for the nations of the earth? For Israel, Zion is the center of Israel's faith and of its religious and political life. For this reason, it would serve as the source for the global community of shalom that God desires and intends.

But all families of the earth desire the same sort of peace and justice that Israel seeks. Psalm 72 describes the hope of Israel for what might be possible when the anointed one appears on the scene. They hope for a king who would "judge your people with righteousness and your poor with justice" (72:2), "defend the cause of the poor of the people," and give "deliverance to the needy and crush the oppressor" (72:4). They yearn for one who will "deliver the needy when they call" from oppression and violence (72:12-14). Israel is not the only family of the earth who desires such justice and freedom from oppression. All the families of the earth desire the same thing.

Psalm 110 is quite helpful in offering some insight into the nature of God's anointed one as a king whose lineage stems not so much from Israel as from the order of Melchizedek: "The LORD has sworn and will not change his mind, 'You are a priest forever according to the order of Melchizedek'" (110:4). This priestly role for God's anointed one emerges not out of the priesthood of Israel but rather out of the lineage of the priesthood of this king of Salem who provided bread and wine to Abraham and blessed him. This blessing of Abraham comes from beyond Israel and not from within Israel. It is a blessing offered by the representative of one of the many families of the earth to the father of Israel. If the anointed one of God is of the order of Melchizedek, then the source of his priestly calling, while certainly coming from "God Most High," is not a calling that emerges from his roots in Israel. In similar fashion perhaps, his reign over the earth from Zion is a symbolic reference rather than a geographical or political one.

Is it possible that Israel's hope for the anointed one who will bring about the community of shalom is again an archetypal hope? It reflects the hopes and dreams of all the families of the earth for peace and justice in the world. It presents that hope through the lens of its own experience. Israel understands God's promised king to be a Jewish king. The center of that kingly reign is the holy city of Israel, Jerusalem or Zion. In what other way could Israel possibly understand God's intentions? Any family of the earth would envision its hopes and dreams as emerging from within its own history and tradition. Israel's conviction would be that the blessing of the families of the earth would come from within Israel and be represented in Israel's understanding of human community.

"Righteous Gentiles"

The Hebrew Bible is filled with instances in which "righteous Gentiles" offer blessings to Israel or receive blessings from Israel. Barbara Brown Taylor in *Holy Envy* has pointed out the role of righteous Gentiles in both the Hebrew Bible and the New Testament as the means by which Judaism and Christianity encounter the holy and sacred within other religions. The idea is that mutual blessing occurs in the context of interreligious relationships and experiences. She documents many of the stories in the Hebrew

Bible and the New Testament in which righteous Gentiles like Melchizedek bless and affirm Israel from outside its own community or are blessed and affirmed by the God of Israel even though they are not Jewish or Christian themselves. She concludes that often

> God works through religious strangers. For reasons that will never be entirely clear, God sometimes sends people from outside a faith community to bless those inside of it. It does not seem to matter if the main characters understand God in the same way or call God by the same name. The divine blessing is effective, and the story goes on.[32]

So if the coming Messiah or king is a priest in the order of Melchizedek, why should that king's identity be restricted to a Jewish identity? Certainly, Melchizedek was not Jewish. The coming king is to bring peace to all the families of the earth, not just Israel, enabling humanity to bless itself by accomplishing God's original intentions for it, intentions predicated as much upon the gifts of our cultural differences as upon our common human yearning for peace and justice.

A number of other stories in the Hebrew Bible point toward this notion of "righteous strangers" who come from outside the Jewish faith to bless Israel with gifts they bring to the table or to be blessed by Israel and by its God. Solomon prays for them in his prayer at the dedication of the temple. Naaman the Aramean, the sailors on the boat with the prophet Jonah, the people of Nineveh to whom Jonah is sent, and Cyrus, the Persian king whom God describes as God's anointed one, are all "righteous strangers" who bless Israel or are blessed by Israel.

Solomon's Prayer at the Dedication of the Temple

The prayer of Solomon at the dedication of the temple in 1 Kings 8 provides one example of the relationship God intends between Israel and the other families of the earth as they seek to bless each other. In the middle of his prayer, Solomon asks God to hear the prayers of "foreigners" who come to Jerusalem because they have heard "of your great name, your mighty hand, and your outstretched arm" (8:42). Solomon has already offered petition in earlier parts of the prayer that God would protect, nurture, forgive, and bring peace among the Israelites when they pray toward the temple. He anticipates that God will judge between neighbors in the temple, providing clear evidence of fault, that God will bring victory in battle against Israel's enemies, and that God will receive the confession of the people when they suffer defeat or famine because of disobedience.

In the midst of this litany of temple benefits for Israel, Solomon also prays that God will hear and answer the prayers of the righteous strangers or foreigners who come from outside Israel. He asks God to "Do according to all that the foreigner calls to you, so that all the peoples of the earth may know your name and fear you, as do your people Israel" (8:43). Solomon's plea for the stranger fits the pattern of the Hebrew Bible in that his hope is that other families of the earth might know God and fear God in the same way that Israel knows God and fears God.

But the prayer is not specific about the particular connection between Israel and the stranger. Is the hope that the strangers will receive a blessing from the God of Israel and then return to their own homes to worship their own gods? Or is the hope that the strangers will embrace the faith of Israel and forsake their own particular faiths? Solomon's prayer for the foreigner seems intended not as an effort at conversion of the Gentiles or strangers but as a means whereby the God of Israel might bless people outside the Jewish family who would then carry the story of that blessing back into their own cultural contexts.

Naaman the Aramean

The story of Naaman the Aramean (one from the area known as modern-day Syria) in 2 Kings 5 provides a powerful example of one such righteous Gentile who seeks a blessing from the God of Israel and who returns to his own context with the intention of integrating his worship of the God of Israel within that context. A number of interesting details mark this rather humorous story. First, Naaman's king respected Naaman as the commander of his army because "by him the LORD had given victory to Aram" (5:1). Here another family of the earth is victorious in battle over Israel specifically because God has ensured that victory. God has blessed the Arameans.

Despite his battle prowess, Naaman has contracted leprosy and is desperately seeking a cure. A servant girl from Israel, one among a number of lowly characters in the story who move it along in powerful ways, mentions a prophet in Samaria who could heal his leprosy. Naaman leaps at the possibility for healing. His king writes a letter to the king of Israel, imploring him to heal Naaman of his disease. Believing that the king of Aram is trying to encourage another fight with Israel, Israel's king tears his clothes out of frustration and fear. Hearing of the king's distress, the prophet Elisha asks, "Why have you torn your clothes? Let him come to me, that he may learn that there is a prophet in Israel" (v. 8). When Naaman arrives, Elisha does not even bother to come to the door. He sends a messenger telling Naaman to go and bathe seven times in the Jordan River. Furious at the slight, Naaman protests that he could have washed in the rivers of Damascus instead of the tiny Jordan River.

Again, a servant intervenes. "Father," the servant says, "if the prophet had commanded you to do something difficult, would you not have done it? How much more, when all he said to you was, 'Wash, and be clean'?" (5:13). Naaman finally complies and his leprosy disappears. Returning to Elisha, Naaman professes his belief that "there is no God in all the earth except in Israel" (5:15). He offers Elisha a gift that Elisha refuses, perhaps a sign of Elisha's own pride and prejudice against the Arameans and of his refusal to receive a blessing from the Arameans that God might intend for him to receive.

Naaman departs with a single request. He asks for two mule-loads of dirt and insists that he will no longer offer burnt offering or sacrifice to any god except the Lord. He obviously intends to worship God on the dirt of Israel that he will bring back to Aram. His encounter with Elisha ends when he makes a final request: "But may the LORD pardon your servant on one count: when my master goes into the house of Rimmon[33] to worship there, leaning on my arm, and I bow down in the house of Rimmon, may the LORD pardon your servant on this one count" (5:18). Elisha simply replies, "Go in peace."

The story is quite remarkable in at least two ways that offer perspective on the call of the families of the earth to bless themselves by Israel and to offer blessing to Israel. First, Naaman offers a blessing to Elisha in his witness to the unique power and authority of God as the only God in all the earth. He affirms the unique relationship of God and Israel by asking to take the two mule-loads of the dirt of Israel back to Aram. Naaman also asks for Elisha's blessing and counsel when Naaman goes into the temple of Rimmon, the god of Aram's king. He seeks the blessing of Elisha to bow his head in that temple so that he can support his king in the worship of Rimmon. Elisha's response is somewhat ambiguous but certainly falls short of an outright denunciation of such an action. "Go in peace," he says, suggesting that the action is acceptable in light of Naaman's own contextual realities.

This story is a powerful missiological story. Elsewhere in the Hebrew Bible, idolatry is condemned. God insists in the First Commandment that Israel "not make for yourself an idol, whether in the form of anything that is in heaven above, or that is on the earth beneath, or that is in the water under the earth. You shall not bow down to them or worship them" (Exod 20:4-5). So how are we to understand Naaman's request and Elisha's response? Again, the answer depends on whether Israel is an archetypal family of the earth or the particular family of the earth whose stories and laws all families of the earth are to embrace. Is it possible that the commandment against idolatry extends to Israel alone? Is it possible that Elisha as well as God recognize that a particular family must begin its search for the divine from within its own particular stories and mythologies? Does Elisha realize that Naaman's decision to take the mule-load of dirt back to Aram and worship God on it might lead to the integration of the stories of Israel with the stories of Aram and the God of Israel with the God of Aram?

How else are we to understand the human search for God? Both Jewish and Christian theology would affirm that human beings are searching for meaning and purpose in life. We want to understand the reality of suffering and death. We want to know why we are in the world and for what reason. Our mythological stories provide the foundation or roots of that meaning. We build upon the experiences of our ancestors and the particular origin and meaning stories that gave shape to our particular cultural reality. At the same time, we affirm that God is seeking us as much as we are seeking God. To provide meaning and purpose to only one particular people would seem to be a cruel joke on the part of a God who scattered the families of the earth around the world, confused our languages, and nurtured cultural differences that make us unique and often perplexing to each other.

Naaman's story has been a pivotal story in my own experience of teaching the religions of the world to college and seminary students. It implies that entering into a mosque, synagogue, or temple of another religion is something God encourages. We need such a story in a day in which our encounter as Christian people with followers of other religions is often marked by the tendency to objectify such followers as "other" and "different" from us rather than to receive them as "righteous strangers."

I once took a group of college students to the Sri Venkateswara Temple in Riverdale, Georgia. Hindu devotees of Venkateswara, one in a long line of manifestations of Lord Vishnu, had constructed this beautiful temple just south of Atlanta. One particular student did not want to make the trip.

"I don't need to go to a Hindu temple," Jimmy said.

"Why not?" I asked.

He went on to explain that he had seen many Hindu temples in Vietnam when he served in the US military during the Vietnam War.

I patiently responded that Vietnam was primarily a Buddhist country with Buddhist temples.

To his credit, Jimmy showed up. We went to the temple. I asked the priest if we could enter the central shrine that housed the image of Sri Venkateswara. The priest welcomed us in and went through the basic rituals of puja to help us understand the daily worship experience performed by Hindu people all over the world. He shone a candle around our bodies, he recanted the priestly worship chants, and, afterward, he gave us a small gift, an apple, to take with us as we left. I understood it to be a blessing from this particular Hindu priest to us, one family of the earth blessing another family.

As we exited the central shrine, Jimmy turned to me with an intense and angry expression on his face.

"Dr. Nash, did we just worship an idol?" he asked in a tone that was more a definitive statement than it was a question.

I waited through a pregnant pause.

"I didn't, Jimmy. Did you?"

"Good Lord, no!" he shouted. Then he walked over to the shrine to Hanuman, the monkey god, who guards the entrance to the temple, and he took his apple and tossed it through the shrine's gate at the image.

"If that monkey can walk over there and get that apple and eat it, then he can have it," Jimmy said.

Disappointed in his behavior, I decided to make the experience a teaching moment for everyone. I waited until we were back in the van and then I said to the entire group, "You know, in all of my years of taking students to this Hindu temple, Jimmy here is the first one who actually left a sacrifice for one of the gods!"

Of course, the van exploded in laughter and Jimmy experienced a lot of teasing on the ride home. He also spent a couple of hours in my office later that week because now Jimmy believed that he had sacrificed to an idol. I had to assure him that the attitude with which he tossed that apple at Sri Hanuman made it clear that he had no intention to worship Hanuman's image.

I tell this story because of my conviction that by going to the temple we were offering a blessing to the priests and Hindu adherents who worship there, and that by receiving the gift of the apple we received a blessing from them as well. Such mutual blessing is very different from worship, and we have to learn to distinguish between the two—between blessing and worship. Like Naaman after his visit to Israel, we can enter the house of Rimmon, acknowledging the powerful meaning and hope that the followers of Rimmon experience in that place. We can do this to such an extent that the experience blesses us even without obligating us to worship anyone or anything other than God. At the same time, we can offer a blessing, a gift, if you will, from the ground of our own meaning, represented in the story of Naaman by the two mule-loads of dirt from Israel. We can also recognize the power of that particular family of the earth to seek the divine presence in its midst. We can affirm that perhaps they have discovered something about the divine, some knowledge that we do not possess. We can also know because of the power of our own relationship to God that we have something to offer to them in return, some sort of blessing straight from our divine encounters.

The Book of Jonah

The story of the reluctant prophet Jonah offers perhaps the clearest expression of the relationship between God's intentions and hopes for Israel and of Israel's place in God's blessing of the families of the earth. In the story, Nineveh is a kind of representative city, inhabited by one among the many families of the earth who dispersed after the building of the Tower of Babel. Both the city of Nineveh and the prophet Jonah seem disconnected from their respective regions, Nineveh from the larger region of Assyria and Jonah from the larger region of Israel. The only mention of the prophet outside the book that bears his name occurs in 2 Kings 14:25 during the reign of Jeroboam II when God spoke a word through "Jonah son of Amittai." This reference would place the prophet Jonah's story as occurring at some point between 786 BCE and 746 BCE during Jeroboam II's reign. At this time, Assyria was a weak kingdom whose capital was not Nineveh, and so perhaps this is why the book of Jonah speaks of the king of Nineveh as a localized king rather than the king of an empire. In addition, the story presents Nineveh as "an exceedingly large city, a three days walk across" (v. 3), a claim that would belie its historical roots in the mid to late eighth century BCE.

The book addresses Jonah's and, by extension, Israel's reluctance to participate in the work of blessing that God intends for the people of Nineveh. The story becomes one in which the Ninevites, after hearing this reluctant and narrow-minded prophet preach his message of repentance, elect to recognize the blessing of God within their own people and place, and they receive that blessing. In similar fashion, God blesses the Ninevites despite Jonah's hope that God would punish the Ninevites instead.

The story begins with a clear call from the Lord to Jonah that tells him to "Go at once to Nineveh, that great city, and cry out against it; for their wickedness has come up before me" (1:2). Jonah immediately rejects that call and boards a ship at Joppa that is bound for Tarshish. Disappointed in Jonah, God raises up a storm from the sea that threatens to break the ship. This raising up of the storm brings to mind passages in the Gospels of the New Testament when similar storms interrupt the efforts of Jesus and the disciples to cross the Sea of Galilee from the Jewish side to the Gentile side. The storm would seem to represent the cultural challenges that emerge whenever boundaries are crossed and one family of the earth engages another.

In this instance, the mariners who spend so much time on the sea are frightened of the intensity of the storm that they witness. Out of fear, they cry out to their own gods, but the storm does not abate. They discover Jonah in the hold of the ship and realize that at least one person on board is not praying to his particular god, and so the captain says to him, "What are you doing fast asleep? Get up, call on your god! Perhaps the god will spare us a thought so that we do not perish" (1:6). The sailors then cast lots to determine who is to blame and "the lot fell on Jonah" (1:7).

The response of the sailors in the story is remarkable. They ask Jonah a series of questions, all intended to bring to light his personal and cultural identity. We should not overlook the part their questions play in the larger story of Jonah as well as the human story itself: "Tell us why this calamity has come upon us. What is your occupation? Where do you come from? What is your country? And, of what people are you" (1:8). Their questions are questions that get at the very heart of human suffering, of the quest for meaning and purpose in life, and of the need to understand the worldview and perspectives of others.

The book of Jonah expresses the nature of God's relationship with all the families of the earth. Jonah's occupation, region, country and family all have great relevance for the challenge that the sailors and Jonah are facing in the moment. The only possible solution for the crisis is to isolate Jonah's cultural and religious identity, enter into that particular worldview, and, using that worldview and perspective, end the storm. The sailors must know what Jonah has done against his particular god, the god who is visiting this calamity upon them.

Jonah answers their questions. In response, they ask, "What shall we do to you, that the sea may quiet down for us" (v. 11)? The question is grounded in the reality of competing worldviews and perspectives and in the challenge that, somehow, they must find a way to make those world-views and perspectives work together to alleviate the crisis. The sailors know what to do when suffering comes in the context of their own particular worldviews, but they have no idea what to do when the suffering comes from a worldview that they do not know or understand. And even when Jonah does offer a solution from within his own worldview ("Pick me up and throw me into the sea"), the sailors strain at the oars to return to the land without having to sacrifice Jonah's life. When it becomes clear that they have no other choice, they toss Jonah into the sea and immediately "the sea ceased from its raging" (1:15). Having entered into the worldview of Jonah to resolve the crisis, they also realize their obligation to Jonah's god, and so "the men feared the LORD even more, and they offered a sacrifice to the LORD and made vows" (1:16).

In this reading, the experience of Jonah in the belly of the fish pales in contrast to the conversation that occurs on the boat prior to it. The point of the story is to somehow return Jonah to dry land and move him along on his journey to Nineveh. Modern readers focus far too much attention on how Jonah survived in the belly of the fish and miss the cross-cultural engagement that God intends as the main point of the story. Jonah makes his way to Nineveh, enters about a day's walk into the city, and proclaims the judgment of God upon it.

The people of Nineveh immediately "believed God; they proclaimed a fast, and everyone, great and small, put on sackcloth" (3:5), including even the king who "removed his robe, covered himself with sackcloth, and sat in ashes" (3:6). The king then issues one of the most powerful proclamations of penitence in the entire Hebrew Bible:

> No human being or animal, no herd or flock, shall taste anything. They shall not feed, nor shall they drink water. Human beings and animals shall be covered in sackcloth, and they shall cry mightily to God. All shall turn from their evil ways and from the violence that is in their hands. Who knows? God may relent and change his mind; he may turn from his fierce anger, so that we do not perish. (3:7-9)

When God saw that the king and his people were truly penitent, he did exactly as the king had hoped: "he changed his mind about the calamity that he had said he would bring upon them" (3:10).

Jonah is not happy. He protests in anger and frustration that he knew "while I was still in my own country" that God was "a gracious God and merciful, slow to anger, and abounding in steadfast love, and ready to relent from punishing" (Jonah 4:2). The phrase "while I was still in my own country" is an interesting and overlooked phrase. Again, it points to the significance of intercultural relationships within the book of Jonah. Is Jonah's point that he had predicted this action on the part of God while still in Israel, and thus his journey was pointless, or is the writer of the book making the larger point that Jonah's worldview is a culturally conditioned perspective that emerges out of Jonah's own limited understanding? It seems clear that it is the latter. As long as God's people remain "in their own country," they remain largely ignorant of the ways of God as well as of the ways of other families of the earth. It is only in the intercultural engagement with other families of the earth that one can fully understand the ways of God in the context of God's care and concern for all of humanity.

The story does not end there. Jonah's anger and frustration at God's mercy and grace is so debilitating to Jonah that he insists three times that he is so angry he wants to die. He is determined to manipulate God into changing God's mind once again and punishing the people of Nineveh. Like a petulant child, he builds a little booth and sits on a hill to see what will happen. He has turned his call to preach repentance to the Ninevites into a test to see whether God cares more about him (and, by extension, about Israel) or about the Ninevites. He is battling God and Nineveh for God's blessings to be restricted only to those for whom Jonah seeks the blessings. As far as we know, he still sits on the hill above Nineveh awaiting the city's destruction.

Cyrus the Great

Cyrus figures prominently in the writings of 2 Isaiah, an unknown prophet of the Babylonian exile whose work encompasses Isaiah 40–55. This prophet prophesies about the great work of God's chosen king, who will overcome the enemies of God and restore the people to their rightful place in Jerusalem. Isaiah 40 begins with a word from God that God's people are to be comforted in their affliction: "Speak tenderly to Jerusalem," God says, "and cry to her that she has served her term, that her penalty is paid, that she has received from the LORD's hand double for her sins" (40:2). Isaiah reminds Israel of God's care and provision for it and of God's strength as the one who gives "power to the faint, and strengthens the powerless" (40:29).

Through the prophet, God calls on the people to draw near to hear what God is about to do (41:1). God will bring a "victor from the east" to whom God will "deliver up nations and trample kings underfoot" (41:2). This king will be the servant of God; indeed, Isaiah calls Cyrus by name, identifying him as God's "anointed . . . whose right hand I have grasped to subdue nations before him and strip kings of their robes" (45:1). Cyrus is referred to as God's shepherd, "and he shall carry out all of my purpose," including the rebuilding of Jerusalem (44:28). God's relationship with Cyrus is described most intimately when God indicates his love for this great king who will "perform his purpose on Babylon, and his arm shall be against the Chaldeans" (48:14).

Cyrus the Great would rule the Persian Empire during the sixth century BCE, creating the largest empire in the world to that point in history. His reign was marked by respect for the cultures, religions, and languages of the lands that he conquered, including that of the Jewish people whom he allowed to return to Jerusalem to rebuild the city. The book of Nehemiah chronicles the experience of the rebuilding of the city walls and the temple during the reign of Artaxerxes, a successor to Cyrus.

The fact that Cyrus could serve as God's anointed one offers some perspective on the way in which God works in history to accomplish God's purposes in the world. God blesses Israel through Cyrus, but God blesses far more families of the earth than just Israel through this one whom "the LORD loves." Clearly, the empire that Cyrus establishes is a model for the sort of community that God intends on earth. It stands with the community of shalom, the community envisioned by the Jewish Law, as a second example of what that community might look like if it were to find concrete expression in the world. In Cyrus, the Persian family of the earth becomes God's example of goodness and a model for the ways in which human families are to bless each other.

Conclusion

The story of Cyrus as one among a number of "righteous strangers" who bless Israel or who are in turn blessed by Israel brings us to the end of the Hebrew Bible. The "righteous strangers" of the Persian Empire made possible the rebuilding of Jerusalem and the temple. Israel could never have accomplished this on its own. In some ways, this powerful story means that we have come full circle. We have seen how God's intention and purpose from the beginning was for human beings "to be fruitful, multiply and fill the earth." We have seen how humanity frustrated that purpose and intention by remaining together both after the creation and after the flood. In response to the human effort to build the Tower of Babel, God came down and confused human language to drive humanity apart and to ensure that the human perspective on God would achieve the cultural complexities that God intended.

Once those families had dispersed to the ends of the earth, God chose a single family, the family of Abram, as an archetypal family that would model the ways in which God would work within human cultures and languages to help each one discover its own gifts and possibilities that it could then share with the rest of humanity. Throughout Israel's history, God constantly brought other human families into Israel's orbit to bless Israel with their particular gifts as well as to receive the gifts that Israel had to offer. Israel's own prophets recognized these righteous strangers and celebrated the many ways in which Israel benefitted from them.

This perspective supports the conclusion that the biblical vision of the community of shalom can never emerge from a single human family. Such a community would be limited by the perspectives and understanding of that human family. Every family bears within it discontent and discord. Its perspective on God, humanity, and the creation is limited and finite. It was for this reason that God insisted that all human families should go to their own spaces, nurture their own languages and cultures, determine their own perspectives on community, and find meaning and purpose out of their own experiences. God's conviction was that, once this occurred, humanity could gather once again to share the truths that each family had discovered and, in the process, share what they had learned with the other families of the earth. This vision, for Israel at least, is a vision for a New Jerusalem to which all human families would belong. How else could Israel possibly understand the nature of this new community of all the families of the earth?

The concept of the New Jerusalem, however, is a particularly Jewish one. It is a community whose boundaries are shaped by the Jewish perspective. Such a community offers the Jewish vision for such a global community to the other families of the earth. It invites the other families of the earth to full participation in that community. At the same time, though, other families of the earth bring their own perspectives to such community in ways that nurture the Jewish perspective and perhaps enhance it. A community to which all human beings belonged would have to be a community that included the contributions of the perspectives and worldviews of all human families toward what that community should be.

We should understand Israel then as a single earthly family, no more or less blessed than other families of the earth, whom God chose as an example to other families of the earth of God's intention for all families. The stories of the Hebrew Bible provide the contours of the Jewish understanding of the creation, of God's mission in the world, of the nature of community within the Jewish family and with other families, and of the particular calling of the Jewish people to contribute to the ultimate vision of God for all the families of the earth. The Hebrew Bible beckons all families toward deep and honest reflection on their own particular worldviews, cultures, and perspectives in order to discover their unique blessings and to share those blessings with the world. It also beckons all families toward the embrace of other perspectives and worldviews so that the mutual blessing enables as full an understanding of God, the creation, and each other as is humanly possible.

The prophet Habakkuk, writing in the mid- to late seventh century BCE, described the entire earth as "filled with the knowledge of the glory of the LORD, as the waters cover the sea" (Hab 2:14). His words help to explain in a powerful way the universal search for God on the part of every family of the earth and the emergence of religions "as eloquent testimony to the native sense of human beings that there must be a God."[34] The knowledge of God, manifested in every corner of the earth and in every family, is most fully revealed only when we recognize the divine presence in each other and share the knowledge of God with which each one of us has been particularly blessed.

Notes

1. William Carey, *An Enquiry into the Obligations of Christians to Use Means for the Conversion of the Heathen* (Leicester, England: Ann Ireland, 1792), 8.

2. Carey, *An Enquiry*, 82–83.

3. Robert T. Coote, "Twentieth Century Shifts in the North American Protestant Missionary Community," *International Bulletin of Missionary Research* 22/4 (October 1998): 152–53.

4. Coote, "Twentieth Century Shifts," 152–53.

5. Marcus J. Borg, *Reading the Bible Again for the First Time* (San Francisco, CA: HarperSanFrancisco, 2001), 18.

6. I include Genesis 12:1-4 here because of the direct connection between the primeval history in Genesis 1–11 and the call of Abram in Genesis 12.

7. See Cynthia Long Westfall, "The Hebrew Mission: Voices from the Margin," in Stanley E. Porter and Cynthia Long Westfall, eds., *Christian Mission: Old Testament Foundations and New Testament Developments* (Eugene, OR: Wipf and Stock, 2011), 187. Westfall connects mission, vision, and strategic planning to mission as the broad work of God in the world as opposed to the specific work of evangelism.

8. Christopher Wright, *The Mission of God: Unlocking the Bible's Grand Narrative* (Downers Grove, IL: InterVarsity Press, 2006), 22–23.

9. David Bosch, *Transforming Mission: Paradigm Shifts in Theology of Mission* (Maryknoll, NY: Orbis Books, 1991), xv.

10. N. T. Wright, *Surprised by Hope: Rethinking Heaven, the Resurrection, and the Mission of the Church* (New York: HarperCollins, 2008), 193.

11. I am grateful to Nancy deClaisse-Walford in "God Came Down and God Scattered: Acts of Punishment or Acts of Grace?" *Review and Expositor* 103 (Spring 2006): 403–16 for identifying scholars who advocate this particular perspective, including David J. A. Clines, *The Theme of the Pentateuch*, 2nd ed., Journal for the Study of the Old Testament Supplement Series 10, ed. David J. A. Clines and Philip R. Davies (Sheffield: Sheffield Academic Press, 1997), 70; William Sanford LaSor et al., *Old Testament Survey: The Message, Form and Background of the Old Testament,*

rev. ed. (Grand Rapids, MI: Eerdmans, 1996), 30; and Gerhard von Rad, *Old Testament Theology*, vol. 1, trans. D. M. G. Stalker (New York: Harper and Row, Publishers, 1962), 163.

12. deClaisse-Walford, "God Came Down and God Scattered," 414.

13. Bill T. Arnold, *Genesis* (New York: Cambridge University Press, 2009), 118.

14. Arnold, *Genesis*, 120.

15. See Franz Boas, "Language," in *General Anthropology* (Madison, WI: United States Armed Forces Institute, 1938), 124–45 for a summary of Boas' perspective on the relationship between language and culture.

16. Quoted in Benjamin L. Whorf, "The Relation of Habitual Thought and Behavior to Language," in *Language, Thought, and Reality: Selected Writings of Benjamin Lee Whorf*, ed. John B. Carroll (Cambridge, MA: The Massachusetts Institute of Technology Press, 1956, 1974 edition), 134.

17. John R. Stott, *Christian Mission in the Modern World* (Downers Grove, IL: InterVarsity Press, 2008), 31-32.

18. Bosch, *Transforming Mission*, 26.

19. Thomas Cahill, *The Gift of the Jews: How a Tribe of Desert Nomads Changed the Way Everyone Thinks and Feels* (New York: Anchor Books, 1999), 3.

20. Walter Brueggemann, *The Land: Place as Gift, Promise, and Challenge in Biblical Faith* (Philadelphia, PA: Fortress Press, 1977), 3.

21. For a more thorough analysis of the differences between the Niphal and Hithpael forms of *barak* in Genesis 12, see Chee-Chiew Lee, "Once Again: the Niphal and the Hithpael of ברך in the Abrahamic Blessing for the Nations, *Journal for the Study of the Old Testament* 36/3 (2012): 279–96.

22. Popular English language versions with this particular translation form include the New Revised Standard Version, the New American Standard Bible, the King James Version, and the New International Version.

23. Versions with this translation tradition are less popular but include the New English Translation ("all families of the earth will bless one another

by your name") and the Revised Standard Version ("by you all the families of the earth shall bless themselves").

24. James Chukwuma Okoye, *Israel and the Nations: A Mission Theology of the Old Testament* (Maryknoll, NY: Orbis Books, 2006), 6.

25. Ellen Davis, *Scripture, Culture and Agriculture: An Agrarian Reading of the Bible* (New York: Cambridge University Press, 2009), 26.

26. John Rolfe, "A Relation of the State of Virginia" (1616), in *The Virginia Historical Register and Literary Advertiser* 1 (1848): 11–12, quoted in Perry Miller, *Errand to the Wilderness* (Cambridge, MA: Harvard University Press, 1956), 119.

27. For full explorations of this appropriation, see Conrad Cherry, *God's New Israel: Religious Interpretations of America's Destiny* (Englewood Cliffs, NJ: Prentice-Hall, 1971), and William R. Hutchinson, *Errand to the World: American Protestant Thought and Foreign Missions* (Chicago, IL: University of Chicago Press, 1987).

28. See "The Lost Book of the Karens," *neo house church network,* http://www.neohcn.org/resources/articles/the-lost-book-of-the-karens. Website source is Don Richardson, *Eternity in Their Hearts* (Ventura, CA: Regal Books, 1984).

29. Nancy L. deClaisse-Walford, *Introduction to the Psalms: A Song from Ancient Israel* (St. Louis, MO: Chalice Press, 2004), 143.

30. Mark J. Boda, "'Declare His Glory Among the Nations': The Psalter as Missional Collection," in *Christian Mission: Old Testament Foundations and New Testament Development,* ed. Stanley E. Porter and Cynthia Long Westfall (Eugene, OR: Wipf and Stock, 2011), 15.

31. Boda, "Declare His Glory Among the Nations," 16–18.

32. Barbara Brown Taylor, *Holy Envy: Finding God in the Faith of Others* (New York: HarperOne, 2019), 109–10.

33. Rimmon was a god of the cult of Baal.

34. R. Alan Culpepper, "The Knowledge of God: Prophetic Vision and Johannine Theme," in *"A Temple Not Made with Hands": Essays in Honor of Naymond H. Keathley,* ed. Mikeal C. Parsons and Richard Walsh (Eugene, OR: Pickwick Publishers, 2018), 57.

Chapter 4

The New Testament, Mission, and Matthew

[Jesus] stands in the tradition of the prophets. Like them and like John
the Baptist his concern is the repentance and salvation of Israel.
—David Bosch, *Transforming Mission*

I love climbing Mount Tai with my students. It is one of the great Taoist
mountains in China, and the climb to the top is rigorous. Some tourists
take the ten-minute cable car up; my students always prefer the 3,000-step
path that leads up into the clouds and to the Highway of Heaven and the
Confucian, Taoist, and Buddhist temples that wind along the mountain's
ridge.

On one particular climb, a student named Mary was struggling and so
I hung back with her, though I will confess that I was struggling at least as
much as she was. We took our time, pausing to admire the various shrines
that dotted the path. Dozens of elderly Chinese passed us by, laughing
and patting my prominent belly while saying something in Mandarin that
probably resembled, "Hey, buddy, you should have taken the cable car!"

Karen, who played on the college basketball team and was in the best
shape of anyone in our group, raced up the steps to the top of the mountain, walked around a bit, and then ran back down to see what was taking
the rest of us so long. She kept appearing, encouraging us along, and eventually we made it. We looked out over the beautiful mountains and walked
into the temples that lined the Highway of Heaven. We were literally in
the clouds!

Deciding I needed a little time alone to take in the experience, I took a side path away from the temples and the cable car station and my students. It was there that I bumped into Karen, the basketball player, sitting on a rock.

Looking out over the valley, we talked about the Chinese pilgrims we had encountered and of the temples that lined the Highway. We marveled at their faith and of all that we shared with them when it came to hope and to devotion to a power much greater than ourselves.

After a long pause, I asked a question.

"Do you think there are streets in our country that people would describe as highways to heaven?"

She thought for a moment and then said, "The only ones I can think of would be Wall Street or Hollywood Avenue."

We talked about which highways to heaven we would prefer to travel, the one on Mount Tai or the ones she had mentioned. We confessed to each other our constant temptation to take the other highways as opposed to the one that we sat beside at the moment, but we both finally determined that we would rather be on Mount Tai with other pilgrims who were trying to connect with God than on Wall Street or Hollywood Avenue where our ultimate goal might be fortune or fame. She was as much my teacher in the conversation as I was hers. It was a holy moment that helped both of us to embrace the encounter with otherness and difference on top of Mount Tai. It opened our minds and hearts to new possibilities.

My experience with Karen on the Highway of Heaven is one of many such experiences in my life that have helped me to be open to blessings from other religious families of the earth.

I have sat cross-legged under a Bodhi tree in Bodh Gaya, India, where the Buddha experienced enlightenment, and I have listened to student presentations on the ways the Buddha came to such enlightenment and exactly what it meant, not just for India but for humanity.

I have traveled up and down the Yellow River in China from the Islamic mosques of Xi'an to the Longmen Buddhist Caves of Luoyang to the birthplace of Confucius in Shandong, all while reading the sacred texts of each religion and discovering new spiritual insight unavailable to me within my own Christian tradition.

I have wandered the Shinto temples of Japan and Korea, made merit with the Buddhist monks of Laos, and stood at a spirit grove behind a university in Thailand decorated with hundreds of kites left by students who were hoping for the help of the spirits in passing their exams.

I have chatted with abbots in Buddhist monasteries in Cambodia and made my way through a pressing crowd in a Kali temple in Kolkata, India, to catch a glimpse of the goddess.

I have watched the sunset on top of a thousand-year-old stupa on the Bagan plain in Myanmar with a student who had never been outside the United States before, and heard him exclaim as we looked out over dozens of other stupas silhouetted in the sun, "Dr. Nash, we're a long way from Atlanta!"

In every single one of these religious experiences, I have encountered that ultimate force and reality in the world that we call God. Each one has caused me to acknowledge the limitations of my own Christian perspective and to wonder about the tensions within the Christian faith between an exclusivity that insists that Jesus is the only way to God and the universal pronouncement that God created the world with all of its diversity and loves every family of the earth. These tensions have led me to ask the question, "Is there something about Jesus that I, and by extension my particular evangelical and Christian tradition, are missing as a result of the formulations of previous centuries of Christian tradition and history?"

Did Jesus come into the world to offer to humanity a single path to redemption and salvation grounded in the acceptance of certain propositional truths about him, or was his purpose to point us back toward an ancient path from which we had strayed? Was his real intention to remind us of divine truth that we had ignored or overlooked, encourage us toward the embrace of otherness and difference as a means toward the full understanding of God, and help us to live fully and faithfully into God's future?

Is this so hard to imagine? Is it possible that we have been viewing the life of Jesus through the prism of a modern lens that used to be sufficient for a superstructure that has collapsed and is no longer viable? Have we spent so much time defending doctrinal positions about the divinity of Jesus or the humanity of Jesus that we have lost our way? Is there a new way of understanding the life of Jesus and of the earliest followers of Jesus that can provide meaning and purpose as we construct a new superstructure for a new day? Can we locate the equator in a new center?

I know my own religious tradition quite well. I am the product of American evangelicalism, and particularly of a Baptist tradition, that champions the importance of Scripture as a primary source of divine revelation. For that reason, the discernment of any new perspective on God for me and for my tradition must receive some sort of validation in Scripture and particularly in the New Testament, which tells the story of Jesus and of the early church. There are few other sources to help us uncover the meaning of Jesus' life, death, and resurrection. The books of the New Testament were written at particular moments in time to particular churches and people who were struggling to bring meaning and purpose to their lives. For this reason, every book in the New Testament is a missionary document, written with the intention of deepening a particular community's perspective on God, humanity, and the creation and inviting it toward participation in God's mission to accomplish the divine vision. The New Testament continues to be a missionary document for the church today, though the shift in context enables new interpretations that have never been available to us before.

Remember that *mission* is the work that we do *now* in the world. For this reason, we can understand the books of the New Testament as missionary documents. Each book is encouraging a faith community or group of communities in the first century and perhaps the early second century to participate in God's work both inside and outside the community. This perspective moves us beyond our tendency to restrict the work of God in the world to the church. God works beyond the church in intentionally missionary ways that have everything to do with God and perhaps nothing to do with the church. This fits well with the previous chapter of this book in which we explored the mission of Israel in the world. God's mission was not dependent on Israel any more than God's mission in the world is dependent on the church. God's mission is God's work now to bring about God's future vision. As Israel and the church, we are free to participate in it or not.

We have read the New Testament through a lens that says God was establishing a new religion, Christianity, a religion that God intended from the beginning to be the source of the world's salvation. In the process, we have made Judaism little more than a prelude to God's work of salvation in Jesus Christ and have branded other ways to God as wrong at best and as evil at worst. This cannot be right. It simply cannot. There must be a different way of understanding the role and work of Jesus in the midst of the diversity of cultures and religions. Perhaps Jesus' purpose in the world was to affirm that diversity and call us back to the original purpose of God that the families of the earth separate into their various cultures and languages and then come back together to bless each other.

Whether intentionally or not, the framers of the biblical canon arranged the Gospels of the New Testament in a way that affirms diversity, especially in the wake of the Hebrew Bible that precedes them. The Gospel of Matthew addresses a Jewish community of Jesus' followers late in the first century CE that was wrestling with its mission in light of the Gentile world that surrounded it and of the Gentile Christians who had joined it. Matthew calls us to know our particular cultures and ourselves fully, acknowledging our strengths and weaknesses and the contributions we can make to humanity's understanding of the divine. The Gospel of Mark, written to a group of Jewish and Gentile followers of Jesus who were struggling with their respective cultural and religious differences, encourages this diverse group to embrace each other as a single community. Mark calls us beyond our own particular cultures and worldviews and toward engagement with other cultures and people. The Gospel of Luke and the Acts of the Apostles address Gentile followers of Jesus who are encouraged to claim the message of Jesus as their own and to take it beyond Jerusalem, Judea, and Samaria and into the rest of the world. Luke-Acts calls us into the context of otherness and difference that surrounds us, acknowledging that the embrace of the other can reverse our perspectives about life in our own context and enhance our understanding of the divine. The Gospel of John, farthest removed in both time and location from Jerusalem, merges Hellenistic philosophical perspectives with the message of Jesus in a way that contextualizes that message with powerful new insights and offers a model for the integration of divine truth gained from other religions and philosophies. John calls us to become a New Humanity that embraces concepts and ideas from the wider culture with its many understandings of God, humanity, and the creation.

Every single congregation addressed by Matthew, Mark, Luke, John, Paul, and the other New Testament writers faced some sort of challenge, crisis, and/or possibility. Generally, by addressing these challenges and possibilities, the author encouraged the particular faith community to deepen its understanding of God and of Jesus Christ and, as a result, to renew its purpose and mission in its context. The key word here is *context*. Each faith community inhabited a particular space at a particular time. Each writer brought to the table a set of life experiences that then merged in each Gospel, letter, or book with the life of the community. The community took what it received and reimagined its own *mission* in light of the writer's perspective and God's larger mission and purpose. For this reason, we can say that the New Testament documents contain all sorts of particular *missions* of various communities who participate in the *missio dei* or mission of God that is always at work in the world.

This now brings us to a point of engagement with the texts of the New Testament. God is at work in the world in many different sorts of ways. The diverse perspectives on Christian mission in the Gospels make this clear. Moreover, while the Christian faith makes every effort to connect with God's intentions and purposes in the world, God's work is not limited to Christianity as an institutionalized religious system. We have to understand Jesus in the context of the New Testament documents as one who calls us toward a vision for all of humanity. The calling and mission of Jesus is a calling to make all earthly families aware of the unique ways in which God has blessed them and to encourage them toward sharing their blessings with each other. In similar fashion, Jesus calls each particular family of the earth to embrace otherness and difference as a means by which it can fully understand and acknowledge its own failures and engage in the hard work of transformation.

Such a calling is particularly important in our own day. We must somehow open ourselves up to new possibilities and new truths in a diverse world, overcoming our reluctance to understand new realities about God, humanity, the world, and ourselves. The next few chapters explore the Gospels of Matthew, Mark, Luke, and John along with Luke's companion volume, the Acts of the Apostles, and a small portion of Paul's letters to the Romans and the Galatians in order to understand the particular ways in which each writer joined together context and text to renew their community's vision and mission. As we embark on this journey, I hope we can be open to new ways of seeing and understanding the reality that we inhabit.

Matthew: Jesus as Rabbi Reclaiming an Ancient Way

The Gospel of Matthew is the most Jewish of the four Gospels in that it grounds the story of Jesus in the history and prophetic traditions of Israel while also analyzing that tradition through the lens of the Gentile world that surrounds it. It is a literary and linguistic masterpiece, written between 80 and 90 CE in the region of Antioch of Syria and by a highly educated Christian, probably a Jew or perhaps a Gentile convert to Judaism, who wanted to encourage the Jewish members of his community to embrace their Gentile counterparts.[1] For this reason, Matthew offers a powerful model for the church of our own day. He reflects the history and faith of Israel through the lens of Gentiles, reminding it, and by extension the church throughout history, that such reflection is the only means by which we can see and acknowledge our own particular cultural strengths and weaknesses.

God has known this from the very beginning and, for this reason, has insisted on cultural diversity as the means for transformation. Each family of the earth must first know itself and seek its own transformation before it can ever offer a word of hope to other families of the earth. Darrell Guder points out in his book *The Continuing Conversion of the Church* that the church never "arrives" at a moment of full conversion. We are on a path that demands constant humility, confession, and repentance. This process is both individual and communal. Every individual and every family of the earth must be willing to turn the cultural mirror upon itself in order to see itself for who it is. Guder says that "this is perhaps the most profound reason for ecumenical exchange: the continuing mutual conversion of Christian communities in diverse cultures."[2]

Matthew's Gospel accomplishes this for Jewish followers of Jesus because it provides a bridge between the story of Israel and the story of Jesus, reminding Matthew's Jewish community of the ancient path from which some in Israel had strayed. Matthew utilizes the powerful subtext of the Gentile mission of Israel to serve as a pounding refrain throughout the Gospel, providing for that reflection in the Magi who visit Jesus, the Canaanite woman who exhibits faith, and the centurion who pronounces upon Jesus' death that Jesus is the Son of God. Obviously, a tension exists between some in Matthew's community who champion a mission of Jesus to the Jews and others who encourage a mission that includes both Jews and Gentiles. As Michael Knowles points out, "Matthew is conscious that Jesus and his followers alike have failed to win over people of the land of Israel."[3] So Matthew encourages a mission to both, calling his disciples at the midpoint of the Gospel to "Go nowhere among the Gentiles, and enter no town of the Samaritans" (10:5), while insisting at the end of the Gospel that they "make disciples of all the nations" (28:19).[4]

Matthew's Jewish Christian community had lost its way in the same sense in which a second- or third-generation immigrant community often struggles to find the connection between the culture of its country of origin and the culture of the place that it inhabits. Matthew's intention is to encourage his community to celebrate God's obvious blessings upon Israel and the Jewish faith while also discovering again the reasons that God called the Jewish people in the first place: to be a light to the nations and a model for the ways in which God had blessed all the families of the earth.

Matthew 1-4—The Blessing of the Gentiles upon Jesus' Jewish Roots

To this end, Matthew first establishes Jesus' credentials as a child of Israel. He traces Jesus' genealogy from Abraham to David, from David to the Babylonian exile, and then from the exile to Jesus' birth into the family of Abraham's descendant, Joseph. He grounds Jesus' life in the history of Israel and in the context of its particular language, place, and culture. Notice that Matthew spends very little time describing the birth of Jesus. He simply says that Joseph had no "marital relations" with Mary "until she had borne a son; and he named him Jesus" (Matt 1:25). No angels or shepherds appear in the sky. There is no effort to find room in Bethlehem. Joseph has a simple dream and then Jesus is born.

Matthew draws our attention instead to the strange story of the wise men (or Magi) who come from the East. Like the righteous strangers of the Hebrew Bible, they appear out of nowhere seeking "the child who has been born king of the Jews" (2:2). When Herod asks the chief priests and scribes of the people about this king, the religious leaders quote the prophet Micah who said that the "one who is to rule Israel" would come from Bethlehem (Matt 2:6 and Mic 5:2).

Significantly, Jesus the Messiah is described by Matthew and the wise men as the "king of the Jews" and not as the Messiah of the world. It is not a future king of the whole earth that the wise men seek but rather the king of a particular family of the earth. Once they find that king, Matthew reports, "they paid him homage" (v. 11), recognizing his importance as a king of the Jews. Scholars have mostly understood this story from the perspective of the wise men. The assumption has been that Jesus is the savior of the world and so the world comes to worship him and to honor him. But what if this strange story is a reminder to Israel of its own calling that "the families of the earth are to bless themselves by Israel" as well as to reinforce God's intention that Israel is to receive blessings from the other families of the earth who are similarly blessed?

When viewed through this lens, the story becomes a very different one. Matthew is reminding his community of its own mission, the work that it does at that moment in the world, which is to model for the world the blessing that God intends for all families of the earth while at the same time reminding it of God's desire that it should accept the blessing of other families of the earth. God has sent Jesus to Israel just as God sent the prophets to Israel, to call Israel back to God's original intention and purpose for it. That intention and purpose is a uniquely Jewish intention and purpose; thus Jesus is identified here as the king of the Jews and not as the Savior of the world.

Just as important, Matthew is reminding Israel that the families of the earth will bless it as much as Israel will bless them. For this reason, the story is a gentle critique of Israel's preoccupation with itself as God's elect people. The gifts of gold, frankincense, and myrrh are representative gifts in the same way that the Magi are representative of all families. Here God affirms the blessing of Israel as having its source in the blessing it receives from others, so the Magi come seeking "the King of the Jews" in order to pay homage to him and to leave a blessing or gift for him.

The story of the Magi is a story of hospitality, though it is also a story about how to be a good guest in a strange land. The representative gifts from the Magi acknowledge the contributions of the Jewish faith to God's work in the world while at the same time affirming that other families of the earth have contributions to make to that same work. It is a story that reminds Israel that it is only one among many families and nations whom God has chosen, each of which has received God's blessing, and extends that blessing beyond itself. Israel is as dependent on the goodness, grace, and gifts of other families, tribes, and ethnicities as those families are dependent on Israel.

In the immediate aftermath of the visit of the Magi, an angel warns Joseph in a dream that Herod will try to kill the child, and so Joseph and Mary flee with Jesus to Egypt. Matthew says this is to fulfill a prophecy of Hosea that "out of Egypt" God will call God's son (2:15). Here the opposite kind of hospitality occurs. Now, instead of serving as hosts who receive gifts, Mary and Joseph, and by extension Israel, become guests along with Jesus in the nation of Egypt where the pharaohs had enslaved the Israelites. Even the nation of Egypt, the source of Israel's own oppression, is quite capable of offering the blessing of safety and security to Jesus and his family.

In his first two chapters then, Matthew grounds the birth of Jesus within the specific history and prophetic tradition of Israel even as representatives of the various families of the earth travel to Bethlehem to bring gifts to Jesus and as Jesus and his family travel to Egypt to receive the blessing of safety and security from the Egyptians. These foundational chapters contain the particular calling of Jesus in the context of Israel while also hinting at a universal mission of blessing that gets at the ultimate purposes of God for all the families of the earth. God has not forgotten Israel, nor has God forgotten God's promise that "the families of the earth would bless themselves by Israel."

Matthew 4 develops these two themes of the Gospel by pointing Israel toward the recovery of its mission and purpose in the world and by declaring to the Gentile families of the earth beyond Israel the reality of their blessing. John the Baptist warns the Pharisees and Sadducees who come to him for baptism that their ancestral connection to Abraham is meaningless apart from their faithfulness to God's covenant with Abraham and, indeed, that "God is able from these stones to raise up children to Abraham" (3:9). And after his temptations in the wilderness and John's arrest, Jesus makes his home in Capernaum by the Sea of Galilee in the land of Zebulun and Naphtali, a region that the prophet Isaiah had called "Galilee of the Gentiles" and about which he prophesied that "the people who sat in darkness have seen a great light" (4:15-16).

Now Jesus is ready to preach this twofold message: to call Israel back to God's original covenant with it and to proclaim to Jews and Gentiles alike that other families are also blessed and that the light of God extends as much to them as it does to Israel. The call to Israel and the Gentiles is a call to bless as well as to receive blessing. By the end of Matthew 4, Jesus' fame has spread "throughout all Syria . . . and great crowds followed him from Galilee, the Decapolis, Jerusalem, Judea, and from beyond the Jordan" (4:24-25). His ministry to Jews and Gentiles included the healing of diseases and pains and the curing of demoniacs, epileptics, and paralytics.

From this point through the end of the Gospel, five sections of discourses or sermons by Jesus help Matthew's church identify its mission and purpose as part of the mission and purpose of God in the world. Some scholars suggest that these five sermons parallel the five books of the Law. The Sermon on the Mount reminds Matthew's community of God's original intention that Israel live by the spirit of the Law and not its letter. The other sermons focus on the mission of the community (Matt 10), the way God works in the world (Matt 13), church discipline (Matt 18), and eschatology (Matt 24 and 25).[5] The narrative passages in the Gospel hint at God's blessing of the families of the earth beyond Israel, a message that God had intended for Israel to convey from the moment of the implementation of the covenant but that it had periodically ignored.

Matthew 5-7—The Sermon on the Mount: Jesus' Interpretation of Jewish Law

The Sermon on the Mount in Matthew 5–7 contains Jesus' encouragement of Israel toward a different understanding of the Law. Clarence Jordan interpreted the Beatitudes in Matthew 5:1-11 as a ladder into Jesus' perspective or worldview about the kingdom of God on earth.[6] Taken together, the Beatitudes summarize the basic content of the Sermon on the Mount. Here Jesus calls for an individual descent into humility of spirit, followed by deep mourning and grief over the reality of one's own spiritual condition and of meekness and gentleness in light of this inadequacy. From this point, Jesus calls his listeners to ascend toward righteousness, mercy, purity, and peacemaking in the world. The result, he assures them, will be persecution for the sake of righteousness. One cannot live in the world according to a proper understanding of the Law of Moses without encountering intense persecution.

In the Sermon on the Mount, Jesus introduces absolutely nothing that is uniquely Christian. Every word in the Beatitudes and in the rest of the sermon focuses attention squarely on what it means to live as a follower of the Law of Moses. Jesus expounds upon the themes of the Beatitudes throughout the sermon, assuring his listeners of his respect for the Law and the Prophets and addressing the ways in which the Law should be interpreted when it comes to anger, adultery, divorce, oath-taking, retaliation, love for enemies, almsgiving, prayer, fasting, and material possessions. He concludes by reassuring his listeners of God's provision for them, reminding them of the need to treat others as they themselves would want to be treated, and warning them about false prophets and against doing evil in the world. Always for Matthew, the focus is on action and the doing and living out of the Law by blessing others as a manifestation of faithfulness to the Law. To this end, Jesus concludes the sermon with the words, "Everyone then who hears these words of mine and acts on them will be like a wise man who built his house on a rock" (7:24).

The Sermon on the Mount is a missionary text in the sense that it encourages Israel, and by extension Matthew's community, toward the full embrace of its calling to be a community in the world that models God's intention for all of humanity from the very moment of creation. By living out its life in full commitment to the Law as Jesus interprets it here, Israel becomes again the example to other families of the earth of life together in a community of wholeness or shalom.

Matthew 8-9—The Faith of the Gentiles

The story of the centurion's servant in Matthew 8 is part of Matthew's subtext that subtly hints at the reality of God's blessing those outside of Israel by drawing attention to the faith that Gentiles possess. The Gentile centurion asks Jesus to heal his servant. When Jesus says, "I will come and cure him," the centurion insists that there is no reason for Jesus to go to his house to perform the miracle (8:7-8). He believes that Jesus can simply speak the words of healing and the healing will occur. In response, Jesus addresses Israel's lack of faithfulness, saying to the crowds, "in no one in Israel have I found such faith," and adding "I tell you, many will come from east and west and will eat with Abraham and Isaac and Jacob in the kingdom of heaven, while the heirs of the kingdom will be thrown into the outer darkness, where there will be weeping and gnashing of teeth" (8:10-12). This great reversal of Israel's expectations parallels the judgment upon some in Israel by the prophets of the Hebrew Bible. Other stories in Matthew 8 and 9 document Jesus' fulfillment of the words of the prophets in the Hebrew Scriptures and the efforts of the scribes and Pharisees to brand him as a heretic.

Matthew 10–14—The Jewish Mission

In Matthew 10 (the mission discourse), Jesus prepares his disciples for their first *mission*, this one a mission *specifically to Israel*. Again, *mission* refers to any effort by a human being in the world or a family of the earth to work together with God at that moment to accomplish God's intentions and purposes for the creation. Here Jesus tells the disciples to "Go nowhere among the Gentiles, and enter no town of the Samaritans, but go rather to the lost sheep of the house of Israel" (10:5-6). By designating Israel as the "lost sheep," Jesus expresses his conviction that Israel, or at least some portion of Israel, has strayed from the path that God intended for them to follow. The twelve disciples are charged with the doing of certain miracles including healing, raising the dead, and casting out demons. They are to take nothing for the journey and to depend on their hosts for whatever they need.

In this commission, Jesus reflects more deeply on the reality of the persecution that the disciples will experience, a reality to which he had first drawn their attention in the Sermon on the Mount. He warns them that the initial persecution will come from within Israel itself. "Beware of them," Jesus says, "for they will hand you over to councils and flog you in their synagogues; and you will be dragged before governors and kings because of me, as a testimony to them and to the Gentiles" (10:17-18). He adds, "You will be hated by all (Jew and Gentile alike) because of my name" and warns them that they will be persecuted in every town of Israel that they enter.

These are not encouraging words. Jesus reminds the disciples that they should not fear those who can kill the body and that they should acknowledge him before others here on earth knowing that then Jesus will acknowledge them "before my Father in heaven" (10:32). Jesus affirms the revolutionary nature of his own message, knowing that in Israel that message will not bring peace but rather will bring a sword that separates family members from each other, perhaps in the same way that the remnant of Israel as designated by the prophets of Israel signaled a separation. He concludes this second sermon by returning to their mission and reminding the disciples "whoever welcomes you welcomes me" (10:40). Significantly, the original mission of the twelve Jewish disciples of Jesus is a Jewish mission to the Jewish people.

Jesus' words and actions confuse even John the Baptist. He sends messengers to Jesus to ask if Jesus is "the one who is to come, or are we to wait for another?" (11:2). Jesus seems on a mission to divide Israel rather than to unite it, which is exactly the opposite of what Israel expected of the

Messiah. Jesus points to what he has accomplished: the blind see, the lame walk, the lepers are cleansed, the deaf hear, the dead are raised, and the poor have good news brought to them (11:5). He reproaches the cities of Chorazin, Bethsaida, and Capernaum in Israel for their lack of repentance and suggests that the Gentile cities of Tyre and Sidon and Sodom "would have repented long ago in sackcloth and ashes" (11:21).

In Matthew 12, the Pharisees and scribes, threatened by Jesus' interpretations of the Law, constantly challenge him. They point out that he and his disciples work on the Sabbath (plucking heads of grain and healing), thus breaking the commandment that the Sabbath is a day of rest. They condemn the casting out of a demon as the work of Beelzebul. Once again Jesus lifts up Gentile families, including the Ninevites and the "Queen of the South" (a reference to the Queen of Sheba in 1 Kings 10:2) who are identified as repentant families of the earth (12:38-42). Nineveh and the Queen of the South "will rise up at the judgment with this generation and condemn it" (12:41-42). Consistently through the chapter, Matthew reminds his community that Jesus fulfills the prophecies of the Hebrew Scriptures.

Matthew 13 and 14 contain parables of Jesus related to the kingdom of God and more miracles of Jesus, including the feeding of the five thousand and the account of Jesus and Peter walking on the water. Significantly, after Jesus and Peter walk on the water, "those in the boat worshiped him, saying, 'Truly you are the Son of God'" (14:28). Matthew repeats the title "Son of God" for Jesus at several points in the Gospel and by Jews and Gentiles alike.

Matthew 15–17—Recovering the Jewish Calling through a Mission to the Gentiles

The central story in Matthew 15 is the story of the Canaanite woman's faith. Jesus has departed to the region of Tyre and Sidon, a region that Jesus has already described in Matthew 11 as a place that would have repented in sackcloth and ashes long ago if it had been aware of God's blessings upon it and the reality of its own sin. Again, like the wise men, the Canaanite woman identifies Jesus with Israel, this time as "Son of David" instead of "king of the Jews." Jesus ignores her plea to remove a demon from her child, pointing out that his mission is only to the lost sheep of the house of Israel (15:24). She responds that "even the dogs eat the crumbs that fall from their master's table" (15:28), and Jesus acknowledges the depth of her faith and heals her daughter.

The only way to explain Jesus' response is to acknowledge that Jesus' primary mission in Matthew is to focus his work among the people of Israel in order to help Israel recover its divine mission and purpose. There is nothing universal about this text. Jesus refers to the Canaanites as "dogs," signaling his own perspective as a Jew toward Gentiles. Here he identifies fully with his own Jewish mission to such an extent that he shows little empathy for the woman and her child.

What could possibly cause such apparent callousness on the part of Jesus? How are we to understand the fact that a universal Savior for all of humanity would refer to a person outside the Jewish faith as a "dog" and, initially at least, refuse to grant her request? The only answer is that, for Matthew, Jesus' focus is solely on his own people and family and the recovery of their mission and purpose in the world. He recognizes that his opportunity to transform Israel's perspective and renew its commitment to the mission of God in the world is limited, and he prefers not to turn his attention in a different direction, at least not in this instance. Here Matthew makes clear Jesus' primary focus on Israel. Any focus beyond Israel, even one as worthy as that expressed by the Canaanite woman, detracted from Jesus' particular mission and purpose. By reminding him of the universal nature of his divine mission, she models the depth of faith that Gentiles also possess. His experience with her makes clear that even Jesus can become so preoccupied with Israel's blessing that he ignores the reality of God's blessing upon every earthly family.

In chapters 16 and 17, Matthew juxtaposes the condemnation of Jesus by the scribes and Pharisees with the affirmation of Jesus by Peter, Moses, Elijah, and God at the Mount of Transfiguration and with Jesus' own words about his call to his followers to "deny themselves and take up their cross and follow me" (16:24). The experience on the Mount of Transfiguration with Moses and Elijah once again signals the connection between the mission of Israel and the mission of Jesus. Jesus stands within the tradition of the Law and the Prophets as one who calls Israel back toward a proper understanding of both.

Matthew 18–20—The Ecclesia as a Jewish/Gentile Community

Matthew 18 represents a transition in the Gospel. In the particular sermon in this section (the third of the five discourses in Matthew), Jesus turns his attention to the church. The first mention of the word "church" in Matthew occurred in chapter 16 when Jesus responded to Peter's confession that he was the Messiah with words of blessing: "You are Peter, and upon this rock I will build my church, and the gates of Hades will not prevail against it" (16:18). The institutional church seized upon the word to refer to itself and to justify its existence in the world and its own authority vested in its hierarchical structures.

This is not how Matthew would have understood the word. The word Matthew uses is the Greek word *ecclesia*, a word that simply means "the called-out ones" or those who commit to the way of Jesus as expressed in Matthew's Gospel. The word *ecclesia* calls to mind the faithful remnant of Israel whom the Hebrew prophets had praised as opposed to the faithless people of Israel who continued to oppress the poor and to engage in other acts of injustice. In Matthew 18:15, Jesus says to the disciples, "If another member of the *called-out ones* sins against you, go and point out the fault when the two of you are alone." Jesus then outlines a process for reconciliation among the *ecclesia* who obviously are part of Matthew's community. They are encouraged to forgive each other "seventy-seven" times. They are also advised earlier in the chapter that, "unless you become like children, you will never enter the kingdom of heaven" (18:3) and that they should not cause each other to stumble (18:6-7).

The concept of the *ecclesia* provides Matthew with a powerful identity for his particular community. By identifying the followers of Jesus as "the called-out ones," Matthew offers them a designation for themselves that is neither Jewish nor Christian and that allows them to move beyond the Jewish-Gentile divide that had become a problem for the community. They were simply those who had been called out to embrace the way of Jesus and to live their lives out of that conviction and embrace.

Chapters 19 and 20 provide further evidence of Jesus' primary concern for Israel. A rich young man asks a question that gets right to the heart of the Law of Moses: "Teacher, what good deed must I do to have eternal life?" (19:16). Jesus responds with a very Jewish answer: "If you wish to enter into life, keep the commandments" (19:17). He responds out of the context of the Jewish worldview in a way that recognizes and affirms the keeping of the Law and specifically the Ten Commandments as a path toward eternal life. But he also recognizes that the young man's wealth stands in his way and so he advises him to "sell your possessions and give the money to the poor . . . then come, follow me" (19:21).

When the young man leaves because such sacrifice is impossible for him, Jesus says to his disciples, "it is easier for a camel to go through the eye of a needle than for someone who is rich to enter the kingdom of God" (19:24). At the end of the chapter, Jesus praises the disciples for their willingness to abandon material wealth for the good of his kingdom and he promises them twelve thrones from which to judge the twelve tribes of

Israel, a hundredfold in blessings, and eternal life as well (19:27-30). Note that the disciples are to judge the twelve tribes of Israel as opposed to other families of the earth.

Gentiles are mentioned twice in chapter 20, first as the ones to whom Jesus will be handed over by the chief priests and scribes to be "mocked, flogged and crucified" (20:19) and then as the ones whose rulers "lord it over them" as tyrants. Jesus reminds the disciples as his Jewish followers "whoever wishes to be first among you must be your servant" (20:26), the only conclusion being that Matthew wants to treat Jews and Gentiles equally. Jesus is about to condemn Jewish leaders upon his entry into Jerusalem, so now he condemns the ways in which Gentiles lead as well. No one lives up to the standards or expectations of God. The chapter ends as Jesus heals two blind men on his way to Jerusalem. At the point of the triumphal entry, they beg mercy from the "Lord, Son of David" (20:30).

Matthew 21–28—The Mission to Every Earthly Family

The large crowd who welcomes Jesus to Jerusalem in chapter 21 takes up the cry of the blind men as they shout, "Hosanna to the Son of David!" Matthew describes Jesus' entry into Jerusalem as the fulfillment of the words of the prophet Zechariah in Zechariah 9:9: "Tell the daughter of Zion, Look your king is coming to you, humble, and mounted on a donkey, and on a colt, the foal of a donkey" (21:9).

Upon entering Jerusalem, Jesus goes to the temple where he turns over the tables of the moneychangers, thus symbolically upending the perversion of the Law by the chief priests and elders. In the parable of the two sons (21:28-32) and in the parable of the wicked tenants (21:33-41), Jesus contrasts the righteousness of the chief priests and the elders with the righteousness of tax collectors and prostitutes who produce "the fruits of the kingdom" and will enter that kingdom ahead of the chief priests and elders (21:43 and 21:31). The tension with the chief priests and elders and the scribes and Pharisees intensifies in chapters 22 and 23 to the extent that Jesus refers to the scribes and Pharisees as "hypocrites" who "lock people out of the kingdom of heaven" (23:13) and as "blind guides" and "blind fools" (23:16-17). He charges them with "neglecting . . . justice and mercy and faith" (23:23) and with being full of "greed and self-indulgence" (23:25). His condemnation reaches a climax with the words "upon you may come all the righteous blood shed on earth, from the blood of righteous Abel to the blood of Zechariah son of Barachiah, whom you murdered between the sanctuary and the altar" (23:35).

Sensing that, after this diatribe, his end is near, Jesus predicts the destruction of the temple in Matthew 24 as the introduction to his fourth sermon. He predicts the persecution that will come upon his followers and then announces the pounding refrain that the "good news of the kingdom will be proclaimed throughout the world, as a testimony to all the nations" (*panta ta ethne*), literally, among all the families of the earth (24:14). In this refrain is the distant echo of the promise of God to Abraham, that the families of the earth will bless themselves by him. Once this proclamation occurs, "the Son of Man will appear in heaven, and . . . all of the tribes of the earth will mourn, and 'they will see the Son of Man coming on the clouds of heaven' with power and great glory . . . and they will gather his elect from the four winds, from one end of heaven to the other" (24:30-31).

Jesus' words in Matthew 24 communicate the powerful message that the perversion of the Law by the scribes and Pharisees is going to give way to a recovery of God's original intention and purpose for the covenant that God made with Abram and the proclamation of the good news that God has blessed all the families of the earth. At the end of time, all the families of the earth will mourn the great suffering that has occurred, and the Son of Man will gather his elect from "one end of heaven to the other," a clear indication that the righteous will include representatives from every family of the earth. In the meantime, Matthew 25 calls for Jesus' disciples and Matthew's community to prepare themselves for that day (the parable of the ten bridesmaids), to work on behalf of the kingdom by investing them-selves in it (the parable of the talents), and to do justice and mercy in the world (the parable of the sheep and the goats).

The parable of the sheep and the goats is perhaps the most revealing in the entire Gospel. It refers to the criteria for the judgment of all the families of the earth (*panta ta ethne*) (25:32) who had been dispersed at the point of the Tower of Babel story. The families of the earth come back together, each to give an account of their particular contributions to the blessing of all humanity. The story of the Magi bringing their gifts of gold, frankincense, and myrrh also comes to mind. In this parable, the Son of Man "will separate people one from another as a shepherd separates the sheep from the goats," putting the sheep on his right hand and the goats on his left (25:32). The criteria at the judgment is determined not by assent to doctrine or commitment to a particular belief about the Son of Man but rather by each family's contributions or gifts of justice and mercy to the world: to feeding the hungry, giving drink to the thirsty, welcoming the stranger, clothing the naked, and visiting those in prison. The hope is that each family and each individual has contributed to the community of shalom, of wholeness and peace that God intended from the beginning.

The parable makes clear that those at the judgment are not of any one particular religion or faith. The Son of Man gathers all the families of the earth to give account of their particular contributions to justice and mercy in the world as evidenced by their acts of kindness and goodness. God's mission in the world is inclusive of those beyond Israel and the church who follow "the law written upon their hearts" to accomplish God's original intention of a diverse community of peace (the *ecclesia*) that lives in harmony with itself, with other families of the earth, and with the rest of the creation.

This parable offers a prophetic word to the church today that often shuts itself off to partnership in mission with people of other faiths and religious traditions. I once served as president of a community ministry composed of Christian churches. A Jewish synagogue applied to become a member congregation. One church, the largest contributing financial partner to the community ministry, refused to allow the synagogue to join, stating as its reason that it only collaborated with people who ministered "in the name of Jesus." Ultimately, the community ministry lost the opportunity for partnership with the synagogue who, for good reason, felt unwelcomed at the table. It also lost its largest contributing church. The parable of the judgment in Matthew offers a compelling call toward partnership with any family of the earth seeking to do justice and mercy in its community.

After the parable of the judgment, Jesus makes a solemn announcement to his disciples: "You know that after two days the Passover is coming, and the Son of Man will be handed over to be crucified" (26:2). Matthew 26 and 27 tell the horrific story of the betrayal of Jesus by Judas Iscariot, the denial of Jesus by Peter, the abandonment of Jesus in the garden by Peter, James, and John, and the betrayal and death of Jesus at the hands of the chief priests and the Roman leaders. Throughout this entire section of the Gospel, Matthew refers to Jesus as "rabbi" and "teacher" (26:17, 25, 49). He claims the words of the prophets Zechariah and Daniel to legitimate Jesus as the Messiah of Israel (26:31, 64), including the prophecy of the abandonment of the shepherd by the sheep. Just at the point of his arrest, Jesus points out that "all this has taken place so that the scriptures of the prophets may be fulfilled" (26:56), and, at this point, his own disciples abandon him.

As they prepare him for the crucifixion, the soldiers of Pilate, the governor of Judea, mock Jesus by calling him "King of the Jews," and, once they crucify him, they put a sign over his head that says, "This is Jesus, King of the Jews" (27:29, 37). Even the scribes and elders join in with the taunt, "He is the King of Israel; let him come down from the cross now, and we will believe him" (27:42). Only a centurion, a Gentile, and those with him, frightened by the darkness and the earthquake that followed Jesus' death, cry out, "Truly this man was God's son" (27:54).

Joseph of Arimathea requests the body of Jesus, buries it in his own tomb, and seals it with a rock. On the third day, an angel of the Lord rolls the rock away and proclaims to Mary Magdalene and Mary that the tomb is empty. Jesus appears to the two Marys and instructs them to tell Jesus' disciples to meet him in Galilee. He then appears to his disciples on a mountain in Galilee, announcing, "All authority in heaven and on earth has been given to me." He instructs the eleven remaining disciples to "Go . . . and make disciples of all the nations (*panta ta ethne*), baptizing them in the name of the Father and of the Son and of the Holy Spirit, and teaching them to obey everything that I have commanded you. And remember, I am with you always, to the end of the age" (28:16-20).

Here the disciples receive their particular mission, a mission that is among the most misunderstood passages in all of the New Testament, largely because of the interpretation of it across the last three hundred years of Christian mission. First, the mission to which Jesus calls the disciples is a mission to teach and to make disciples. It is not a calling to convince others to intellectual belief in Jesus as the Son of God and to baptize those who have "believed" in this propositional truth. Rather, it is a calling to teach other families of the earth to embrace the way of Jesus expressed in the Sermon on the Mount and refined in his teachings throughout the other four sermons in Matthew's Gospel. Once they have taught this way, the disciples are to baptize other families of the earth who acknowledge their commitment to it. The evidence of this commitment comes at the point of their willingness "to obey everything that I have commanded you" (28:20).

Jesus' disciples in Matthew's Gospel do not teach until they themselves have embraced these teachings to such an extent that they live them out in their own lives. As Michael P. Knowles points out, "Their teaching is a distinctly post-Easter activity."[7] Once they have been able to grasp Jesus' teachings about the mission and purpose of God in the world in the light of his resurrection, they encourage others to join the *ecclesia*, the called-out ones, who embrace the way of love, grace, and peace that he modeled. Baptism is an acknowledgment of the full embrace of this way rather than simple mental assent to propositional truth about Jesus' identity as the Son of God. It is baptism into the way that he proclaimed and not baptism into belief about him.

Again, this calling to teach all the nations or families of the earth adds a deeper element to the Tower of Babel story. At Babel, God dispersed human families to the various corners of the earth. Now Jesus sends the disciples as bearers of the message of God's intentions to that dispersed humanity. The disciples have received the gospel or good news of God, expressed through a Jewish cultural lens, and are now to baptize all families of the earth in the ways of love, mercy, and grace that God intended from the beginning and has now fully expressed in the life and words of the rabbi Jesus. Having received the full authority of heaven and earth, Jesus sends the disciples forth into other cultures and families in the same way that God sent him into the Jewish family. Each culture possesses within itself the same possibility for love, mercy, grace, and justice that existed within the Jewish faith. The teachings of Jesus, experienced and proclaimed by his Jewish disciples through the lens of their own particular culture, serve as the foundation for the message of love and grace that they now share with other earthly families. The disciples have the same obligation as Abram: to enable the families of the earth to bless themselves and, in time, to offer their own gifts of blessing to the common human family.

The subtext within Matthew's Gospel is equally significant. The gifts of the Magi, the faith of the Canaanite woman, Jesus' elevation of Gentile families of the earth over the Jewish family at various points in the Gospel, and the parable of the great judgment in Matthew 25 remind Matthew's community that the Jewish family receives a hundred-fold in blessing what it gives away in blessing. God's blessings do not flow in a single direction. Every family of the earth contributes in significant ways to the full realization of God's vision and mission for all the earth. In the hands of the Gentiles, the teachings of the rabbi Jesus will take on much deeper and more powerful meaning and clarity than if they had simply retained their Jewish ethos. The Gentiles will bless Israel and the church with deeper insights about God, the creation, and humanity than would have otherwise been possible.

Conclusion

The twofold purpose of the Gospel of Matthew then was to assist Israel to rediscover its calling to be a blessing to other families of the earth as well as to accept the reality that God had blessed other families and intended for them to become the source of blessing to Israel and to each other. Matthew is a particularly Jewish Gospel that bridges the story of the Hebrew Bible with Jesus' role as the Son of Man who calls Israel to return to God's original intentions for it. In Matthew, Jesus is the rabbi or teacher who reimagines the Law for a new day, pointing out the many ways in which its letter has replaced its spirit and condemning those like the Pharisees, Sadducees, and scribes who have misinterpreted it. From start to finish, Matthew's Gospel is a gospel to the Jewish family that has embraced the way of Jesus, calling it to share with the world its particular gifts that unlock a message of hope and possibility for all of humanity. It is a call to Israel to join God on mission in the world to create the community of shalom. It is a call to Israel to reject the worst of itself by embracing the best of its neighbors.

Matthew's message is as universal as it is particular. At the heart of the gospel is a message to all the families of the earth. The call of God to each family is a calling to embrace the law written on its heart by recognizing its own inadequacy, its need for repentance, mercy, and forgiveness, and its need to live pure and righteous lives of grace and mercy and to seek justice, reconciliation, and peace both within the family and beyond. In Israel, all families of the earth find a model for the ways that God works through their particular cultures and histories to accomplish God's mission in the world. Jesus' message to Israel through Matthew then is a message of blessing to all the families of the earth. It is also a call to acknowledge the ways in which we have twisted that blessing and turned it into a curse upon others rather than a blessing.

So what new insights emerge for the church today in light of Matthew's Gospel? How do we read it differently than our forebears read it two or three centuries ago? Where has the equator of Matthew's Gospel shifted in light of the new context that we inhabit? A reading of the Gospel in a multicultural context raises questions for other families of the earth as well as for ancient Israel. What have our own cultures, religions, and faith perspectives offered to us in the past that we have now lost? How do we recover ancient truths that might bring us to a point of repentance and a deeper faith in God?

I will use my own earthly family as an example. I recently sent a DNA sample to Ancestry.com for analysis. In the meantime, I began working on my genealogy and made some interesting discoveries. My particular family of the earth is Scotch-Irish and English with a sprinkling of German. I belong squarely in the Anglo-Saxon tribe. That tribe's particular early religious expression focused, like many first religions,[8] on a relationship to the earth itself and to harmonious relationships between the tribe and the gods, within the tribe, and beyond the tribe. In the fifth century, Anglo-Saxons migrated from the northern coast of Germany and into Great Britain. Over time, Anglo-Saxons would become the dominant political power in Great Britain and the ancestors of the British people.[9] They also became primarily Christian because of their conversion to the Christian faith, and they became the source of much of the tradition of Western and particularly Protestant Christianity. There is much to celebrate in the history of Anglo-Saxon Christianity as well as much for which to repent.

The Euro-tribal churches to which I have referred throughout this book have been the source of much pain and suffering for other families of the earth as they have enslaved other families, justifying that oppression by appealing to Christian Scripture. Our sin has been the sin of colonialism, of cultural domination, and of extracting the resources of other peoples and nations for our own benefit. We tend to be insular and to assume our own superiority over other families; as a result, our strength often serves to expose our weakness. Despite our obvious cultural sins and limitations, our missionary efforts in the last three centuries have resulted in the emergence of the Christian faith as one of the major religions of the world, albeit one that is twisted and perverted by the original sin of White cultural domination and superiority.

I once joined a group of representatives from various ethnic backgrounds in writing a book about ministry to our particular ethnicity. My assignment was to describe for my readers from other families of the earth how they should minister to Anglo-Americans.[10] After wrestling for days with the assignment, I finally concluded that the only way to minister to Anglo-Americans was to forgive us for this sense of superiority over other families of the earth and to minister to us despite it. My assumption was that Anglo-Americans will only realize the absurdity of our sense of superiority when persons of other races and cultures reflect it back to us by relating their experience of it.

My conclusions were short-sighted and erroneous. The reflections of ourselves through the lens of others is not enough to overcome our own self-interest. Some thirty years later I have reached a different conclusion, one helped along by the work of womanist theologian Chanequa Walker-Barnes, who argues that racial reconciliation is only possible when it focuses its efforts *"upon dismantling White supremacy, the systemic evil that denies and distorts the image of God inherent in all humans based upon the heretical belief that White aesthetics, values, and cultural norms bear the fullest representation of the* imago Dei" (italics hers).[11] It is not enough to expect Anglo-Americans to act differently because they have been forgiven by those whom they have wronged. Instead, the racist structures that perpetuate such legitimacy must be demolished and rebuilt. Only in this way can the heresy be eliminated. Walker-Barnes points out that such a process must include the reconstruction of every public system from political structures to educational structures to the criminal justice system to healthcare to religious institutions and structures because these institutions in their current forms "create and reproduce patterns of racial injustice over time."[12]

To put it another way, we cannot simply appropriate the history of Israel for ourselves, especially as Euro-tribal followers of Jesus, branding ourselves as the New Israel, a Chosen People, and ignoring the unique realities of our own cultural heritage that have been a curse to so many other families. My Euro-tribal cultural identity matters as much to me as to others. It is both curse and gift, as are the facts that I am a US American male, that my family roots run deep in the American South, and that my families on both sides migrated from Scotland, Ireland, England, and Germany into the Appalachian Mountains. My cultural blessings are many. History for me is linear, I value common sense and a practical approach to life, I champion individualism and democracy, and I believe in hard work and that there is no such thing as fate. My curse, however, is a devastating curse. Deep down within me is that sense that my race is superior to all others. The challenge for me is to fully acknowledge that curse and to work together with other families of the earth to dismantle its pernicious effects and continued existence in nearly every area of global life.

I recently listened to two podcasts that focused on murder cases in the American South during the Civil Rights era. *Buried Truths* explored events surrounding the murder of Isaiah Nixon in Alston, Georgia, by two White men in 1948 and the shooting of A. C. Hill by two White police officers in 1962 in Macon, Georgia.[13] *White Lies* focused on the murder of the Rev. James Reeb, a White Unitarian minister, in Selma, Alabama, in 1965.[14] The complicity and solidarity of the White community that either refused to identify the people who had carried out the murders or refused to convict those charged with the murders deeply disturbed me and exposed once again the lengths to which a particular family of the earth will go in protecting its own privileged place. White eyewitnesses liberally sprinkled references to God and faith throughout hundreds of interviews, most far more concerned with protecting people of their own race than with acknowledging the injustices that occurred.

I came away from those podcasts convinced again that it is only at that common human table that I can confess the sins of my own earthly family, work to dismantle the structures by which it has elevated itself, rediscover my calling to bless others with the gifts that my family does possess, and, with humility, receive the blessing that other families of the earth offer to me. Matthew's Gospel beckons me to that table as Matthew reminds his own earthly family, and by extension the church in its Euro-tribal expression that has usurped Israel's mythologies, that we see ourselves most clearly only when we acknowledge the curse that we have visited upon other families of the earth, embrace the otherness and difference that is their gift to us, and work together to create a global community that reflects the full power of God's blessing upon all of us. The Gospels of Mark, Luke, and John and the teachings of the Apostle Paul help us toward a full understanding of the challenges and possibilities of such embrace.

Notes

1. John P. Meier, *Matthew* (Wilmington, DE: Michael Glazier, Inc., 1980), xi.

2. Darrell Guder, *The Continuing Conversion of the Church* (Grand Rapids, MI: Eerdmans Publishing, 2000), 90.

3. Michael P. Knowles, "Mark, Matthew, and Mission: Faith, Failure and the Fidelity of Jesus," in *Christian Mission: Old Testament Foundations and New Testament Developments*, ed. Stanley E. Porter and Cynthia Long Westfall (Eugene, OR: Wipf and Stock, 2011), 81.

4. James LaGrand, *The Earliest Christian Mission to "All Nations" in the Light of Matthew's Gospel* (Grand Rapids, MI: Eerdmans, 1999), xiii–xiv. Note that it is Richard Bauckham who mentions this tension in the foreword.

5. Robert H. Mounce, *Matthew* (San Francisco, CA: Harper and Row, 1985), xv.

6. Clarence Jordan, *Sermon on the Mount* (Valley Forge, PA: Judson Press, 1952, 1970 edition), 19.

7. Knowles, "Mark, Matthew, and Mission," 80.

8. I use the term "first religions" to refer to the original religious practices of ancient tribal families across the earth. These first religions were generally animistic, sharing a belief in a high god or gods, a particular tribal emergence mythology, shamans or holy people who assisted the tribe to cross life and geographic boundaries, a high regard for dreams and visions as sources of spiritual insight, kinship with all of creation, and ancestor veneration.

9. Kelly Brown Douglas, *Stand Your Ground: Black Bodies and the Justice of God* (Maryknoll, NY: Orbis Books, 2015), 7. Douglas traces the development of the Anglo-Saxon race from Tacitus's *Germanica* written in 98 CE to the incorporation of Anglo-Saxon mythologies in the structures and

worldview of White persons in the United States and the notion of American exceptionalism (see pp. 3–47).

10. See Robert N. Nash, Jr., "Anglo-Americans," in *Many Nations Under God: Ministering to Culture Groups in America*, ed. Ele Clay (Birmingham, AL: New Hope Publishing, 1997), 55–73.

11. Chanequa Walker-Barnes, *I Bring the Voices of My People: A Womanist Vision for Racial Reconciliation* (Grand Rapids, MI: Eerdmans, 2019), 11.

12. Walker-Barnes, *I Bring the Voices of My People*, 44.

13. *Buried Truths*, podcast, National Public Radio, https://www.npr.org/podcasts/577471834/buried-truths.

14. *White Lies*, podcast, National Public Radio, https://www.npr.org/podcasts/510343/white-lies.

Chapter 5

Mark and Mission— Bridging the Families of the Earth

> The open space of Galilee symbolizes a freer spirit than that represented by the walled city of Jerusalem. The Kingdom is open to "all the nations," Jews and Gentiles, as well as to both males and females. It is not hierarchical in structure but egalitarian in nature . . . . Most importantly, its central authority is Jesus, who was enthroned not by the power of the resurrection but in the humiliation of the cross. (94)
> —Werner H. Kelber, *Mark's Story of Jesus*

The Gospel of Mark is the oldest Gospel in the New Testament, composed at some point in the decade of the 60s CE, and thus a primary source for Matthew and Luke. For this reason alone, its message is significant. The other Gospel writers will either add to Mark's account or subtract from it, giving clues to the particular concerns of the churches to which they write. While the exact location of Mark's community is difficult to discern, many scholars assume that it is somewhere outside Palestine and perhaps just north of Galilee in the area of Syria, a predominately Gentile region.[1] Authorship and location, however, are far less important than the themes of the Gospel, especially those related to Mark's church, which, like Matthew's community, faced considerable challenges. The lack of unity between its Jewish and Gentile members threatened to overwhelm and sink it beneath the waves of its own aversion to otherness and difference. This alone was enough to distract it from full and faithful participation in the mission of God in the world.

Mark writes to a community that is probably some distance from the center of the Jewish faith and the emerging Christian community, and it includes both Gentiles and Jews. His purpose is twofold: to bridge cultural and religious differences between the two groups and to encourage a geographically isolated community by reminding it of its central place as a unified community in God's mission in the world. He calls it to move beyond the divide between Gentile and Jew in order to offer a compelling witness to the presence of the resurrected Jesus in its midst.

How does the Gospel of Mark encourage the relocation of the equator of interpretation in our own day? It offers a compelling and prophetic word to the church in the twenty-first century that challenges the church toward multicultural faith, unity, and witness. It also encourages the church toward otherness and difference, as much for the purpose of its own transformation as for the transformation of those outside it. Finally, the Gospel of Mark encourages a church that exists on the margins of a dominant culture to learn what it means to engage in mission from the margins instead of from the center.

Interestingly, Mark prioritizes the region of Galilee and Nazareth over Jerusalem and Judea in his interpretation of the life and ministry of Jesus. I play a little game with my classes when I teach about mission and the Gospel of Mark. I call it "Gospel Geography," and I encourage my students to boo and hiss when they hear the words "Jerusalem" or "Judea" in the Gospel and to cheer when they hear the words "Nazareth" or "Galilee." I then point out that Matthew and Luke both contain narratives about the birth of Jesus, but that Mark has no interest in Jesus' birth. Jesus was born in Bethlehem *of Judea* ("boo and hiss"), so perhaps this is the reason Mark ignores it. Instead, Mark begins with the appearance of John the Baptist in the wilderness *outside* Jerusalem and Judea ("boo and hiss"), presumably near the Jordan River, preaching "a baptism of repentance for the forgiveness of sins" (1:4). The people *of Jerusalem and Judea* are coming out into the wilderness for baptism by John perhaps because, being from the region, they are unrepentant people who need it.

Mark then reports, "Jesus came from Nazareth of Galilee [resounding cheers] and was baptized by John in the Jordan" (1:9). Immediately after the baptism, the Spirit "drove him out into the wilderness" where he spent forty days with the wild beasts and angels and where Satan tempted him. Mark captures Jesus' entire experience in Jerusalem and Judea in thirteen short verses. He reports that "Jesus came to Galilee, proclaiming the good news of God" and the coming kingdom (1:14). Mark's word choice communicates the powerful reality that centers the Gospel in Galilee. Jesus "came" to

Galilee; he did not "go" to Galilee. In the same way, at his baptism he came "from" Nazareth of Galilee and not to the wilderness of Judea.

The entire ministry of Jesus will then unfold in Galilee, where Jesus will call the first disciples (1:16-20), heal the sick and demon possessed, and proclaim the kingdom of God. The Sea of Galilee plays a central role in the Gospel as Jesus moves back and forth across the water, performing similar miracles on both its Jewish and Gentile sides. Werner Kelber and E. S. Malbon have carefully documented Mark's distinction between the Jewish culture of the Jewish side of the sea and the Gentile culture(s) of the non-Jewish side of the sea.[2] The Sea of Galilee serves as a metaphor in the Gospel for what occurs whenever followers of Jesus cross a cultural divide. Storms ensue. People become frightened in the boat. Jesus then appears to denounce the lack of faith of those who are crossing the divide and to calm the storms. It is the sea that "exposes the disciples' lack of faith and the formidable boundary between Jew and Gentile."[3]

Jesus' encouragement of the crossing of cultural divides offers deeper perspective on the reasons for God's displeasure at the point of the Tower of Babel story when the families of the earth clung together. Now, with the Jewish family firmly entrenched in its particular culture, Mark's Jesus encourages it to cross the divide to engage otherness and difference. In the same way, he empowers Gentiles in the Gospel by encouraging them to receive him as well as his disciples despite the broken relationships that exist between the two groups. Mark's call is for a community of Jewish and Gentile followers of Jesus to learn to get along with each other and, in the process, to learn from each other.

To accomplish his purpose, Mark divides his Gospel into several sections that help to make his point about cultural difference through the lens of "Gospel Geography." Here are the sections along with their distinctive geographical foci:

1. Mark 1:1–13—Jesus in Judea
2. Mark 1:14–4:34—Jesus in Jewish Galilee
3. Mark 4:35–5:20—The Gentile Side of the Sea
4. Mark 5:21–6:44—The Jewish Side of the Sea
5. Mark 6:45–8:21—The Gentile Side of the Sea
6. Mark 8:22–10:52—The Prediction of Suffering on the Journey to Jerusalem
7. Mark 11:1–13:37—Jesus in Jerusalem
8. Mark 14:1–15:47—Jesus' Crucifixion in Jerusalem
9. Mark 16:1-8—Jesus' Resurrection in Galilee

Jesus and the disciples cross over to the Gentile side of the sea twice, and each time a storm rises on the sea and Jesus confronts his disciples with their lack of faith. Interestingly, no storms occur when the disciples and Jesus travel from the Gentile side of the sea back over to the Jewish side. Similar miracles also happen on each side of the sea, as do the feedings of the five thousand on the Jewish side and then of the four thousand on the Gentile side.

Mark 1:14-4:34—Jesus in Jewish Galilee

The second section (Jewish side) and the third section (Gentile side) of the Gospel offer striking contrasts. On the Jewish side, Jesus casts out a demon, heals numerous people including Simon's mother-in-law, and attracts followers from among both Jews and Gentiles with some coming from as far as Tyre and Sidon to witness his miracles and hear his teachings. Perhaps the greatest contrast occurs at the point of Jesus' encounter with the demon-possessed men on their respective sides. On the Jewish side (1:23-28), the demon-possessed man is in the synagogue with the other Jewish men who are praying there. He says to Jesus, "What have you to do with us, Jesus of Nazareth? Have you come to destroy us? I know who you are, the Holy One of God" (1:24). Jesus commands the demon to come out, and immediately it does. The man convulses and cries out with a loud voice, and the incident is over. Everyone marvels at the authority of Jesus and the fact that even the demons obey him.

Mark 4:35-5:20—The Gentile Side of the Sea

Mark reports that "A great windstorm arose, and the waves beat into the boat, so that the boat was being swamped" as the disciples and Jesus crossed from the Jewish side to the Gentile side and made their way toward the Gerasene demoniac (4:37). Despite the storm, Jesus falls asleep on a cushion in the stern of the boat. His disciples wake him up, incredulous that he can sleep while "we are perishing" (4:38). In this first crossing, Jesus rebukes the wind and the waves as opposed to rebuking the disciples, and immediately "the wind ceased, and there was dead calm" (4:39). He asks the disciples why they were afraid and questions the depth of their faith. In awe, they say to one another, "Who is this, that even the wind and the sea obey him" (4:41).

For the disciples, a journey to the region of the Gerasenes offered enough reason to be afraid. They were entering an unclean and unholy place beyond the boundaries of their own religion and people and one that their own Law forbade them to enter. Like their forebears at the point of their enslavement in Egypt, they were moving beyond their own space, where real demons and danger lurked. Their response was to be expected. They had assumed that ethnicity and purity determined both access to God and the blessing of God; now Jesus was implying that such spiritual access and blessing was available, indeed that it had already been extended, to every family of the earth.[4]

On the Gentile side, in the country of the Gerasenes, the demon-possessed Gentile, in a very different place from his Jewish counterpart, is among the tombs and occasionally restrained with chains that are unable to hold him. Night and day, he sits there, howling and bruising himself with stones. Seeing Jesus in the distance, he runs to him and says, "What have you to do with me, Jesus, Son of the Most High God? I adjure you by God, do not torment me" (5:7). The demons in him protest that they are many, and Jesus agrees to send them into a herd of swine feeding near the sea. Immediately, two thousand swine "rushed down the steep bank into the sea, and were drowned" (5:11-13).

The contrasts between the two stories are powerful and significant. In both instances, Jesus casts out the demons. The Jewish story is a tame story in which Jesus and the demon exchange words in the synagogue and Jesus orders the demon out of the man. The Gentile story is much more colorful, dripping with impurity and filthiness, at least as Mark's Jewish readers would hear it. Standing among the Gentile tombs, the demon-possessed man refers to Jesus as the "Son of God Most High" (5:7) as opposed to "the Holy One of God" (2:24). The Jewish law would have prohibited swine on the Jewish side of the sea, but on the Gentile side pigs feed among the tombs, and thousands rush into the sea when the demons enter them, creating what had to be a horrible sight in the water.

The disciples and, by extension, Israel, are not the only group to respond to the engagement with otherness and difference with fear and aversion. I will speak only for my particular family of the earth, Euro-tribal Christians, who are often guilty of similar behavior, assuming ethnic or at least national and religious superiority over the very people to whom they seek to minister. These attitudes of superiority, as subtle as they may be, are nevertheless real. They are especially evident as churches move outside their own cultural and national spaces on short-term mission trips and without sufficient orientation to make them aware of their cultural blinders. Sometimes, fear and aversion are the ways attitudes of superiority are expressed.

Several years ago, I found myself in a hotel in Quito, Ecuador, having breakfast with a colleague from my university. We were there to meet with university officials in Ecuador to promote faculty and student exchanges. As we ate our breakfast, a mission team from a church in the United States came thundering down the stairs and noisily took their places at a table. We could easily overhear their conversation because they were talking so loudly.

The waiter came up with a pitcher of orange juice and offered it to every person at the table. One of the group members addressed his colleagues: "Remember that we aren't supposed to drink anything in these countries that isn't in a sealed bottle because it might be made with dirty water." Other group members nodded, and, one after another, they refused the orange juice.

By this point, many Ecuadorans in the restaurant had lifted their heads to observe the exchange. Shaking his head in confusion at the fact that all ten people had refused the orange juice, the waiter retreated to the kitchen.

In a few moments, a woman, obviously the team leader, joined the group. Cautiously, the waiter made his way over to her and timidly asked, "Would you like some orange juice?"

"Absolutely," she responded, and she lifted up her glass so that he could easily pour the orange juice into it.

The entire table thundered, "We thought you said we weren't supposed to drink the orange juice in these countries because it's made with dirty water!"

For the briefest moment, I thought we had made progress.

"Oh, yes," she said. "We can drink the orange juice in a nice restaurant like this. It's only out *in the jungle* that we can't drink the orange juice."

I turned to my South American colleague and apologized for the behavior of my particular family of the earth. Being gracious, Linda nodded, grinned, and simply continued eating her breakfast.

Storms ensue whenever we leave our own space to inhabit the space of others. Mark knows this. For him, the storms on the Sea of Galilee are as much metaphorical storms as they are real. The disciples are entering into a region that, for them, is unclean and where impurity abounds. The storms represent the turmoil and challenge of any intercultural engagement and symbolize the fear of otherness and difference that often paralyzes the church today. We fear what we do not understand. We are most comfortable with those who are part of our own cultural and religious family. We demonstrate the superiority of our culture by demonizing another culture, its religion, and even its food.

Mark's storms represent the demonic and evil forces that perpetuate such attitudes and increase our separation from the other families of the earth rather than our intentional engagement with them. No family of the earth is immune from such destructive attitudes. For the disciples, the sea represents a tomb of darkness that threatens to overwhelm them.[5] The overcoming of fear is a recurring theme for Mark and perhaps the very point that Mark is trying to impress upon his community. In Mark's Gospel, Jesus overcomes our fears, calling us to embrace otherness and difference rather than to avoid it, and he attributes avoidance to demonic and evil attitudes of the heart.

Mark 5:21–6:44–The Jewish Side of the Sea

In Mark 5:21, Jesus and the disciples return to the Jewish side, this time without storms or other incidents. Mark simply says, "When Jesus had crossed again in the boat to the other side, a great crowd gathered around him." The disciples and Jesus head back to their own place and people. No storms ensue. The wind and the waves remain calm. They arrive back in a familiar context where their particular worldview is the dominant one. They know the landscape and feel at home in the space.

We should not minimize or discount the ease with which this return occurs; the power of it rests in the relative simplicity with which it happens. We speak of "the comfort of home." Such comfort emerges from a common language, places with which we are familiar, and people who are very much like us in terms of allegiances and worldviews. We long for home. The experience of being in strange places exhausts us and requires far more intensity and energy than we think we can sustain. This was as true for the disciples of Jesus when they returned to the Jewish side of the sea as it is for us when we return into our own cultural space from an encounter with otherness and difference. For this reason, we should pay as much attention to what happens to the disciples on the return voyage as we do to what happens to them on the outbound one.

In the summer of 1980, I decided to travel around the world by myself, flying west from Atlanta. After spending about three weeks in Manila with my missionary parents, I set out on the longest part of my journey. For about eight weeks, I did not see a single person that I had known previously. In those days, there was no email or internet, no Facebook or Twitter. Telephone calls were too expensive. Mail was slow to catch up with me, and the postcards I sent home arrived long after I did. For eight weeks, I traveled alone on an Air India "around-the-world" ticket that cost me $600. I spent time in Hong Kong, Thailand, India, Greece, Germany, France, Switzerland, Holland, Spain, and the United Kingdom.

Storms emerged constantly on the journey. I lost my way in a maze of streets in Mumbai, India, and had real difficulty getting back to my hotel. I spent time at the Taj Mahal in Agra but found myself frustrated by a taxi driver who was determined to take me to carpet factories that I had no desire to see. I could not find a hotel room in Rome after arriving in the city around midnight, so I spent the night in the train station with one leg drooped through the handle of my backpack and one eye open.

My mood alternated between exhilaration and intense loneliness and frustration. I enjoyed the sights of Rome with an Austrian farm boy who was studying architecture at the University of Vienna. I walked the streets of Paris with a group of Greek students who were staying at the same youth hostel. I sat on the steps of the British Museum as a Japanese neurosurgeon who had just finished his residency in Scotland apologized to me for Japan's actions in World War II.

I finally arrived back in the US at JFK airport in New York City and made my Delta connection to Atlanta. As I sat back in my seat, the flight attendant announced in a deep Southern drawl that we should buckle our seatbelts and return our trays to their upright position. The cadence of her voice and the Deep South in it caused my entire body to relax. I knew I was home. The various storms that had come up on my journey were over. I was in my own space where the dominant worldview and language were my own and where most everything was familiar. I imagine that this is how it was for Jesus' disciples as they crossed back again to the Jewish side of the sea. There were no storms because they were headed home.

Mark's point is that home demands the least of us. It is the journey across the sea toward *the other side* that reminds us of our obligations as followers of Jesus. The journey to the other side heightens our dependence on those who live there as much as it heightens our dependence on the One who encourages us toward the encounter. The visit to the other side forces us to see ourselves as we really are. I often tell my students during a study abroad visit or during a mission immersion experience in another country that I never want to hear anyone say, "I learned to appreciate the United States so much more because of this experience." This is not the point. The point is to allow the encounter with otherness and difference among other families of the earth to expose our cultural blemishes at least as much as it validates and reinforces what we believe to be our cultural blessings.

After the return journey, Mark sets up an intentional parallel between Jesus' words and actions on the Jewish side of the sea and Jesus' words and actions on the Gentile side of the sea (6:45–8:21). On the Jewish side, Jesus heals a woman with a hemorrhage and raises the daughter of Jairus, a synagogue official, from the dead. He also returns to his hometown in Nazareth where his own townspeople "took offense at him" and "he could do no deed of power" (6:4-5). This story of Jesus' reception in Nazareth signals the hesitancy of Jesus' own friends and family to embrace his message of inclusivity. Mark also tells the story of the sending of the twelve into nearby villages, though, unlike Matthew, Mark does not emphasize that this is a mission to the lost sheep of Israel. For Mark, Jesus' mission is not simply to Israel. From the very beginning, it is to the Gentiles as well.

The section reaches its climax in the story of the feeding of the five thousand on the Jewish side of the sea just as the next section will end with the feeding of the four thousand on the Gentile side of the sea. Jesus' first question to the disciples in both stories is, "How many loaves do you have?" (6:38 and 8:5). On the Jewish side, the disciples find five loaves and two fish, and on the Gentile side, they locate seven loaves and "a little fish." In both instances, Jesus blesses the loaves and then later distributes the fish. The loaves, and not the fish, play the central part in the story.

Mark 6:45–8:21—The Gentile Side of the Sea

After the feeding of the five thousand on the Jewish side of the sea, Jesus sends his disciples across the sea again to Bethsaida on the Gentile side while he departs to a mountain to pray. This particular crossing of the sea is one of the most revealing passages in all of Mark's Gospel and perhaps its climax. I often use it as an ordination text for ministers preparing to serve Christ's church in the context of the diversity and multicultural realities of the twenty-first century. Notice that this time Jesus instructs the disciples to make the passage without him. He has already accompanied them once on the journey from the Jewish side to the Gentile side. His hope now is that they will be able to cross the great divide toward the encounter with otherness and difference without him.

Significantly and perhaps symbolically, the disciples are literally hugging the shore of the Sea of Galilee as they make their way toward Bethsaida. Jesus is "alone on the land" and he sees that the disciples are "straining at the oars against an adverse wind" (6:47-48). He determines at that point to walk across the water in the general direction of the boat, but "he intended to pass them by" (6:48). He does not intend to stop to help the disciples. He was with them in the boat on the previous crossing. Surely they can make the trip without him this time. They are fighting a headwind, but the boat is in shallow water, a scant few hundred feet off the shore.

Once again, the disciples are frightened, but this time not by the wind. They are terrified instead by the sight of Jesus crossing the water toward the Gentile side of the sea. They think he must be a ghost (6:50). Is it their assumption that only ghosts can walk on water, or is it their assumption that only ghosts would head toward the unclean Gentile side of the sea? They know of the demon-possessed swine who ran off the cliff into the water. They remember the cemetery where the demon-possessed Gentile man lurked. The sea is a terrifying place for them. They fully expect ghosts to emerge out of it. To allay their fears, Jesus ceases his journey toward the Gentile side and climbs into the boat with the disciples. Immediately, he lets them know who he is ("Take heart, it is I"), and his presence in the boat causes the winds to cease. To explain their astonishment, Mark inserts the curious line, "for they did not understand about the loaves, but their hearts were hardened" (6:52).

This interesting statement by Mark again shows Mark's interest in the loaves that play such a prominent role in both feedings. What point is Mark trying to make to his community somewhere up north of the Sea of Galilee? It must be that the loaves on the Jewish side of the sea and the loaves on the Gentile side of the sea have some bearing on the experience of the disciples as they cross from one side to the other. The answer to these questions will emerge in Mark 8 upon the return journey to the Jewish side.

The fact that Jesus made every effort to avoid climbing into the boat with the disciples reveals so much about Mark's purpose and intention in writing the Gospel. Jesus' desire is to be on the Gentile side of the sea with the Gentiles when the Jewish disciples arrive. Instead of encouraging him in his intention, the disciples frustrate his mission out of their own fear, not of the wind but of Jesus. They are as frightened by the sight of Jesus headed to the Gentile side without them as they are by the sight of Jesus walking on the water. The text reflects the constant challenge that has disturbed God from the very moment God ordered humanity to "be fruitful and multiply and fill the earth." Evading this directive, humanity has tended to cling to itself, preferring the comfort of its own particular culture, language, and worldview to the challenge of engaging otherness and difference in the world.

When Jesus arrived in Gennesaret on the Gentile side, "people at once recognized him" and brought the sick to him to be healed (6:54). Jesus had been to Gennesaret before. The Gentiles there knew him. The fact that his disciples had forced him back into the boat to reassure them in the midst of their terror must have been terribly frustrating. Despite the time they had spent with him and the healings and miracles they had witnessed, they were not capable of making the journey alone. They still needed Jesus to be with them in the boat when they arrived on the Gentile side.

This text is such a powerful ordination text because it reminds ministers in the twenty-first century in a global context of diversity and multiculturalism that it is the calling of the minister to sit in the boat with the church, offering encouragement as Jesus passes by on his way to the other side. A minister of the Gospel must be ready to say, "Don't worry. That's just Jesus passing by. He is on his way to the people on the other side. We have spent time with him, as have they. Let him go where he needs to go. We will join him soon." The leadership calling of a minister in the context of a diverse world requires a willingness to cross cultural divides and to assist churches toward those places where Jesus already is, even if the church has difficulty recognizing Christ's presence there. This calling is true for ministers in Euro-tribal churches, but it is also true for churches to which other families of the earth belong. The need to embrace otherness and difference is at the core of God's intention for humanity.

I once had the privilege of serving as the interim pastor of a large church in an inner suburb of Atlanta. This predominately White congregation had approached a large Black Baptist church about joining in a Palm Sunday afternoon worship service together. On the designated Sunday, the White congregation made its way toward the Black church. The initial plan called for the White deacons and the Black deacons to meet together for prayer while the Black ministers and White ministers did the same thing in a separate room. As the ministers gathered, a Black deacon entered the room and announced to his pastor, "Preacher, we have a problem!"

My Black pastor counterpart responded, "Well, brother, what seems to be the issue?"

The deacon plunged ahead. "Preacher, this White church has women deacons!"

I have to confess that I panicked, believing that our carefully planned worship service might not happen and that I would have to gather up my church members and head home.

Not to worry.

Without missing a beat, the Black pastor looked at me, rolled his eyes, and then turned to his deacon. "We're here to work on diversity," he said. "What did you think? That they were the only ones who had to do it?"

With that prophetic word from his pastor, the deacon turned and left the room and the service proceeded without incident. We two pastors, one Black and one White, would stand by the altar table and pass the elements of the supper, first to a woman, then to a Black man, and then to a White man in one of the most powerful Communion services of which I have been part.

This crossing of the sea brings to mind the great theological and missiological challenge for Euro-tribal churches as well as for congregations of other ethnicities in the twenty-first century. This challenge is the inordinate fear of otherness and difference that twists and perverts the gospel. Again, I will speak only for my own family of the earth. Euro-tribal churches, having drunk deeply from the cup of White patriarchy, mourn the loss of our own place and space in a rapidly changing culture. Fighting the headwinds of such change, we insist that Jesus remain in the boat with us and we cling more tightly to our privilege and prominence. We believe that we possess Jesus, and, in the process, we compromise the good news of God's love for all the families of the earth.

Mark then pushes the matter of inclusivity forward in his Gospel. First, he shifts the understanding of purity from an external purity under the Law to an internal purity of the heart. Approached by Pharisees and scribes who have noticed his disciples "eating with defiled hands," Jesus condemns them by charging them with holding to human tradition instead of the commandment of God. He then calls the crowd to him and says, "There is nothing outside a person that by going in can defile, but the things that come out are what defile" (7:1-14). Here the matter of Jewish purity, so important to the Jewish family, gives way to an internal purity that is possible for all of humanity.

The story of the Syrophoenician woman and her demon-possessed daughter in the region of Tyre in Lebanon follows this one about Jewish purity. The contrast of this story with Matthew's account is as striking as the earlier contrast in Mark's Gospel between the casting out of demons on the Jewish and Gentile sides of the sea. Mark's account does not contain the words that Matthew uses: "I was sent *only* to the lost sheep of the house of Israel." Instead, Jesus says, "Let the children be fed first" (7:27), a much gentler assertion of the priority of Jesus' mission to the Jews. In both instances, Jesus exorcises the demon from the daughter because of the woman's faith and without the need for Jesus' actual presence. Here Mark pushes beyond both the Jewish and Gentile divide as well as the divide between men and women as two women benefit from Jesus' healing power.

Mark then focuses on the feeding of the four thousand people on the Gentile side. Werner Kelber points out one significant difference and one significant similarity between the feeding of the five thousand on the Jewish side and this feeding of the four thousand. The significant difference comes at the point of the amount of food collected afterward, twelve baskets on the Jewish side and seven baskets on the Gentile side. In Kelber's estimation, the numbers recall the early Christian and Jewish community in Jerusalem that "was presided over by the leadership structure of the Twelve but also by a group made up of seven Hellenists under the supervision of Stephen (Acts 6:1-6)."[6] These symbolic numbers signal that the two groups are about to become one loaf.

In both feedings, Jesus insists that the disciples should be the ones to share the loaves and the fish with the gathered crowds. In this way, he draws attention to their responsibility to provide for the physical and spiritual needs of both Jews and Gentiles. Again Kelber points out that "their feeding of the Jews and of the Gentiles should enlighten them with respect to their own future roles and the kind of community for which they were to carry responsibility."[7] They are ministers to Jews and Gentiles alike, and their calling is to encourage diverse groups from among the families of the earth to embrace each other. Only in this way can the families of the earth fully grasp God's intentions for all creation.

Jesus reemphasizes the matter on the next journey on the sea, again to another location on the Gentile side. Despite the fact that they had taken up seven baskets full of food from among the Gentiles, they "had forgotten to bring any bread" and end up with only a single loaf in the boat to share. The general interpretive approach to this passage has been to point to the lack of faith of the disciples when it comes to Jesus' ability to multiply the loaves and fish. This interpretation misses the point of the feedings. Jesus has no concern about whether his disciples are hungry or whether they have enough faith to believe that he can perform another multiplication miracle. Instead, Jesus wants his disciples to grasp the much greater miracle that his Jewish and Gentile followers are a single loaf and thus one body. In Christ, each family brings its perspective to the common table where the two groups become one.

Here Jesus speaks to the disciples as if they are children. Frustrated by their lack of understanding, he asks a series of rhetorical questions intended to expose their ignorance: "Why are you talking about having no bread? Do you still not perceive or understand? Are your hearts hardened? Do you have eyes, and fail to see? Do you have ears, and fail to hear? And do you not remember?" (8:17-18).

Then, perhaps rolling his eyes, he asks a simpler question: "When I broke the five loaves for the five thousand, how many baskets full of broken pieces did you collect?"

The disciples respond, "Twelve."

Jesus continues, "And the seven for the four thousand, how many baskets full of broken pieces did you collect?"

They respond, "Seven."

Jesus' last question is the most damning: "Do you not yet understand?"

This is the entire point of Mark's Gospel. Somewhere on the northern edge of Galilee, perhaps in Syria, sits a church that includes among its membership both Jews (twelve disciples) and Gentiles (seven deacons). This church is a harbinger of God's original intention for the creation. It is a community of faith composed of representatives from among the families of the earth. It represents the world as God intended it to be from the beginning, a community in which various cultures share together their perspectives on God, the creation, humanity, love, and faith. Jews and Gentiles alike compose a single loaf in the vision that God has for humanity.

Mark 8:22–10:52—The Prediction of Suffering on the Journey to Jerusalem

The blindness of the disciples to this unified vision becomes clear in the healings of the two blind men that frame the next section of the Gospel. First Jesus heals a blind man at Bethsaida in Mark 8:22-26 just prior to Peter's confession of Jesus as Messiah, and then he heals blind Bartimaeus in Mark 10:46-52 just prior to his triumphal entry into Jerusalem. In between the two healings, Jesus makes his way together with his disciples from Caesarea Philippi and toward Jerusalem. Along the way, Jesus clarifies for his disciples exactly what it means that he is the Messiah. They thwart his efforts at every turn because of their blindness about his coming death and resurrection. On three different occasions and in three different geographical locations, Jesus talks of his suffering and death and of its implications for his followers. He addresses the matter first in Gentile Galilee at Caesarea Philippi at the beginning of the journey (8:31–9:1), second on the way through what is presumably Jewish Galilee on the way toward Jerusalem (9:30-32), and finally as he is about to enter Jerusalem (10:32-34). Repeatedly, the disciples in both Gentile and Jewish regions reveal the depth of their own blindness about his mission and purpose as they argue among themselves about their own greatness (9:33-37), the depth of their sacrifice for Jesus (10:28), and their right to sit at his right hand in his kingdom (10:35-45).

Mark intends for this particular section to offer a contrast between the increasing blindness of Jesus' disciples on the way to Jerusalem (boo and hiss) with the increasing faith and sight of Jesus' new disciples in Mark's own faith community to the north of Galilee (cheers). They can see what the disciples cannot see. They are privy to a truth that Jesus' own disciples do not perceive. Jesus is the Messiah, not just for the Jews but for the Gentiles as well. His mission is to bring the families of the earth back together again as a single human family that encompasses Jew and Gentile alike.

Mark 11:1–13:37—Jesus in Jerusalem

Several unique features mark this section of Mark's Gospel, all intended to drive home for Mark the reality that the mission of Jesus has nothing whatsoever to do with being the Messiah of Israel, nor does it have much to do with the temple in Jerusalem. The city and its temple represent for Mark the worst features of a Jewish faith that has lost its way. As Jesus makes his way into Jerusalem, it is the people of Galilee ("those who went ahead and those who followed") who sing hosannas, but even they misunderstand his purpose and mission, believing him to be the one who will restore "the coming kingdom of our ancestor David" (11:9-10).

Kelber points out that Jesus never worships in the temple on the three occasions that he visits it in the Gospel.[8] On his first visit, he "looked around at everything" (11:11) as if he were on a reconnaissance mission to assess the state of the temple. On the second visit, he drives the moneychangers away (11:15-19) in a passage that is filled with symbolism, especially as it relates to the function of the temple. Citing the prophet Isaiah (Isa 56:7), Jesus reminds his listeners that the house of God was to be a "house of prayer for all the nations" ("all the peoples" in Isaiah). Here the obvious implication is that worship and prayer in the temple has been restricted to the Jewish people while people from other families of the earth stand outside, perhaps figuratively as well as literally. This alienation of the other families of the earth flies in the face of Solomon's prayer at the dedication of the temple when he asked God to hear the prayers of foreigners who would pray toward it. God's intention has been that Israel enable the families of the earth to bless themselves by Israel. The behavior of the chief priests, scribes, Pharisees, elders, temple sellers and buyers, and moneychangers are frustrating God's intention.

On his third visit, Jesus teaches in the temple, contrasting his own authority with that of the temple and its administrators. One by one, Pharisees, Herodians, Sadducees, and scribes test him by asking questions designed to trap him. Each time, he frustrates their efforts by responding with open-ended questions or direct confrontation. At the end of all the questions and testing, he predicts the destruction of the temple (13:1-2) and instructs his followers to prepare themselves for the suffering that is to come. He speaks of the coming of the Son of Man who will "send out the angels, and gather his elect from the four winds, from the ends of the earth to the ends of heaven" (13:27), again an obvious reference to the fact that those whom God has chosen extend far beyond Israel and include all families of the earth.

Mark 14:1–15:47—Jesus' Crucifixion in Jerusalem

It should be clear by now that nothing good happens in Jerusalem in Mark's Gospel. The passion narrative in Mark chronicles the growing divide between Jesus and the disciples, and in the end the disciples remain in Jerusalem, separated from Jesus, while the resurrected Jesus returns to Galilee. Mark describes this growing divide in a series of stories that include the woman with the jar of ointment (14:3-9), Judas's decision to betray Jesus

(14:10-11 and 14:43-50), the terrible story of the Passover meal with its themes of alienation and betrayal (14:12-25), and Peter's denial of Jesus (14:26-31 and 14:66-72). In each instance, the disciples clearly misunderstand Jesus' intentions and purpose, distance themselves from him, and fail to stand with him when he most needs their support and encouragement. Modeling their behavior on the second journey toward the Gentile side of the Sea of Galilee, they symbolically try to force him back into the boat with them rather than move along toward the place where he is waiting for them to join him. This time, however, he "passes them by" and makes his way to the far side of Galilee.

Mark takes only a single chapter of his Gospel to narrate the story of Jesus' crucifixion. Pilate washes his hands of him. The soldiers mock him as "King of the Jews," a real irony in Mark's Gospel since we have already seen that Mark understands Jesus to be much more than a Jewish king, and Jesus himself in Mark would see this as a misstatement of his mission and purpose. Passersby taunt him. Even God forsakes him.

When he takes his last breath, the curtain in the temple tears into two pieces from top to bottom, signaling the end of the temple as the seat of God's presence on earth and of the division between Jew and Gentile that had so disturbed Jesus and that is such a powerful theme of Mark's Gospel. Significantly, it is a Roman centurion, a Gentile, who notices that Jesus has taken his last breath and who proclaims, "Truly this man was God's Son!" (15:33-39). Jesus' only remaining disciples at the point of his death are the women who "used to follow him and provided for him when he was in Galilee" (15:41). Everyone else has abandoned him, and it remains to Joseph of Arimathea, "a respected member of the council," to claim Jesus' body and bury it. Perhaps here, Mark balances the confession of the Gentile centurion with the courage of a Jewish member of the council.

Mark 16:1-8—Jesus' Resurrection in Galilee

Mark reports that "when the Sabbath was over, Mary Magdalene, and Mary the mother of James, and Salome bought spices, so that they might go and anoint him" (16:1). When they arrive at the tomb, they discover that the stone that covered the entrance has been rolled back and that "a young man, dressed in a white robe" is waiting for them (16:5). He announces to them that "Jesus of Nazareth, who was crucified . . . has been raised; he is not here" (16:6). Then he adds, "Go, tell his disciples and Peter that he is going ahead of you to Galilee; there you will see him, just as he told you" (16:7).

Many readers of the Gospel of Mark are disturbed that it contains no resurrection appearance by Jesus. Without such an appearance, it appears at first glance to be a Gospel of suffering in which a forsaken Jesus identifies with those among his followers who have also been abandoned and forsaken. The apparent lack of a resurrection narrative was so disturbing that later manuscript editors added a longer ending to the Gospel that included an appearance to Mary Magdalene, to two anonymous disciples, and finally to the eleven themselves. This addition misses the point of Mark's Gospel. Of course the resurrected Jesus does not manifest himself in Jerusalem. Nothing good happens in Jerusalem in the Gospel. Jesus' ministry and focus throughout Mark has been in Galilee, and so it is in Galilee that the resurrected Jesus will appear.

At the conclusion of Mark's Gospel, Jesus is in Galilee. He stands with the faith community that lives not in the center or heart in Jerusalem but out on the edge in that place where people who are different from each other somehow manage to become one faith community composed of many families of the earth. This community on the margins deserves to know that the resurrected Jesus stands in its midst. The struggle for this community is the very real struggle and challenge of somehow becoming a single loaf despite its diversity and difference.

Conclusion

For these reasons, Mark's Gospel is a powerful Gospel for a church now that is struggling in the midst of diversity to find its way toward wholeness and community. This Gospel calls us toward the embrace of the other to such an extent that we are able to receive his or her blessing and to offer a blessing in return. Mark calls us beyond exclusion and toward embrace because his Gospel asks us to open our arms to the other not so that we crush them but so that we make them part of who we are and we become part of who they are.[9] It is a powerful Gospel in a day in which families of the earth who embrace Jesus Christ as Lord are seeking to worship and share life together despite their differences. It is a powerful Gospel in a day in which we are seeking common ground with our friends of other religions and worldviews who are working in concert with God's intentions and purposes for the world. It begs us to see the world from their perspectives and to understand their faith traditions from within.

I said at the beginning of this section on Mark's Gospel that Mark's purpose is twofold:[1] to bridge cultural and religious differences between Jews and Gentiles and to encourage a geographically isolated community by reminding it of its central place in God's mission in the world as a unified community of various earthly families. Mark takes a realistic approach to the challenges of such community by allowing us to see the deep struggle of the disciples as they cross the Sea of Galilee from the Jewish side to the Gentile side. The crossing is stormy and difficult, and heavy winds threaten the small boat. The effort to engage other perspectives and worldviews with open hearts and minds will often overwhelm anyone who seeks to make the crossing. Mark, however, is uncompromising in his call to his faith community to rise to the challenge. The point of his Gospel is not that we must take *our message* of Jesus to the world. Rather, his hope is that we will embrace the world with the blessings that we have received while being open to receive the blessings that others want to share with us. Mark's Gospel holds this out as the central hope and mission for his community.

For Mark, it is the willingness of his community to overcome its fear of otherness and difference that bears witness to the presence of the risen Lord in its midst. Its monocultural expression as purely a Jewish Christian community or a Gentile Christian community flew in the face of God's original intention and purpose for humanity. Jesus had gone ahead of his disciples into Galilee and toward that community of people who had embraced each other despite their differences. The risen Lord had no good reason to appear in Jerusalem (boo and hiss) in Mark's Gospel. The Jerusalem church was composed of people of a single religious and cultural heritage. Instead of appearing to this group, Jesus had "gone ahead" to that church beyond Galilee (resounding cheers), the one on the margins, the one that understood that a full grasp of the good news of God is impossible apart from the full embrace of otherness and difference.

Notes

1. Werner H. Kelber, *Mark's Story of Jesus* (Philadelphia, PA: Fortress Press, 1979), 13.

2. Werner H. Kelber, *The Kingdom in Mark: A New Place and a New Time* (Philadelphia, PA: Fortress Press, 1974), 60–63, and E. S. Malbon, *Narrative Space and Mythic Meaning in Mark* (San Francisco, CA: Harper and Row, 1986), 42.

3. Kelly R. Iverson, *Gentiles in the Gospel of Mark: "Even the Dogs Under the Table Eat the Children's Crumbs"* (New York: T&T Clark, 2007), 21.

4. Donald Senior and Carroll Stuhlmueller, *The Biblical Foundations for Mission* (Maryknoll, NY: Orbis, 1983), 222.

5. Joan L. Mitchell, *Beyond Fear and Silence: A Feminist-literary Reading of Mark* (New York: Continuum Publishing, 2001), 70–71.

6. Kelber, *Mark's Story of Jesus*, 39.

7. Kelber, *Mark's Story of Jesus*, 39.

8. Kelber, *Mark's Story of Jesus*, 58–59.

9. Miroslav Volf, *Exclusion and Embrace: A Theological Exploration of Identity, Otherness, and Reconciliation* (Nashville, TN: Abingdon Press, 1996), 30.

Chapter 6

Luke-Acts and Paul— Gentile Communities and Mission

The Promise is a gift accepted in faith. This makes Abraham the father of believers. The Promise was first made to him (cf. Gen. 12:1-3; 15:1-16) that he and his posterity would be, as St. Paul says in a vigorous and fertile expression, "the heirs of the world" (Rom. 4:13). For this reason, Jesus, John the Baptist (Luke 3:8; 13:16; 16:22; 19:9), and Paul (Gal. 3:16-29; Rom. 4; Heb. 11) place Abraham at the beginning of the work of salvation.

—Gustavo Guitierrez, *A Theology of Liberation*, 1973

Among all the Gospels, Luke and its companion volume, the Acts of the Apostles, offer the clearest connection between the mission of Jesus and the mission of the church.[1] Luke-Acts addresses the matter of how a community, composed primarily of Gentile followers of Jesus, should merge their particular perspective on the message of Jesus with the Jewish roots of that message and, empowered by the Holy Spirit, carry it *beyond* Jerusalem, Judea, and Samaria and into the rest of the world. The two-volume work encourages the church to embrace otherness and difference with intentionality and purpose, emboldened by the Holy Spirit to participate in God's mission in the world.

The Gospel of Luke

Like Matthew, Luke writes long after the completion of the Gospel of Mark, perhaps as much as thirty years later. Where Matthew had been primarily concerned with the mission of a community of Jewish Christians and Mark had encouraged unity between Jews and Gentiles, Luke reminds a church, located somewhere in the area of Antioch of Syria and composed mostly of Gentiles, about its particular calling and the spiritual revitalization that was necessary to accomplish it.

For this reason, Luke's Gospel is particularly missionary and urban in its major themes and concerns, addressing the theological and practical realities of Christian mission as lived out by third-generation Gentile and Jewish followers of Jesus outside Palestine.[2] Luke's community probably inhabited an urban context that was highly pluralistic and diverse. He contextualizes such accounts as Jesus' Sermon on the Plain (Sermon on the Mount in Matthew) among a very diverse crowd that included "a great multitude of people from all Judea, Jerusalem, and the coast of Tyre and Sidon" (6:17). He also locates the feeding of the five thousand in "a city called Bethsaida" as opposed to the "deserted place" in which Mark and Matthew place it (Mark 6:35 and Matt 14:15).

The major themes of Luke carry through to Acts, and the two volumes chronicle the journey of Jesus and the disciples into Jerusalem (Luke) and then the witness of the disciples (Acts) "in Jerusalem, in all Judea and Samaria, and to the ends of the earth" (Acts 1:8). The movement of the two-volume set is toward Jerusalem in Luke and then into the world in Acts. The Holy Spirit accomplished this work by constantly breaking down barriers in Luke-Acts, specifically geographical boundaries as well as those between Jews and Gentiles, rich and poor, and the leadership of Luke's community and its followers. Luke-Acts signals that a great reversal rests at the heart of God's community on earth, one in which the poor, the marginalized, and the oppressed receive the full benefit of God's goodness and grace at the expense of those who have deprived and oppressed them.

Luke structures his Gospel and its companion volume in a way that motivates his community toward missionary revitalization through the power of the Holy Spirit at work in its midst. John Michael Penney has pointed out the symmetry in the two books. Both begin with the Holy Spirit's empowerment of and presence with the key characters of the books. This empowerment is demonstrated then in powerful preaching, the performance of miracles that confirm the work of the Spirit, early successes, increasing opposition, an extended travel narrative, an arrest and trial, and a powerful resolution marked by joy and celebration.[3] In both volumes, "the Holy Spirit . . . is the Lord of mission who directs its progress and also enables its achievements."[4]

The books utilize narrative as instruction, seeking to encourage a new paradigm for mission engagement in the last decades of the first century.

Eugene LaVerdiere describes their primary audience as "the leaders of missionary communities" who "were shaken in their missionary approach to the gospel by problems from within as well as from without."[5] By pointing toward Jesus and the disciples as examples in the Gospel and Acts, Luke reminds these leaders that the Holy Spirit empowers them for their work, ensures the success of their efforts, encourages them in the midst of disappointment and suffering, and ultimately ensures a joyful and unhindered celebration of all that the Spirit has accomplished through them.

For these reasons, Luke-Acts deserves a fresh reading for the light it might offer to the leaders of missionary communities today who minister in diverse and multicultural contexts marked by small successes and huge challenges and disappointments. How do we as leaders of such communities discern the ways in which the Spirit is motivating us beyond social, religious, ethnic, and geographical boundaries that trap the very gospel we are seeking to proclaim? How do we encourage a marginalized church to embrace the opportunities that such marginalization affords? What might we learn from the ways in which Jesus and the disciples communicated the gospel in a diverse world? How might we locate the equator of interpretation in a new place for the diverse world that we now inhabit?

Luke structures his Gospel in the following way:

1. Luke 1:1-4—The Preface
2. Luke 1:5–2:52—The Prologue
3. Luke 3:1–4:13—The Preparation
4. Luke 4:14-44—The Mission of Jesus
5. Luke 5:1–9:50—Church Leadership and Mission
6. Luke 9:51–21:38—The Journey to Jerusalem
7. Luke 22:1–24:53—The Crucifixion, Resurrection, and Ascension of Jesus

Luke directs his preface to Theophilus, a name that simply means "lover of God" and one who has been "instructed," perhaps in a catechetical fashion, about Christian theology and practice. The name itself sounds like one that might belong to a righteous stranger of the Gentiles who worshiped God but was not of the Jewish family. Luke seems concerned that the lack of "an orderly account of the events that have been fulfilled among us" (1:1) hindered Theophilus's instruction in the faith. To this end, Luke constructs a careful narrative about the events surrounding the life of Jesus that is packed full of instructions to Theophilus and, by extension, to Luke's community and its leaders.

Luke 1:5–2:52—The Prologue

In his prologue, Luke narrates events surrounding the births of John the Baptist and Jesus, Jesus' presentation at the temple shortly after his birth, and his question-and-answer session with temple rabbis when he is twelve years old. He packs these narratives with rich detail and theological depth, acknowledging and affirming the Jewish religious context into which Jesus and John are born. He wants his Gentile church to appreciate these Jewish roots as the foundation for their own mission alongside God in the world. He also challenges them to build on this foundation through the power of the Holy Spirit in their midst, overcoming ethnic, gender, and geographical boundaries between men and women, rich and poor, and Jew and Gentile and encouraging their embrace of marginalized peoples.

Many events in the prologue occur in the temple and in the context of the established Judaism of the early first century. The first characters in the Gospel, Zechariah and Elizabeth, the parents of John the Baptist, are descended from established priestly families (Abijah and Aaron respectively). Luke describes the couple as "living blamelessly *according to all the commandments and regulations of the Lord*" (1:6), thus indicating their commitment to living righteous Jewish lives. As Zechariah performs his priestly duties in the temple, the angel Gabriel appears and tells him that his wife Elizabeth will bear a son who will "be great in the sight of the Lord" (1:15). Zechariah balks in disbelief due to their ages, and the angel strikes him mute (1:18-20). Once the child John is born, Elizabeth and Zechariah return to the temple for his circumcision and naming, and Zechariah, no longer mute, proclaims John's role as "the prophet of the Most High" who will "go before the Lord to prepare his way" (1:76).

Luke connects both John and Jesus to the covenant of God with Abraham and to the teachings of the prophets of Israel. Mary also acknowledges God's faithfulness to Israel and the Abrahamic covenant. Later, Jesus' parents will take him to the temple where Simeon will announce Jesus' role as "a light for the revelation of the Gentiles and for glory to your people Israel" (2:32). Then, at the age of twelve, Jesus will impress teachers in the temple with his understanding of the Law and the prophets (2:41-51).

Even as he acknowledges the Jewish credentials of Jesus and John, Luke also introduces a phrase in his prologue that is unique to his Gospel and to Acts. He describes John the Baptist, Elizabeth, and Zechariah as all being "filled with the Holy Spirit," while Simeon, another devout Jew who holds the infant Jesus in the temple, is described as having the Holy Spirit rest upon him (2:25). The phrase "filled with the Holy Spirit" is repeated three times in Luke (1:15, 41, and 67) and seven times in Acts (2:4; 4:8,

31; 7:55; 9:17; 13:9, 52) and appears nowhere else in Scripture.[6] It points to the powerful Lukan theme of the role of the Holy Spirit in helping humanity toward a deeper understanding of God's purposes (Luke) and in breaking down barriers that hinder the work of God in the world (Acts). The Spirit's presence within and upon these particular people certifies that in John the Baptist and Jesus, God is doing something new and different.

The prologue makes clear Luke's intention to include women and other generally overlooked individuals as significant people in the life story of Jesus and to allow his readers to hear their voices and innermost thoughts. Elizabeth proclaims, "This is what the Lord has done for me when he looked favorably on me and took away the disgrace I have endured among my people" (1:25). Mary sings eloquently and powerfully about the great reversal that God will accomplish through her child (1:46-55). And Anna, a widow of eighty-four years old when she sees the infant Jesus in the temple, "began to praise God and to speak about the child to all who were looking for the redemption of Jerusalem" (2:38). The powerful role these women play in Luke's story foreshadows Luke's concern for the marginalized and oppressed throughout his narrative.

Luke's story of the birth of Jesus reinforces the themes that he has already introduced. Just as he acknowledged the Jewish world into which Jesus was born, Luke now draws attention to the larger Roman and Gentile context. When the Roman emperor Augustus orders a census, Joseph and Mary make their way to Bethlehem because Joseph was "descended from the house and family of David" (2:4). Upon their arrival, Mary gives birth to Jesus in the humble context of a manger, again signaling Jesus' identification with the poor and oppressed of the world and the reality that his life will be lived on the margins of the political and religious power centers. Angels appear to humble shepherds, announcing Jesus' birth, and the shepherds make their way to Bethlehem to "see this thing that has taken place which the Lord has made known to us" (2:15). Once they have seen Jesus, they "made known what had been told them about this child" (2:17). Unlike Matthew, Luke reports no visit by strange wise men from the East nor any concerns of Herod about the child.

By the end of the prologue, Jesus has "increased in wisdom and in years, and in divine and human favor" (2:52). Luke has certified Jesus' Jewish credentials by the several stories that occur in the temple itself. He has also documented the high regard that Jewish priests and rabbis have for him. Finally, he has drawn attention to the work of the Holy Spirit in his understanding of God's mission in the world and to the elevation of the poor and oppressed that the Spirit will accomplish. To put it simply, even as Luke establishes Jesus' Jewish heritage by connecting Jesus to the temple, he also signals through his constant reference to the Holy Spirit that God is about to do something significant and unanticipated. That something will focus primarily on the work of God among the Gentiles.

Luke 3:1–4:13—The Preparation

Like Mark, Luke makes powerful use of geography at certain points in his Gospel and especially here at the beginning of Luke 3 when he describes the context of Jesus' baptism by John the Baptist and John's message of repentance for the forgiveness of sins. With a historian's attention to detail, he marks the exact time and place at which "the word of God came to John son of Zechariah." It occurred "in the wilderness" and "in the fifteenth year of the reign of Emperor Tiberius, when Pontius Pilate was governor of Judea, and Herod was ruler of Galilee, and his brother Philip ruler of the region of Ituraea and Trachonitis, and Lysanius ruler of Abilene, during the high priesthood of Annas and Caiaphas" (3:1-2). At this moment in a wilderness context, separated from and yet still in the center of all these regions of Palestine and these rulers, John preached the word he had received from God and baptized those who repented. *In the wilderness*, the Holy Spirit descended upon Jesus at his baptism and a voice from heaven attested, "You are my Son, the Beloved; with you I am well pleased" (3:32).

With this masterful use of history and geography, Luke points out the continuity of Jesus' mission with what has gone before as well as the interruption that Jesus' ministry will bring to the prevailing notions about God's work in the world. The Holy Spirit has interrupted history by situating John and Jesus outside the power centers with a prophetic message of repentance for the forgiveness of sins disconnected from particular political and religious contexts. Here Luke signals that the *word* of God as received by John *in the wilderness* will become a prophetic word that moves first into Jerusalem and then from Jerusalem into Judea and Samaria and across the Roman Empire, confronting and challenging political and religious authority. This rootless *word* enters into each particular context by the power of the Holy Spirit and beckons the families of the earth toward repentance for the forgiveness of sins and toward wholeness in community.

Luke follows his account of Jesus' baptism with the lineage of Jesus, tracing Jesus' ancestors all the way back, not just to David and Abraham as Matthew did, but also to Adam and God. Again, Luke's point is to separate Jesus from the particular history of a single family of the earth, in this case the family of Israel, and to point to his connection to Adam as the father of all humanity and to God as the source of all human life. Interestingly, Luke acknowledges Joseph as the father of Jesus but adds the parenthetical phrase, "as was thought," to indicate that Jesus is both of Israel and not of

Israel in the same way that Jesus is both the son of a man and not the son of a man. He is the son of God as much as he is the son of Adam. No particular human family has full claim to the lineage of Jesus.

This section ends with Jesus' temptations in the wilderness by the devil (4:1-13). Luke places the temptations immediately after his account of the lineage of Jesus to make concrete the relationship between the humanity of Jesus and his divinity. Unlike the children of Israel in the wilderness and Adam and Eve in the garden, Jesus withstands every common temptation and, in the process, signals the completion of his preparation for the challenges ahead. Luke uses the temptations as a teaching device for his own church, reminding its leadership to temper physical desires with spiritual vitality, to avoid spiritual pride in their own accomplishments, and to be prepared for violence and persecution because of their attention to the leadership of the Holy Spirit. The rest of Luke-Acts will give testimony to what happens when a community's leadership, filled with the Holy Spirit, is faithful to its calling.

Luke 4:14-44—The Mission of Jesus

In this brief text, Luke identifies Jesus as the Son of God and summarizes the mission of Jesus as a mission to the marginalized and oppressed among the Gentiles. Following his baptism and the temptations in the wilderness, Jesus returns to Galilee in order to announce his mission in the world and to begin his ministry. Luke describes Jesus as "filled with the Holy Spirit" as he prepares to teach in the synagogues of Galilee and Judea. His first stop is his own hometown of Nazareth, where his sermon in the synagogue on the Sabbath foreshadows his mission, not just to Israel but to the Gentile families of the earth as well. First, Jesus reads from the prophet Isaiah and proclaims his mission to "bring good news to the poor," "release to the captives," and "the recovery of sight to the blind" as well as "to let the oppressed go free" (Isa 61:1-2 and Luke 4:18). The crowd receives his words with openness and anticipation.

Then Jesus announces the Gentile mission. Using the stories of the widow of Zarephath in Sidon in the time of Elijah and of Naaman the Syrian leper in the time of Elisha, Jesus points out that both prophets ignored the needs of widows and lepers in Israel while performing miracles for a widow and a leper who lived outside of Israel. As this focus on Gentiles becomes clear, the crowd, "filled with rage," chases Jesus out of town and to a cliff intending to hurl him off, "but he passed through the midst of them and went on his way" (4:24-30). In one short text, Luke presents the major themes of his Gospel and the Acts of the Apostles, pointing toward the elevation of the marginalized as well as of the Gentile families of the earth.

The rest of Luke 4 tells the story of two miracles of Jesus and of Jesus' intentional decision to engage in ministry beyond Galilee. In Capernaum, he encounters a demon-possessed man who affirms Jesus' human and divine identities by referring to him as both Jesus of Nazareth and the Holy One of God (4:34). Jesus then moves from the synagogue to Simon's house, perhaps signaling the movement of the church from synagogue to house in Acts. There he heals many people of various diseases even as the demons he exorcises proclaim him "the Son of God" (4:41). This time the crowds try to prevent his departure from Capernaum, but he insists that he must "proclaim the good news of the kingdom of God to the other cities also" (4:43), in this instance the cities of Judea but eventually the cities of the Gentiles as well.

Luke 5:1–9:50—Church Leadership and Mission

This section of Luke's Gospel focuses attention on the disciples of Jesus and, by extension, the mission leaders of Luke's community. LaVerdiere points out that the nature of leadership in Christian mission unfolds in four major sections, each of which opens with a narrative about the disciples of Jesus: Luke 5:1-11; 6:12-16; 8:1-3; and 9:17.[7] Jesus selects leaders from among his followers, including a number of women. He instructs them about the nature of discipleship and about how to lead the church on mission in the world. He sends the twelve disciples out "to proclaim the kingdom of God and to heal" (9:2), giving specific instructions about what they should take on the journey. At the end of the section, the disciples feed five thousand people in response to Jesus' command, "You give them something to eat" (9:13).

Section 1: Luke 5:1–6:11.

The call of Simon Peter is the central story in this text and establishes Peter's position as the first among the disciples. It also foreshadows Peter's role in Acts when he will become the one who proclaims the meaning of Jesus' life, death, and resurrection to the Gentiles at the home of Cornelius (Acts 10). For this reason, the story is didactical, pointing the mission leaders of Luke's church to Peter's faithfulness and to this future moment of leadership when the Holy Spirit will fall upon the Gentiles. Luke's intention is that Peter's approach in Acts 10 should be the approach of a Gentile church in a Gentile world.

Here in Luke, Peter becomes an example of faithful obedience to Jesus by allowing Jesus to use his boat as a place from which to address the crowds on the shore and then by following Jesus' advice to drop his fishing net into deeper water. The symbolism in these two acts is the main point of the story. Peter's primary role is to help Jesus address a primarily Jewish crowd, but his willingness to "put out into deep water" and let down his nets for a catch is a uniquely Lukan way of signaling that, despite his initial reluctance, Peter will also play a major role in the Gentile mission (5:4). In the end, Jesus makes the point that the days of Peter, James, and John as fishermen have ended, and "from now on you will be catching people" (5:10)—Jewish people in the shallow water and Gentile people in the deeper water.

The miracles that Jesus performs in the rest of this section prefigure the Gentile mission of the church. He cleanses a leper "in one of the cities" (5:12), he stands up on three separate occasions to the challenge of the Pharisees and teachers of the Law about his authority to forgive sins, and he exposes their hypocrisy as it related to the observance of the Sabbath. By the end of the section, Jesus has reinforced his primary mission to preach repentance for the forgiveness of sins. He has also demonstrated that, because "the Son of Man is lord of the Sabbath," his call to discipleship and mission is the interpretive lens for the Mosaic Law. At this point, the scribes and Pharisees considered "what they might do to Jesus" (6:11).

Section 2: Luke 6:12–7:50.

Now Luke presents the call of the remaining disciples to the path of discipleship that Jesus has just defined as the new interpretive lens for the Law. Choosing twelve apostles, perhaps representative of the twelve tribes of Israel, Jesus signals the emergence of a New Israel. The twelve new apostles join him on a "level place" with "a great multitude of people from all Judea, Jerusalem, and the coast of Tyre and Sidon" (6:17). Here a diverse crowd gathers as equal families of the earth to hear Jesus and to witness miracles of healing; indeed, Luke reports that Jesus "healed all of them" (6:19).

After the healings, Jesus addresses the crowd, beginning with the twelve disciples, and provides a specific set of instructions to them. These instructions are again didactical and directed at the mission leaders of Luke's congregation. Jesus draws attention to the physical and spiritual deprivation that the disciples and other leaders will experience as well as to the persecution that will come to them because of the path they have accepted. Interestingly, he warns them of their branding as false prophets if they stray from the path, an obvious effort by Luke to address leadership challenges in his church.

Jesus then turns his attention to the crowd who represent for Luke the larger Christian community. The sentence "Do unto others as you would have them do unto you" serves as the major theme of his sermon (6:31). Discipleship means loving one's enemies (6:27-30), refraining from judgment and hypocrisy (6:37-42), and acting in ways that conform to the inner righteousness that ought to mark a follower of Jesus (6:42-49).

Immediately after the Sermon on the Plain, Jesus performs two miracles that demonstrate that his ministry is to both Gentiles and Jews respectively. First, he heals the slave of a Roman centurion, a close friend of Jewish elders. Struck by the faith of the centurion who insists that Jesus does not even need to enter his home in order to perform the healing miracle, he simply says, "not even in Israel have I found such faith" (7:9). In the second instance, Jesus enters the town of Nain where he encounters a funeral procession for the son of a Jewish widow. He touches the bier and commands, "Young man, I say to you, rise!" (7:14). Immediately the young man speaks and the witnesses declare, "a great prophet has risen among us! And God has looked favorably upon his people" (7:16). In both instances, Luke identifies Jesus as Lord of both groups and as having authority in the Gentile community to accomplish healing as the result of faith and in the Jewish community to raise a young man from the dead as the result of the young man's own compassion for his mother, and, by extension, for his own people.

The confirmation of the mission among both Jews and Gentiles causes John the Baptist to inquire if Jesus is "the one who is to come" (7:18-35). In this section, Luke reminds his readers of Jesus' description of his own mission in the synagogue at Nazareth (4:18-19) and points out that the "Pharisees and lawyers" rejected both the baptism of John the Baptist and the path of discipleship to which Jesus called them. The story of the forgiveness offered by Jesus to the sinful woman in Luke 8:36-50 serves as a contrast to the false righteousness of the Pharisees and lawyers and as a warning even to Simon and the other disciples and the leaders of Luke's church, driving home Luke's main theme that Jesus' primary mission is the forgiveness of sins.

Section 3: Luke 8:1-56.

Here Luke addresses the twelve disciples with specific instruction about the nature of the mission to which they are called, and he expands their circle to include "some women who had been cured of evil spirits and infirmities" (8:2). Again, Luke is speaking to mission leaders in his own church through this teaching and instruction. The presence of women in the group reinforces Luke's theme of inclusivity even as it prepares Luke's readers for the pivotal role of women at the cross, at the empty tomb, and in the life of the church in the book of Acts. Significantly, these women are not simply marginalized people with little standing apart from their relationship to

Jesus; among them is Joanna, the wife of Herod's steward, and other women "who provided for them [the disciples] out of their resources" (8:3).

The parable of the seed in Luke 8:4-15 and the calming of the storm on the Sea of Galilee in Luke 8:22-25 speak powerfully to the loss of mission and purpose that gripped Luke's church by providing the opportunity for Luke to remind it of its calling. Church leaders were confused. Why was the proclamation of the gospel falling on deaf ears? Why had the church lost the fire and passion that had marked its early years? Luke's answers are quite simple. Through the parable of the seed, he points out that a continuum of commitment to discipleship exists in the faith community, ranging from those who lack any commitment at all to those who, "when they hear the word, hold it fast in an honest and good heart, and bear fruit with patient endurance" (8:15). In other words, some receive the seed and do nothing with it; others embrace it fully and express it in faithful action that bears fruit in the world.

Luke uses the story of the storm on the Sea of Galilee to ask his own church a powerful question: "Where is your faith?" (8:25). In the midst of the challenges of life in the late first century, Luke's church was adrift in the sea with little direction and without a sense of how to get back to dry land. Like the disciples in the boat, the church feared that it was perishing and had no idea how to respond to this reality. In this sense, Luke's church is very much like congregations today who have little idea how to stem the tide of loss of place, membership, and mission passion. Luke calls his church to "patient endurance" (8:15), a listening spirit (8:18), and faithful action (8:21, 25). When Jesus' mother and brothers show up to see him, Jesus puts it quite simply: "My mother and brothers are those who hear the word of God and do it" (8:21).

The rest of this section draws attention again to the mission of Luke's church as one primarily to Gentiles while also acknowledging the importance of Jesus' relationship to Judaism. Unlike Mark, Luke is less concerned with the notion of the church as a single loaf of both Gentiles and Jews. In the story of the healing of the Gerasene demoniac (8:26-39) on the Gentile side of the sea, Jesus instructs the man from whom the demons have been exorcised to "return to your home and declare how much God has done for you" (8:39). Back on the Jewish side, Jesus encounters Jairus, "a leader of the synagogue," who begs him to heal his dying daughter. Jesus' words to Jairus and his wife when he raises their daughter from the dead are in marked contrast to his words to the demoniac; he instructs them "to tell no one what had happened" (8:56). This seems a clear signal to Luke's church that the focus of its mission and calling is among the Gentiles.

Section 4: Luke 9:1-50.

At this point, Jesus calls the Twelve together, empowers them for the work that they are to do, and dispatches them into the villages "to proclaim the kingdom of God and to heal" (9:2). He gives specific instructions about how to pack for the journey. They are to take nothing with them, leaving behind staff, bag, bread, money, and extra tunic. In other words, they are to be completely dependent on the people who receive them. Alan Roxburgh points out the reverse nature of hospitality that the disciples are to practice and emphasizes the link "between being in the place of the stranger in need and being able to discern God's working in the world . . . . one is the precursor of the other."[8] Rather than offering hospitality to others, the disciples are to accept the hospitality of the villages that they enter. They are to become guests in the world rather than hosts in their own homes. Luke insists that the mission leaders of his own church should learn to receive hospitality outside the church at least as much as they offer hospitality from inside it.

Jesus' instructions to the disciples call to mind my own upbringing in my family of origin. My mother spent considerable time teaching me how to be a good guest and a good deal less time teaching me how to be a good host. She probably assumed that if I could guest well, I could probably also host well. The rules she taught me are ones that are seared into my mind:

1. Watch your hosts and do what they do.
2. Put your napkin in your lap.
3. Eat what is put in front of you.
4. Write a thank-you note.
5. Make your bed.
6. Listen more and talk less.
7. Obey the rules of the house.
8. Make yourself useful as well as ornamental (my personal favorite).

On and on the list goes. Good guesting is hard work. It puts us at the disposal of others. It forces us to ask for what we need or to do without. It heightens our sensitivity to the needs of others. It forces us to acknowledge our own dependency.

For Luke, this forced dependency is essential to effective mission. It nurtures a deep spirit of humility and an attention to the needs of others. It forces a leader to listen more attentively to the leadership of the Spirit than to one's own sense of what action to take. Disciples who guest well in the world know that good leadership is shared leadership and that one must adjust to the needs of a particular context rather than force the context to adjust to the needs of the leader.

Significantly, Jesus instructs the disciples to go into a house and remain there as opposed to moving around from place to place (9:4). Mission leadership is focused and intentional rather than sporadic and temporary. A long-term commitment to a context is essential for lasting transformation of a community. Jesus is also clear that if a house or village refuses to welcome the disciples, then they should simply wipe the dust of the place from their feet and proceed along on the journey to a different place. Once they have received these instructions, the disciples set out for the villages, "bringing the good news and curing diseases everywhere" (9:6).

Luke places the story of the feeding of the five thousand in the city of Bethsaida, an obvious effort to present the ministry of Jesus and the disciples in an urban context. The disciples, having guested in the villages, now serve with Jesus as hosts for the community of Jesus' followers. Jesus welcomed the crowd (9:11) and invited them to sit down in groups of fifty. After blessing five loaves and two fish, he "gave them to the disciples to set before the crowd" (9:16). Here the disciples perform the essential task of ministry within the community, a ministry that is equally important to the work of mission in the world. The community must be fed both physically and spiritually in order to accomplish its work. The meal then is a Eucharistic meal in which the leaders whom Christ has selected nurture the community of faith with spiritual bread and fish. Within a short period, some among that community of 5,000 people will also go into the world on mission (10:1-12).

Luke 9:18-50 represents the climax of the Gospel as Peter makes his declaration about Jesus as the Messiah of God, as Jesus describes the sacrificial nature of the path the disciples have chosen, and as Jesus is transfigured on the mountain and validated by a voice from a cloud that says, "This is my Son, my Chosen; listen to him!" (9:35). Even in the midst of these high and holy moments, the disciples disappoint Jesus in their failure to cast out demons (9:37-43), their lack of understanding of his coming death (9:44-45), their argument over who is the greatest (9:46-48), and their jealousy over those who do manage to cast out demons in the name of Jesus (9:49-50). Always Luke is addressing his own church and its leadership as he narrates the story. His call is to discipleship, servant leadership, and the avoidance of petty jealousy and pride. To accomplish this, Luke's church should listen to the instructions of Jesus about mission and ministry in the world and follow the sacrificial path to which Christ calls it.

Luke 9:51–21:38—The Journey to Jerusalem

Luke signals the transition of his Gospel with a simple sentence: "When the days drew near for him to be taken up, he set his face to go to Jerusalem" (9:51). Significantly, the focus for Luke is not so much on Jerusalem as it is on Jesus' ascension into the clouds at the end of the Gospel. This, for Luke, is the ultimate destination; Jerusalem is simply another step along that path. What Jesus intends to do along the way toward his ascension is to instruct his church about the nature of the mission to which he has called it and to proclaim the age of the Gentiles after the destruction of Jerusalem and its temple.

Luke 9:51–13:21.

This first section of missionary action and teaching serves as a manual for Luke's church as the community seeks to live out its mission in the world. What characteristics should mark its inner life? What should it be doing in the world as a faithful witness to Christ? Using the disciples and followers of Jesus as examples, Luke offers a series of stories and teaching moments that characterize the nature of Christian mission. Obviously, Jesus' instructions reflect challenges that Luke's church was facing. In 9:57-62, Luke reminds his community that it must detach itself from the normal obligations of life, namely concern for food and shelter and family obligations. Apparently, such concerns had caused Luke's church to lose its way.

Having drawn attention to the urgency of the mission calling, Jesus then sends seventy of his followers out into "every town and place where he himself intended to go" (10:1). His instructions to them are much like the instructions he gave to the twelve disciples earlier in chapter 9. They are sent out as "lambs into the midst of wolves," carrying no provision for themselves and not stopping along the way until they reach their destinations. They are to enter a single house and remain in it, eating what is set before them and proclaiming, "the kingdom of God has come near to you" (10:9). If a town refuses to welcome them, then they are to wipe the dust from their feet and leave its judgment in the hands of God. Apparently, their mission was quite successful because they report to Jesus, "Lord, in your name even the demons submit to us." Jesus cautions them not to rejoice in their own power but to rejoice that their names are written in heaven (10:17), again a cautionary word by Luke to his church.

The parable of the good Samaritan immediately follows the story of the sending of the seventy (10:25-37). In this powerful story, a lawyer asks Jesus, "What must I do to inherit eternal life?" Jesus responds by turning the question back on the lawyer.

"What does the Law tell you?"

The lawyer responds, "You shall love the Lord your God with all your heart and with all your soul, and with all your strength, and with all your mind; and your neighbor as yourself."

Jesus praises his answer. "Do this," he says, "and you shall live."

The lawyer presses the matter: "And who is my neighbor?"

Jesus then shares the parable about the traveler from Jerusalem to Jericho who fell among thieves. A priest and a Levite passed him by, but a Samaritan cared for him.

"Which of these three was a neighbor to the man who fell into the hands of robbers?" Jesus asks.

The lawyer had asked a different question: "Who is my neighbor?" Jesus responds with another question that is intended to help the lawyer answer his own original question: "What must I do to inherit eternal life?" The path to eternal life is the path of loving one's neighbor as much as one loves oneself. For Luke's community, the mission calling required the community to embrace its neighbors with loving and boundless intentionality, a challenging word for a church that existed in a diverse urban context. Again, they are to guest well in the world by embracing those who are other and different from them. In this way, they become good neighbors. In this way, they inherit eternal life.

I recently heard Krista Tippett, a renowned journalist and creator of the National Public Radio show *On Being*, talk about the "adventure of civility." She spoke of the importance of the questions we ask each other and of the fact that an honest and sincere question leads both the one who asks the question and the one who answers it to deeper and more profound perspectives on life, God, and truth.[9] Here Jesus asks a powerful question that leads the lawyer and Luke's church to a wholly different understanding of their obligations. What does it mean for Luke's community to be good neighbors in its context? What attitudes should a good neighbor have? What does a good neighbor do? Here the matter of how to engage people who are other and different from the community becomes the primary concern. Luke's community must exhibit the same attitudes and actions as the good Samaritan. They must have compassion and empathy for the other, interrupting the flow of their own lives in order to care for a person whom they might want to ignore.

In a very powerful way, Jesus has shifted the burden of the question onto the one who has asked it. The neighbor is not the only one who needs help. The lawyer and Luke's community also need help. Paul Bergman points out that, for Luke, "scrutiny of motive and action should always be self-directed, not other directed."[10] Luke's community has missed the point of the Law. Their challenge is not simply one of determining whom they should help; rather, their challenge is to recognize that they need help because they have failed to grasp the full obligations that are upon them as they seek to participate in God's mission in the world.

Jesus' words to the disciples in Luke 12 and 13 call them to be courageous (12:4-12), prepared (12:35-40), and faithful (12:41-48) in the face of the challenges of such ministry and mission. They are not to worry about material possessions but to put their trust in God and to "strive for his kingdom" (12:31). The message they proclaim will be a message that divides father against son and mother against daughter (12:49-53). Persecution will be intense, but "the Holy Spirit will teach you at that very hour what you ought to say" (12:12). He cautions patience as the kingdom of God emerges in their midst like yeast that leavens the loaf (13:20-21). For Luke, Jesus' words remind his community that participation in God's mission on earth requires them to stand against injustice and oppression by being good neighbors to those around them and to be prepared for the inevitable backlash that will come. To embrace God's mission in the world is to experience a life that is difficult and challenging as opposed to the harmonious and peaceful life they had come to associate with it.

Luke 13:22–21:38.

This section of the Gospel focuses first on the radical nature of discipleship (13:22–17:10) and then on Jesus' journey up to Jerusalem (17:11–19:48). Jerusalem's role in Jesus' death is foretold at the beginning of the section (13:31-35) when even the Pharisees warn him to "Get away from here, for Herod wants to kill you" (13:31). The challenges facing Luke's community are obvious in the way Luke constructs the section. He teaches them again through the words of Jesus to serve as good hosts and guests and reinforces the need to leave family and possessions behind (14:7-33). He reminds them of the need for reconciliation, especially with those who have been lost to full fellowship in the community (15:1-32). He cautions them to use their wealth wisely (16:1-31). Finally, he warns them of the importance of forgiveness in their relationships with each other (17:1-10).

Now that he has dealt with the important obligations upon his own community, Luke shifts his focus to Jesus' journey to Jerusalem. On his way, Jesus performs a miracle by healing ten lepers (17:11-19), warns against hypocrisy (18:9-14), and reminds his disciples and followers to wait patiently for the arrival of God's kingdom and to invest wisely in it (19:11-27). He continues with his theme of the sharing of wealth in the story of Zacchaeus (19:1-10). By the end of the section, he makes his triumphal entry into Jerusalem where he cleanses the temple even as "the leaders of the people kept looking for a way to kill him" (19:47).

Luke 20 and 21 represent a single day in the life of Jesus, a day that Luke presents as one of teaching and prophecy about the destruction of Jerusalem and its temple. Constantly the chief priests, scribes, and Sadducees seek ways to trap him "so as to hand him over to the jurisdiction and authority of the governor" (20:20). Jesus frustrates all of their efforts, using their questions to reinforce the nature of discipleship and to warn his followers again about the persecution that they will experience. He concludes with a prophecy that Jerusalem will soon be surrounded by armies and the people of Judea "will fall by the edge of the sword and be taken away as captives among all nations; and Jerusalem will be trampled on by the Gentiles, until the times of the Gentiles are fulfilled" (21:24). Luke penned his words in hindsight as these words of Jesus had already happened. The "times of the Gentiles" marked the fulfillment of God's original intention to bless all the families of the earth either with Israel's assistance, which Luke would certainly have welcomed, or without it.

Luke 22:1–24:53—The Crucifixion, Resurrection, and Ascension of Jesus

Luke focuses on the cosmic implications of Jesus' death and resurrection in ways that connect powerfully to the creation story in Genesis, to the Abrahamic covenant, and to God's intention to make God's blessing known to every family of the earth. For Luke, the death of Jesus is the result of evil, embodied in Luke-Acts as Satan; Jesus' resurrection then represents the triumph of good over evil as the Holy Spirit descends upon the church. He reports at the beginning of this section that "Satan entered into Judas called Iscariot," and Judas then betrayed Jesus.

Luke documented this conflict between good and evil earlier in Luke 9:18 when the seventy returned from their mission and Jesus indicated that he had given them "authority . . . over all the power of the enemy" and later in Luke 10:18 when Jesus warns that division in the kingdom of God is brought about by Satan. Luke describes Satan in Luke 13:16 as binding those who are free. In Acts, Satan enters into Ananias (5:3) and frustrates the work of Paul (26:18). Ultimately, Luke describes Paul's conversion as the moment Jesus called him to the Gentiles "to open their eyes so that they may turn from darkness to light and from the power of Satan to God, so that they may receive forgiveness of sins and a place among those who are sanctified by faith" (Acts 26:17-18). These two verses represent the best summary of Luke's purpose in writing his Gospel and Acts.[11] His church needs to know that it is fighting a cosmic battle together with the Holy Spirit to ensure that the Gentiles receive forgiveness and the affirmation of God's blessing, something Satan is seeking to deny to them.

Luke makes clear that Jesus is the sacrificial lamb of the Passover and that the Passover meal represents his last meal with the disciples prior to his death. Significantly, Jesus' words at the Passover point forward to the coming kingdom of God and to the new covenant, and not backward to the exodus as was the point of the Jewish meal. This new covenant represents the blessing of God upon all of humanity in ways that go far beyond God's provision for a particular people. Unfortunately, far too many church leaders today make the Lord's Supper an exclusive meal for Christian people as opposed to a universal meal for all of humanity that points toward the realization of God's blessing with the advent of the kingdom of God.

The meal and the betrayal that follows (by both Judas and Peter) provide opportunity for Luke to offer further instruction about mission to his community. Again, leaders are called to serve (22:24-27), something the leaders in Luke's community have apparently forgotten. Jesus' instructions in Luke 22:35-38 are often misinterpreted. The reference is to Luke 9 and 10 when Jesus sent out the twelve and the seventy into surrounding villages. Jesus instructed them at that point to take nothing for the journey; here Jesus implies that they will need support in the journey, but the reference to purses and bags and even a sword is probably symbolic and not literal. This becomes obvious when the disciples hand two swords to Jesus and he quickly dismisses the effort with the simple statement "that's enough," a phrase that points to his frustration with their reliance on themselves as opposed to God. Again, Luke is offering a word to his community about its tendency toward such self-reliance.

In the garden, Jesus prays that God might "remove this cup from me" and yet affirms his determination to do "not my will but yours" (22:42). He reminds his disciples, who have slept through his prayer, that they also will soon enter into "a time of trouble" (22:46). Jesus' own time of trouble quickly comes. He is mocked and beaten. Pilate and Herod interrogate him and find him to be innocent of the charges against him. Giving in to the desires of the crowds, Pilate releases Barabbas, an insurrectionist himself, and delivers Jesus over for crucifixion. Luke reminds his readers of their calling to carry the cross of Christ (Simon of Cyrene in 23:26), of the reality of their own coming persecution (the weeping daughters of Jerusalem in 22:28), of the forgiveness that Jesus offers to them (the soldiers in 23:34 and the thief on the cross in 23:43), and of the faith of the Gentiles (the centurion in 23:47). Joseph of Arimathea, a Jewish leader who opposed the crucifixion, takes Jesus' body and buries it in his own tomb (24:50).

The tomb is quite incidental to Luke's story of the resurrection. He focuses his attention instead on the living community of God to whom the Lord appears after his resurrection, including the two followers on the road to Emmaus and the disciples themselves in Jerusalem. The Emmaus story is unique to Luke's Gospel. Here Luke exposes for his readers their own blindness to the presence of the Risen Lord in their midst and their inability to recall the teachings of Moses and the prophets about the Messiah. He also reminds them of the power of the Eucharistic meal to reveal the presence of Christ among them and calls them to follow in the way of Jesus. Jesus' identity and presence emerge only when they take him in as a stranger and share their bread. In this selfless action, accomplished in the midst of their own disappointment and pain (the suffering church), they take a stranger into their midst (good neighborliness) and share a meal with him (Eucharistic meal), thus taking upon themselves by their own actions the mission of Jesus. Once they do this, Jesus "vanished from their sight" and they race to Jerusalem to report "what had happened on the road, and how he had been made known to them in the breaking of bread" (24:35).

Luke has now accomplished his purpose in the Gospel, which was to set out an orderly account for Theophilus "about all that Jesus did and taught from the beginning until the day when he was taken up into heaven" (Acts 1:1). Jesus' final act is to stand among his disciples so they can bear witness to his resurrection and to remind them of their calling to meet the physical and spiritual needs of people in their earthly lives. To drive this point home, he takes a piece of fish "and ate it in their presence" (24:43). He then reinforces the teachings of the Law of Moses, the prophets, and the Psalms and "opened their minds to understand the scriptures" (24:45). Finally, he calls them to the work of proclaiming repentance and forgiveness of sins in the name of the Messiah "to all nations, beginning from Jerusalem" and promises "power from on high" with the gift of the Holy Spirit (24:47-49). Once Jesus withdrew from them up into heaven, they returned to Jerusalem and to the very temple in which Zechariah had been performing his duties when an angel of the Lord appeared to him to announce the birth of John the Baptist.

Remember that in Luke 8, Luke called his church to "patient endurance" (8:15), a listening spirit (8:18), and faithful action (8:21, 25). These characteristics seem to be the necessary ingredients for congregations now who often struggle for relevancy in a context in which they feel marginalized and ineffective. Patient endurance is not enough. Such endurance by itself can lead to a siege mentality that refuses transformation of attitudes, structures, and ritual. Congregations must cultivate listening spirits that are open to the cultural realities that exist around them and willing to hear the tug of the Holy Spirit that beckons them in new directions. They also must risk their own future in faithful actions balanced by patient endurance and listening spirits.

I recently taught a course on the theology and practice of mission in which one of my students presented a case study on the congregation that he served in downtown Atlanta. This congregation had dwindled in recent years to only about twenty-five people. They met faithfully for worship, patiently enduring the challenges of an aging church and the fact that they had lost touch with their own community. One of the members of the church suggested that they begin a feeding ministry to people in the neighborhood so that at least they were doing some good and faithful work on behalf of God's mission in the world.

The church contacted the Atlanta Food Bank and soon about a hundred people lined up every Tuesday at 10 a.m. to receive their allotment of food. My student and other church members would circulate among the assembled crowd until the doors to the fellowship hall opened at 11 a.m. for food distribution. On one particular Tuesday, several people in the crowd asked if they might hold a worship service as they waited. The church agreed to open the doors of the fellowship hall and hold a worship service each week at 10 a.m. Members of the crowd agreed to lead the service. Within a couple of weeks, about 150 people were worshiping every Tuesday morning. To their credit, the older group of 25 people gathered in the sanctuary on Sunday morning realized that the church was meeting on Tuesday and not on Sunday. They dispensed with Sunday worship and joined the Tuesday crowd. A church of 25 people had now become a church of 150.

Patient endurance, a listening spirit, and faithful action led this downtown Atlanta congregation to realize the leadership of the Holy Spirit in their midst. Overcoming racial, economic, and other divisions, they followed that Spirit in a new direction. In the process, they transformed themselves into a new church no longer bound by the old attitudes, structures, and rituals that had marked their long history. Now reconnected with their community, they embraced the mission of God for them, a mission that had come, not from within the old church, but from the new church that stood outside its walls. This is the message of Luke-Acts. By listening to the Spirit, we embrace new possibilities and become the people that God has intended from the beginning.

The Acts of the Apostles

The book of Acts marks a significant transition in Luke's account from describing the implications of Jesus' mission for Luke's church to describing the implications for them of the mission of Jesus' disciples and Paul. Like Luke's church, the disciples remain confused about their mission and purpose at the beginning of Acts. "Is this the time when you will restore the kingdom to Israel?" they ask. Luke's Jesus essentially ignores the question and gets right to the heart of the mission of the disciples themselves. They are to remain in Jerusalem until "the Holy Spirit has come upon you; and you will be my witnesses in Jerusalem, in all Judea and Samaria, and to the ends of the earth" (1:8). For the next twenty-seven chapters of the book, Luke chronicles the emergence of the gospel, first among Jews in Jerusalem, then among Hellenistic Jews and Samaritans outside Jerusalem, then among Gentiles in Palestine, and finally among Jews and Gentiles in Antioch and Europe. This mission begins with the disciples themselves, and especially Peter, but by Acts 15 Paul emerges as the central character in the story and it is his particular approach to mission that becomes the major focus of Luke's narrative.

Again, Luke parallels the account of the experience of Jesus in his Gospel with the account of the experiences of the disciples and Paul in Acts. The first characters in the story receive the Holy Spirit, the "Lord of mission," who directs their work and ensures its success even in the midst of the challenges and difficulties that they face. Their mission begins among Jewish people in Jerusalem and in close proximity to the temple. In the end, though, the Holy Spirit ensures that the Gentile families of the earth receive the powerful message of God's love and grace, a message embodied in Jesus of Nazareth and communicated through the witness of the disciples and Paul.

Luke's account in Acts presents a number of powerful "moments" that helped the church in Jerusalem move beyond its Jewish origins and embrace Gentiles as siblings in Christ. This transition was not an easy one. Luke seems particularly concerned with church leadership throughout Acts, since church leaders must first be convinced of the new direction in which the Spirit is moving. Thus, the first order of business is to replace Judas, thereby ensuring a complete number of disciples for the monumental work ahead. Throughout Acts, leaders will be set aside to enable the orderly work of the Spirit among the earliest followers of Jesus.

The Jewish Pentecost: Acts 2

The first "moment" in Acts occurs when Jewish believers in Jerusalem receive the Holy Spirit at the Feast of Pentecost. The Feast of Pentecost or Weeks was originally a harvest festival, but, after the destruction of the temple in Jerusalem, it became a festival of covenant renewal and eventually of God's gift of the Torah to Moses at Mount Sinai. During the Feast of Weeks, the Jewish people traveled to Jerusalem to bring their firstfruits to the temple. For this reason, "there were devout Jews from every nation under heaven living in Jerusalem" (2:5). The celebration of other covenants, like the covenant with Noah, also figured prominently in the feast.

The disciples' celebration is interrupted by "the rush of a powerful wind" and by the sudden presence of "divided tongues, as of fire" that appeared among them. Luke reports, "a tongue rested on each of them" (2:3) and "all of them were filled with the Holy Spirit and began to speak in other languages, as the Spirit gave them ability" (2:4). Such an event surely brought to the minds of Luke's readers the Tower of Babel account in Genesis 11 when God confused human languages because the families of the earth refused to "be fruitful and multiply and fill the earth" as God had commanded them to do.

Pentecost is not a "reversal" of the confusion that God created at the point of the Tower of Babel story in Genesis. Instead, as Darrell Guder points out, "the Holy Spirit made translation into *all* tongues possible" because "in the gracious economy of God, the joyful message was intended from the very outset to be infinitely translatable and multicultural."[12] Jewish families from every corner of the world, gathered in Jerusalem, suddenly understand the disciples as they speak nearly every known language. The linguistic diversity is quite remarkable, spanning Palestine, the rest of the Middle East, Europe, Africa, and Asia. The disciples become spokespersons of "God's deeds of power" for all the families of the earth, as each family hears that proclamation in its own language (2:11). Luke clearly understands this "moment" as a work of the Spirit that prefigures the movement of the disciples and Paul beyond Jerusalem and into the world. At the same time, those in Jerusalem who hear the disciples speak in their particular languages about these deeds of power can now take what they have heard into their own particular cultural contexts. The fact that the gospel is enculturated in various languages speaks powerfully of God's intention to elicit from those languages and cultures a multiplicity of perspectives on God's mission in the world that would "bless" all of humanity.

Peter's first speech, in Acts 2:14-42, is particularly instructive because it addresses this diverse Jewish crowd, calling them to repentance and baptism. He reminds the crowd of the words of the prophet Joel that in the last days God would pour out God's Spirit upon all flesh, "and your sons and your daughters shall prophesy" (2:17). The word "prophesy" refers not to the fact that the twelve disciples speak in different languages but rather to the fact that they have spoken about God's "deeds of power." Peter reminds them of Jesus' "deeds of power, wonders and signs that God did through him among you" (2:22). He also implies that they are responsible for the crucifixion and death of Jesus of Nazareth, this despite the fact that most of them had not even been in Jerusalem at the time of the trial and crucifixion.

Having established their culpability, he also proclaims that "God raised him up, having freed him from death" (2:24). Now he has been "exalted at the right hand of God, and having received from the Father the promise of the Holy Spirit, he has poured out this that you both see and hear" (2:33). He completes the speech by calling on the crowd to "let the entire house of Israel know with certainty that God has made him both Lord and Messiah, this Jesus whom you crucified" (2:36).

Peter's speech, directed at such a diverse Jewish crowd, results in the conversion of three thousand people and the establishment of the first church, one in which Jewish followers of Jesus share their goods in common (4:32-37). It also leads to more speeches by Peter in Solomon's Portico (3:11-26) and before the council of the high priests (4:8-12), both of which reinforce Peter's message of Jewish guilt to the diverse crowd.

A notable shift, however, occurs once the council releases Peter and John. Luke reports that they joined their friends, meaning perhaps the church in Jerusalem, and the church "raised their voices together to God" and extended culpability for the death of Jesus far beyond the Jewish family to every family of the earth. They insisted that "in this city, both Herod and Pontius Pilate, *with the Gentiles and the peoples of Israel, gathered together* against your holy servant Jesus, whom you anointed, to do whatever your hand and your plan had predestined to take place" (4:27-28). It is as if these friends, through Luke, are reminding Peter and John, and by extension Luke's church, that all families of the earth share the guilt for the death of Jesus and that Peter's focus on Jewish guilt has failed to tell the whole story.

The Gentile Pentecost: Acts 10

A second "moment" of transition occurs in Acts 10 when the Holy Spirit falls upon a group of Gentiles who are members of the household of Cornelius. A Roman centurion who resided in Caesarea, Cornelius is described by Luke as "a devout man who feared God with all his household" and a person of constant prayer and almsgiving (10:2) who is visited by an angel in a vision and ordered to send for Peter in the town of Joppa. Shortly before the envoys arrive from Cornelius's house, Peter falls into a trance in which he sees the heavens open and a large sheet lowered to the ground. Luke reports, "in it were all kinds of four-footed creatures and reptiles and birds of the air" (10:12).

A voice says, "Get up, Peter; kill and eat."

Peter is horrified. "By no means, Lord," he says, "for I have never eaten anything that is profane or unclean."

The voice responds, "What God has made clean, you must not call profane."

While Peter is puzzling over the vision, the envoys arrive and the Holy Spirit insists that Peter accompany them "without hesitation" (10:9-23). When Peter arrives at Cornelius's house, he finds a gathered Gentile crowd eager to hear the message that he has for them. Peter shares with them his initial reluctance: "You yourselves know that it is unlawful for a Jew to associate with or to visit a Gentile; but God has shown me that I should not call anyone profane or unclean" (10:28).

Peter's speech to the Gentile crowd is among the most remarkable speeches in the New Testament. It begins with Peter's assertion "that God shows no partiality" (10:34). This statement is a stunning acknowledgment by Peter of the transformative power of his vision of the sheet with the unclean animals. As a result, he can no longer assume a privileged role for the Jewish people in God's mission and purpose in the world. Rather "*in every nation* anyone who fears him and does what is right is acceptable to him" (10:35). In other words, the God-fearing and righteous among every family of the earth (*en panta ethne*) receive the hospitality, acceptance, and welcome of God. Peter expresses here God's intention from the very beginning that God reinforced in the covenant with Abram and that the prophets of Israel, including Jesus of Nazareth, proclaimed. God's blessing extends to every human family. Peter's assertion is a powerful word to Luke's church, reminding that Gentile church of its right to participate in God's mission in the world and warning it and its leaders of the danger of assuming a privileged role for itself in that mission.

Immediately as Peter was speaking, "the Holy Spirit fell upon all who heard the word" (10:44), and the Jewish believers who had accompanied Peter heard the Gentiles "speaking in tongues and extolling God" (10:46). Just as the church in Jerusalem had extended guilt for the crucifixion and death of Jesus to include Gentiles as well as Jews, so now it affirmed the gift of the Holy Spirit to the Gentiles to communicate God's great deeds of power in various languages. The church in Jerusalem, representing the Jewish family, has now confirmed that God's Spirit has been poured out upon Jew and Gentile alike, affirming the blessing of God on every family of the earth. Peter will return to the Jerusalem church to make his report, and that church will respond first with silence, then with celebration, and then with the affirmation that "God has given even to the Gentiles the repentance that leads to life" (11:18).

The Jerusalem Council: Acts 15

The third "moment" or transition in Acts related to the extension of the gospel from the Jewish family to the Gentile families of the earth occurs at the Jerusalem Council in Acts 15. By this point, Stephen has been martyred for his faith, and Saul, one among those who persecuted Stephen, has converted to the faith after encountering the risen Jesus on the road to Damascus (Acts 9:1-9). Saul is about to emerge in Luke's story as the Apostle Paul who will carry Luke's story to its powerful conclusion. Those followers of Jesus who fled Jerusalem after the martyrdom of Stephen are now living in such places as Phoenicia, Cyprus, and Antioch (11:19). The Holy Spirit calls the church at Antioch to "set apart for me Barnabas and Saul for the work to which I have called them" (13:2). Paul and Barnabas immediately set out for Cyprus, Antioch of Pisidia, Iconium, Lystra, and Derbe, where they preach in synagogues. It is in Antioch of Pisidia that Paul and Barnabas, disturbed by the hostility of the Jewish faithful, declare that "since you reject it and judge yourselves to be unworthy of eternal life, we are now turning to the Gentiles" (13:46).

The stage is then set for the Jerusalem Council that must decide the Jewish obligations upon the newly converted Gentiles. On one side in the debate are "certain individuals" from Judea who insist on circumcision for salvation as well as "some believers who belonged to the sect of the Pharisees" (15:1, 5). On the other side are Barnabas, Paul, Peter, and James. Two arguments sway the council. First, Peter pleas with them not to place "on the neck of the disciples a yoke that neither our ancestors nor we have been able to bear," and then James reminds them of the hope of the prophets "that all other peoples may seek the Lord—even the Gentiles over whom my name has been called" (15:10, 17). In the end, the council sends a letter to the church at Antioch that identifies only four essentials for Gentiles related to the Jewish Law. Three focus on diet. They are to abstain from food sacrificed to idols, from blood, and from eating any strangled animal. They are also to maintain sexual purity by avoiding fornication.

The decision of the Jerusalem Council is significant in that it allows for the contextualization of God's mission in the world in terms of religious observances that are unique among particular Gentile cultures. It removes the "foreign" element of Judaism that had been unique to the Jewish people and part of their particular cultural tradition. Freed from the obligations for Jewish worship and life as well as from the particular prohibitions of the Law, the gospel gains the freedom to take root linguistically and culturally among the Gentile families of the earth. Pentecost, both in its Jewish and Gentile expressions, and the Jerusalem Council provide enough linguistic and religious space for the emergence of radically new perspectives on God, humanity, and the creation, enabling the diversity that was God's intention from the moment of creation. Gentile families can now receive the message of God's blessing upon humanity, enculturate that message in their own traditions, languages, and cultures, and discover in the mix the unique cultural and religious understanding of the divine that emerges as a result. This understanding then becomes their own particular contribution to humanity's understanding of the divine.

Paul at the Areopagus: Acts 17:16-34

The Jerusalem Council sets the stage for Paul's missions among the Gentiles and in the synagogues of Asia Minor and Europe and for the next powerful "moment" in Acts, Paul's dialogue with the philosophers of Athens. Paul's experience at the Areopagus is significant in that it represents the first point of contact between Paul's emerging theological perspective and the philosophical traditions of Hellenism, especially Stoicism and Epicureanism. In the aftermath of Pentecost and the Jerusalem Council, Paul is able to share that perspective with a spiritual, cultural, intellectual, and theological freedom that had previously not been possible. The emerging Christian perspective on the divine that until now has been almost exclusively Jewish is set to engage the radically different perspectives of Hellenistic philosophy.

Paul's experience in Athens is among the most missiologically relevant portions of the New Testament for the diverse global context that we now inhabit. Here Paul's theological perspective with its Jewish roots and emerging Christian consciousness meets two significant Hellenistic philosophical schools—the Epicureans who were highly materialistic and focused on freedom from pain and stress in the world and the Stoics who were pantheists who believed that there was a divine principle or logos within every human being that connected them to God.[13] These two perspectives offer compelling worldviews that many people today embrace. Even as allegiance to particular religions and denominations wanes and the "nones" have emerged as the largest "religious" group in the United States, so now people tend to represent their beliefs in one of two ways: either all we have is this life here on earth to enjoy, so let us make the most of it (Epicureans), or we all have a spark of the divine in us that connects us to ultimate reality and to each other (Stoicism). Paul's other concern in Athens is with the existence of numerous idols in the city, something that causes him deep distress.

Paul speaks in three contexts in Athens—the synagogue, the agora, and the Areopagus. The gathering at the synagogue on the Sabbath to meet with "the Jews and the devout persons" fits Paul's pattern throughout his ministry. His visit to the agora or civic marketplace represents his interest in "third spaces" outside the home and synagogue. In Acts 16, for example, when Paul and his companions were in Philippi, they made their way outside that city to "a place of prayer" where they met Lydia. This place of prayer was perhaps what the Celts referred to as a "thin place" where the divine was experienced beyond any particular religion or worldview. In Athens, the agora was a space where town meetings and other gatherings were held and where intellectuals gathered to share ideas. After listening to him in the agora, a group of civic and religious leaders known as the Court of the Areopagus, who oversaw the political, intellectual, and religious life of Athens, invited Paul to address them.

Luke's account of Paul's speech at the Areopagus is instructive. First, the Athenians seem quite interested in Paul's teaching. They want to hear what he has to say. This openness is evident in the absence of tension and conflict in the story and in the way that they simply ask, "May we know what this new teaching is that you are presenting? It sounds rather strange to us, so we would like to know what it means" (17:19-20). The lack of religious conflict and tension makes this particular story helpful in any context in which relative religious and philosophical freedom exist.

Paul begins his address by identifying points of connection between his Athenian listeners and the divine story that he is sharing. He seizes upon the religious and philosophical curiosity of the Athenians and on the objects of their worship, the many statues of gods and goddesses throughout the city. While many have interpreted Paul's speech as a way of manipulating the Athenians to embrace his perspective on God, I prefer to understand his approach as one that manifests an appreciation for the common human desire to know and understand the divine. Paul is presenting here a common human story to which he and the Athenians can relate. He celebrates their common religiosity and connects the altar to the unknown God in Athens with the particular cultural story that he wants to share.

The fact that the Athenians have built an altar to an unknown God is significant because it represents an acknowledgment by the Athenians of their own limited understanding of the divine. They do not possess all knowledge and they know it. They have cultivated within their worldview an openness to new truth and new understanding. In some sense, this openness, institutionalized in an altar, reminds them to listen to what others have to say.

Such an approach is instructive for the church in our own day. While Christians are quick to acknowledge that God is ultimately unknowable, we are also quick to pronounce whether a particular perspective on God or experience of God is orthodox or unorthodox. I remember a conversation with a Hindu friend in India about the Christian understanding of God. I had visited a number of temples in Kolkata the previous day, and I recounted for him the frenzied worship experience I had witnessed at the Kali temple in that city. Kali, a goddess associated with the destruction of evil, is a fearsome deity. At the temple, people pushed against each other in a frenzied effort to get close to her image.

I commented that, in contrast with the worship of Kali, the Christian perspective on God focused on God's ultimate attributes of power, knowledge, creative energy, and compassion, and that Christian worship generally focused on God's love and not God's wrath.

"Yes," he said. "You Christians manage to keep God under control with your overly simplistic perspectives."

I was slightly offended. "No," I protested. "We believe that God is beyond human knowledge and control."

"Then you should let God be God and make space for some new experience or belief about God to emerge that you can't control."

His words reminded me that the Christian tradition often closes itself off to new experiences of God that do not fit within our existing doctrinal and experiential systems. From Hinduism and from the philosophers of Athens we can learn to make space for the "unknown God" who comes to us from the belief systems and experiences of people of other faith traditions. Paul himself models such an approach in Athens. It is not so much a manipulative approach for Paul as it is a response to an invitation. The Athenians have invited him to the Areopagus. They have extended hospitality to him because their own worldview and perspective compels them to do so. He accepts their invitation and proceeds to share the story that gives meaning and purpose to his existence and that serves as the foundation for his understanding of God, humanity, and the creation. He identifies the unknown God as the Creator God who brought the universe into existence but who stands apart from the created order and "gives to all mortals life and breath and all things" (17:25). This God does not live in shrines or images "made by human hands" (17:24), a point with which many of Paul's listeners probably agreed.

The heart of Paul's speech recounts the primeval history of Genesis in which, from one ancestor, God "made all nations (or families) to inhabit the *whole earth*, and he allotted the times of their existence and the boundaries of the places where they would live" (17:26). Here Paul presents the emergence of diverse families of the earth as a divinely ordained reality grounded in God's mission and purpose for the world. God's intention then was that each family "would search for God and perhaps grope for him and find him" (17:27). The use of the words "search" and "grope" is instructive, suggesting both intentionality in the searching as well as an unintentional stumbling toward God.

Paul then adds that God is not far from any human being or human family, and he even quotes the Stoic poet Aratus of Soli that "we too are his offspring."[14] This quotation is significant in that it shows Paul's respect for the Greek philosophical schools and that he possesses at least some rudimentary knowledge of their poets and particular philosophers. His use of Aratus encourages the church of any age toward at least a basic knowledge of the sacred texts and significant works of other religious traditions. Paul concludes the speech with a gentle reminder to his listeners that God is not captured in images of gold, silver, or stone made by human hands, nor can divine understanding occur solely through human imagination. He then implies that the "times of human ignorance" have ended and calls for repentance prior to the time when all families of the earth are "judged in righteousness by a man whom he has appointed" and raised from the dead as an "assurance to all" (17:31). His listeners respond in three ways: some scoff, some ask to hear more, and some "joined him and became believers" (17:32-34).

Paul's Journey to Jerusalem and Rome: Acts 21–28

The remaining chapters in Acts focus primarily on Paul's journey, first to Jerusalem and then to Rome. Both Acts and Paul's letters make clear that his primary purpose is to carry an offering from the Gentile churches to the church at Jerusalem. He realizes that "imprisonment and persecutions are waiting for me" (20:23) but also insists that he is "a captive to the Spirit" (20:22) in making the visit there. His experience in Jerusalem is remarkably similar to Jesus' experience just prior to his crucifixion. Hauled first before the Roman tribune, Paul informs them that he is a Roman citizen. He then stands before the Jewish council and the high priest Ananias. Several of their number determine to kill him, but the tribune arranges for safe transport to Caesarea. There Paul informs Governor Felix of the nature of his visit to Jerusalem "to bring alms to my nation and to offer sacrifices" (24:17). Later he will share with King Agrippa his primary mission and purpose, to testify to Jew and Gentile alike "that the Messiah must suffer, and that, by being the first to rise from the dead, he would proclaim light both to our people and to the Gentiles" (26:23).

Acts 27 and 28 recount Paul's experience on the journey to Rome where he has appealed his case to the emperor. Once in Rome, he calls the Jewish leaders of the city together and insists, "It is for the sake of the hope of Israel that I am bound with this chain" (28:20). Here he makes clear his concern for both Israel and for the Gentiles. Like Jesus, his focus is on all families of the earth and especially that Israel would recover its calling to bless the families of the earth as well as to receive their blessings. Luke concludes with a summary of Paul's speech to the Jewish leaders and with his quote of the prophet Isaiah about the stubborn refusal of many in Israel to "understand with their heart and turn" (28:27). For this reason, the "salvation of God has been sent to the Gentiles; they will listen" (28:28). Acts ends with Paul in Rome "proclaiming about the kingdom of God and teaching about the Lord Jesus Christ with all boldness and without hindrance" (28:31).

Despite its focus at the end on the mission of Paul among the Gentiles, Luke-Acts is remarkably positive about Jewish culture and religion.[15] Luke's purpose in writing the two-volume work is to connect the Jewish story to the story of the Gentile families of the earth to such an extent that the Jewish family and the Gentile families understand the nature of their respective roles in God's mission and purpose for the creation. To this end, his focus is always on the temple in Jerusalem and on Jerusalem as the place toward which even Gentile families will bring their alms and worship God. It is as if Paul's hope is that Israel would receive the blessing of the Gentiles as Gentile families of the earth make their way to Jerusalem. Paul embodies this focus on Israel in his physical journey to bring the offering of the Gentiles to Jerusalem and his reminder to the Jewish leaders in Rome that he is in chains because of his hopes for Israel. To put it another way, Paul is not just a missionary to the Gentiles; he is a missionary to Israel as well. Graeme Goldsworthy points out that "Paul understands his mission to the Gentiles within the context of his being a Hebrew of the Hebrews."[16] This is especially clear in his Epistle to the Romans that focuses considerable attention on the salvation of Jews and Gentiles alike.

Jews and Gentiles in Luke-Acts and Paul's Letters

Both Luke and Paul then ground the mission of God in the world in the context of God's relationship to Israel. For both writers, the connection is essential. While God's original instruction "to be fruitful and multiply and fill the earth" is a general call to all of humanity, Israel serves as the locus of God's promise of blessing upon all human families. Israel is the example of how God intends to take the language, culture, and worldview of every family and bless the families of the earth by them. God never intended for the divine blessing to become the sole possession of a single family. Instead, God hoped that every family of the earth would see in Israel the reality of their own blessing. Israel's community of shalom, guided by its fidelity to the Law of Moses, exemplified a way in which all families could contribute to the entire human family by virtue of their own respective worldviews and understandings of the divine. Put differently, "fulfillment of the law has to be understood in different terms, as something which Gentiles can do without any reference to whether they are inside the law or outside the law."[17] God's intention was that, whether we lived by the Law of Moses or by the laws God placed in our hearts, we would learn to love God and each other, to treat each other with dignity and respect, and to overcome our fear of otherness and difference. We would then extend to others the unique perspectives God had placed in us by virtue of our particular culture, worldviews, and spirituality.

For Luke, the work of the Holy Spirit in the world made all of this possible. For Paul, Christ accomplished it through the same Spirit. Paul states his perspective clearly in his epistles to the Romans and to the Galatians. In Romans 2, he condemns *all* who judge others, insisting, "There will be anguish and distress *for everyone who does evil, the Jew first and also the Greek*, but glory and honor and peace *for everyone who does good, the Jew first and also the Greek*. For God shows no partiality" (2:9-11). He also acknowledges that Gentiles "who do not possess the law" are able "instinctively" to "do what the law of God requires" (Rom 2:14) because that law "is written on their hearts, to which their own conscience bears witness" (2:15). For Paul, Abraham is the example of the blessing of God upon all of humanity because he expressed faith both as an uncircumcised man (Gentile) and as a circumcised man (Jew): "He received the sign of circumcision as a seal of righteousness that he had by faith while he was still uncircumcised." God's intention then was to make Abraham the ancestor "of all who believe . . . and who thus have righteousness reckoned to them" (4:11). God's promise was that Abraham would become "the father of many nations" (Gen 17:5) and not just the father of Israel.

In the same way, then, that Abraham overcame the division between Jew and Gentile through his faith, blessing all human families and enabling all families to bless each other, so Christ has overcome the division between humanity and God to the extent that "one man's act of righteousness leads to justification and life for all" (5:18). Because of this act of righteousness, "there is no distinction between Jew and Greek; the same Lord is Lord of all and is generous to all who call on him" (10:12). Paul is as concerned for his Jewish family as he is for the Gentiles of the earth, despite his designation as the apostle to the Gentiles. His firm conviction in the end is that "all Israel will be saved" (11:26). Moreover, if all Israel is saved, then why should this salvation not extend to the other families of the earth whom God has also loved and chosen from the very beginning? In Christ, God has extended righteousness to all those who have believed by faith in Christ as well as those for whom the law of God "is written on their hearts, to which their own conscience bears witness." For this reason, Paul tells the church in Galatia,

> For in Christ Jesus *you are all* children of God through faith. As many of you as were baptized into Christ have clothed yourselves with Christ. There is no longer Jew or Greek, there is no longer slave or free, there is no longer male and female; for all of you are one in Christ Jesus. And if you belong to Christ, then you are Abraham's offspring, heirs according to the promise. (Gal 3:26-29)

Luke focuses on far more in his two-volume work than simply the relationship between Jews and Gentiles. He also focuses on the relationship between the Christian faith of his Gentile communities and the surrounding multicultural religious contexts. Throughout the Gospel and Acts, he considers the ways in which his communities ought to approach their neighbors and what their attitudes should be toward other religious traditions. Always, Gentiles who are outside the faith serve as examples to those inside the faith. The philosophers of Athens reflect a similar openness to hear the teachings of Paul about Jesus. Peter responds to the vision of the unclean animals by going to the home of Cornelius and sharing his perspective on Jesus there. Paul goes to "a place of prayer" in Philippi to speak "to the women who had gathered" (16:13). Even Samaritans are cited as examples of good neighborliness, though they were despised even more than Gentiles were (Luke 10:25-37).

The context beyond Israel and Jerusalem demanded an approach by Luke's communities that was marked by openness to the perspectives of others as well as a willingness to share out of their own particular faith and convictions. For Luke, the fear of otherness and difference had to give way to legitimate curiosity and to the open sharing of religious ideas. Only in this way could the Christian faith hope to express itself in a marketplace of languages and cultures. For Luke, his communities could move into the world with the conviction that the Holy Spirit would prepare the way ahead of them, nurturing deep relationships and breaking down barriers between them and people of other faiths and cultures. The ultimate hope for Luke was that his community would be open to new possibilities and perspectives in the same way that Peter had been open to the encounter with Gentiles at Cornelius's house and that Paul had been open to sharing with the philosophers in Athens. Truth emerged in dialogue with others under the leadership of the Holy Spirit, not in the limited perspective on God that Luke's community carried into the encounters.

What do we discover in Luke's Gospel, Acts, and Paul that helps us to locate the equator of the gospel in a new day? First, we learn to pay attention to the work of the Holy Spirit in breaking down the barriers that hinder our engagement with otherness and difference in the world. Luke and Acts contain seventy-three references to the Holy Spirit (seventeen in Luke and fifty-six in Acts). Luke draws our attention to the Spirit's work in enabling the emergence of a powerful global gospel that was marked as much by its connection to the ancient story of Israel as by its enculturation in a variety of contexts far beyond Israel. The Spirit empowered the disciples at Pentecost and the Gentiles in Caesarea by the cross-cultural action of enabling them to speak in various languages. The Spirit pushed Peter toward the house of Cornelius. The Spirit encouraged Philip to speak to the Ethiopian eunuch. The Spirit prevented Paul from speaking in Asia and encouraged him over into Macedonia and Europe. Paul described himself as a captive to the Spirit when he made the decision to return to Jerusalem, knowing that the journey would lead to his imprisonment.

The presence and work of the Spirit marks every significant moment in the Acts of the Apostles and compels us in our own day to nurture a sensitivity to the leadership of the Holy Spirit in breaking down the barriers that separate the church from its primary calling to engage in relationship and connection beyond our own cultural space. Luke's Gospel reminds us to be open to the hospitality of strangers in our engagement with the world and to pay attention to the coincidences that bring us into the orbit of others. Luke encourages us to recognize that we do not possess all that we need, but we must depend on what others offer to us. The Spirit's work in Luke-Acts is devoted to the nurture of open, sensitive, and caring attitudes within the faith community that lead toward deep relationships with people who are different from it. In other words, Luke-Acts compels the people of God through sensitivity to the leadership of the Holy Spirit to embrace otherness and difference. This is as much for the good of the church as it is for the good of the world. It fulfills God's hopes and intentions for humanity when God dispersed it into its various tribes and families at the Tower of Babel.

We learn from Luke-Acts to create space within ourselves for the religious perspectives of others. Both Peter and Paul showed respect for the cultures and religions of the Gentiles of Caesarea and the philosophers of Athens when they preached their sermons in those contexts. Peter acknowledged that God favored Gentiles as much as God favored Jews. Paul showed respect for the philosophers of Athens by citing their own poets. Significantly, both the Gentiles of Caesarea and the philosophers of Athens modeled an openness to dialogue and to what they might learn

from Peter and Paul. Such openness ought to mark Christian communities in the twenty-first century as we engage in dialogue and relationships
with people of other faiths and religions. Such engagement does not
diminish our faith. We learn as much as we teach when we enter into the
marketplace of religious ideas and admit that we do not know all there is
to know about God.

Finally, Paul's understanding of the unique place of Jews and Gentiles
speaks volumes about God's intention for all families of the earth. Paul
offers his churches in Rome and Galatia a theology for both Jews and
Gentiles. Abraham is the common faith ancestor of all humanity by virtue
of the faith that he expresses in the form of obedience to the law written
on his heart. His faithfulness is not tethered to a particular set of doctrines
about God, nor is it connected to the particular rituals that he observes,
including the ritual of circumcision. What is most important for Abraham
is that he follows the law written on his heart, lives his life out of obedience
to God, and determines to accept God's promise that "all the families of the
earth will bless themselves by him." His acceptance of this promise ensures
the blessing, not just of Israel but of all who are faithful to the law written
on their hearts as well as those who have been "baptized into Christ." Such
an understanding of God's blessing upon the righteous of every earthly
family enables the church, composed of those "baptized into Christ," to
move forward in partnership and connection with every tribe, race, nation,
and religion that exhibits the fruits of righteousness. The entire Bible bears
witness to the possibility of such partnership. Indeed, it is only by the
embrace of it that we can experience the full blessing of God and come
closest to understanding God's vision and purpose for the creation.

Notes

1. Several scholars draw attention to this clear connection between the
mission of Jesus and the mission of the church in Luke-Acts, including
Andreas J. Köstenberger and Peter T. O'Brien, *Salvation to the Ends of the
Earth: A Biblical Theology of Mission* (Downers Grove, IL: InterVarsity
Press, 2001), 111; Donald Senior and Carroll Stuhlmueller, *The Biblical
Foundations for Mission* (New York: Orbis Press, 1983), 255; and J. B.
Green, "Proclaiming Repentance and Forgiveness of Sins to All Nations:
A Biblical Perspective on the Church's Mission," in A. G. Padgett, ed.,
The Mission of the Church in Methodist Perspective: The World is My Parish
(Lewiston, NY: Edwin Mellen Press, 1992), 23.

2. Eugene LaVerdiere, *Luke* (Wilmington, DE: Michael Glazier, 1986), xiv–xv.

3. John Michael Penney, *The Missionary Emphasis of Lukan Pneumatology* (Sheffield, England: Sheffield Academic Press, 1997), 16. See also R. C. Tannehill, *The Narrative Unity of Luke-Acts: A Literary Interpretation 1* (Philadelphia, PA: Fortress Press, 1986), xiii.

4. Penney, *Missionary Emphasis*, 17.

5. LaVerdiere, *Luke*, xliv–xlv.

6. See W. Mark Tew, *Luke: Gospel to the Nameless and Faceless* (Eugene, OR: Wipf and Stock, 2012), 8.

7. LaVerdiere, *Luke*, 73.

8. Alan Roxburgh, *Missional: Joining God in the Neighborhood* (Grand Rapids, MI: Baker Books, 2011), 124.

9. Krista Tippett, "The Adventure of Civility," presentation at the Cooperative Baptist Fellowship General Assembly, Birmingham, AL, June 21, 2019.

10. Paul Borgman, *The Way According to Luke: Hearing the Whole Story of Luke-Acts* (Grand Rapids, MI: Eerdmans, 2006), 100.

11. LaVerdiere, *Luke*, 254.

12. Darrell Guder, *The Continuing Conversion of the Church* (Grand Rapids, MI: Eerdmans Publishing, 2000), 79.

13. John B. Polhill, *Paul and His Letters* (Nashville: Broadman and Holman, 1999), 209.

14. Polhill, *Paul and His Letters*, 211.

15. David Bosch, *Transforming Mission: Paradigm Shifts in Theology of Mission* (Maryknoll, NY: Orbis Books, 1991), 92.

16. Graeme Goldsworthy, "Biblical Theology and the Shape of Paul's Mission," in *The Gospel to the Nations: Perspectives on Paul's Mission*, ed. Peter Bolt and Mark Thompson (Downers Grove, IL: InterVarsity Press, 2000), 15.

17. James D. G. Dunn, *The New Perspective on Paul* (Grand Rapids, MI: Eerdmans, 2005), 135.

Chapter 7

John and Mission— The Gospel and the World

The knowledge of Jesus that the disciple gradually achieves is not . . . primarily intellectual or informational. It is the kind of knowledge one has of a friend that makes one say, "We know each other intimately." It is, quite simply, a deep sharing of life with Jesus. And sharing in the life of Jesus is participation in the life of God. (53)
—Sandra M. Schneiders, *Written that You May Believe*

The Gospel of John has been the most widely read and disseminated Gospel in the modern world. Some Christians claim that it is the most inclusive Gospel, providing in its focus on the Logos or Word of God a universal salvation available to all humanity, including even those who do not "profess faith" in Jesus Christ. Others have focused attention on the exclusive claims of the Gospel, insisting that salvation is available only to those who believe in the specific incarnation of this Logos or Word of God in Jesus Christ. To this end, they have passed out millions of copies of the Gospel around the world.

This primacy of John's Gospel has carried such weight that many Christians who advocate an exclusivist perspective (one that insists that Jesus is the only way to God) have read the three other Gospels through a Johannine lens. In John, Jesus declares, "I am the way, the truth, and the life. No one comes to the Father except through me" (14:6). For exclusivists, anyone who dies without professing belief in Jesus Christ or without giving intellectual assent to particular doctrinal statements about him is condemned. Belief in Jesus Christ, in their estimation, is essential to salvation, and apart from such belief human beings are condemned to eternal damnation because they have rejected Jesus. In the modern world and for most evangelical Christians, "belief" means intellectual assent to Jesus' claims about himself and his own divinity against the claims of other religions.

But does this insistence on intellectual assent to beliefs about Jesus give way to a different interpretation when we read the Gospel in light of the challenges facing John's own community and in the context of the diverse and multireligious world that we inhabit? Does the equator shift when we read John's Gospel in a multicultural world and through the lens of the continuing story of God's intention to bless all the families of the earth?

If the church is honest with itself, it must admit that the focus on the exclusivity of Jesus Christ as the only means of salvation for the world is not an effective way of communicating the Christian understanding of God as a God of love. Some very committed churchgoers today entered the faith by way of this path of intellectual assent that guaranteed salvation to them but that did little to emphasize the demands of the faith that they had embraced. In similar fashion, many people who entered the faith in this transactional way have since left the church because of the lack of vital spirituality and commitment to the way of Jesus that they anticipated from it. As my teacher and mentor, Bill J. Leonard, has said repeatedly, "The history of salvation in the United States is a history of salvation happening more and more quickly with less and less fuss." In his recent book, *A Sense of the Heart: Christian Religious Experience in the United States*, Leonard says that "By the late nineteenth and early twentieth century, conversion among many evangelicals was less a transcendent experience than a salvific transaction, a simple belief that provided the forgiveness of sins and entry into eternal life."[1] What was once a powerful and dynamic gateway to Christian discipleship and commitment to the way of Christ has become an end-in-itself and thus an obstacle to the full embrace of Jesus that John intended. It diminishes the power of love that serves as its foundation.

Understanding the worldview and perspective of the theological community that wrote the Gospel helps to resolve the tension between inclusivity and exclusivity that exists in it. Probably written in Asia Minor and far removed geographically from the center of Jewish and Christian faith and practice,[2] it was also the youngest Gospel, having taken final form in the late first century or early in the second and thus the farthest removed in time from the events that it describes. Most scholars generally identify it now as the product of a Johannine School,[3] located in Asia Minor and directed to a group of communities located nearby, rather than as a Gospel written by John, the son of Zebedee and disciple of Jesus. For these reasons, and perhaps more than any other Gospel, John inhabits a Greco-Roman reality. Fernando F. Segovia has argued quite persuasively that John presents Jesus as "a biographical narrative in the Greco-Roman tradition."[4] As the Word or Logos of God, Jesus journeys on both the cosmic and earthly levels in the Gospel.

The Gospel's focus on Logos Christology, grounded in Jewish Hellenism and Middle Platonism, presents Jesus as the Word or Logos, that universal emanation from God that was with God from the very beginning and entered into history as the divine spark of God that sheds spiritual light on reality. This Logos or Word exposes the difference between light and darkness, spirit (or Word) and flesh, life and death, and truth and falsehood. Light, spirit, life, and truth are not the exclusive domains of the Christian understanding of reality. Most Christians would admit that even the Christian understanding of God is a limited perspective. Other religions lead people toward light, spirit, life, and truth. Followers of Jesus are not the only people in the world who lead moral lives and express deep love for others. If this is true, then is it possible that, through this Logos, salvation extends beyond the bounds of institutional Christianity to include righteous people of other religions and worldviews? Is it also possible that this same Word calls John's community, and by extension the church today, to enter into relationships of love with people of other faiths, or of no faith at all, and to leave it to the Word of God to take those relationships in whatever direction it should determine?

First a quick summary of John's Gospel. It begins with a powerful and cosmic theological prologue that identifies Jesus as the Word or Logos who was with God from the beginning. Several people then bear witness to Jesus' identity as the Son of God, including John the Baptist and the first disciples. Jesus himself implies it in his conversations with Nicodemus (3:1-21) and the Samaritan woman at the well (4:7-42). These conversations are followed by seven signs or miracles that witness to Jesus' identity as the Son of God with the climax of the Gospel coming at the point of the resurrection of Lazarus when Martha confesses, "Yes, Lord, I believe that you are the Messiah, the Son of God, the one coming into the world" (11:27).

Following his anointment with perfume by Mary, Jesus washes his disciples' feet and speaks to his followers about his relationship to God and to them, and about their relationship to the Father. This discourse is a message to the Johannine communities in Asia Minor about Jesus' identity, the power of his presence with them, and the particular mission and purpose to which they are called as his followers. The Gospel then moves quickly through Jesus' death and resurrection and concludes with Jesus' post-resurrection appearances to Mary Magdalene and the other disciples whom he commissions for service in the world. Its powerful conclusion includes the confession of Thomas, who insists on seeing and feeling the wounds of Christ before he will believe, and the threefold declaration of Peter of his love for Jesus and desire to follow him even to the point of death. Jesus' words near the end of the Gospel are powerful words for John's church: "Blessed are those who have not seen and yet have come to believe" (20:29).

The purpose of John's Gospel is twofold when it comes to the nature of Christian mission in the world. First, John wants his community to believe that "Jesus is the Messiah, the Son of God, and that through believing you may have life in his name" (20:30-31). Coupled with this focus on belief is the conviction that, in Jesus, God is present with the Johannine communities and that, after Jesus' ascension, God will be present with them through the Holy Spirit. The theme of "presence" in the Gospel is a powerful theme, repeated time and again throughout the Gospel but especially in chapters 13–17 when Jesus speaks intimately to his disciples and, by extension, to the communities, calling them to "abide in me as I abide in you" (15:4).

The second theme of the Gospel concerns the identity of Jesus Christ and the nature of the relationship between God the Father and God the Son. Opponents of Johannine communities in the synagogues charged those communities with worshiping two Gods. Jörg Frey points out that the diaspora Jews of Asia Minor were a self-confident community who enjoyed considerable freedom to maintain the Jewish laws and to assemble.[5] Disturbed by the emerging Christian beliefs about Jesus as the Son of God, they understandably viewed such a perspective as anathema to a Jewish tradition still awaiting the coming Messiah. The Johannine School's theological understanding of Jesus was thus quite reactionary. The hostility between Johannine communities and the synagogue is evident in John's use of the word "aposynagogos," meaning "to be put out of the synagogues," on three separate occasions in the Gospel.[6]

Because of this crisis in the community, John utilizes language that strengthens its identity and unity, reassuring the community that belief in Jesus Christ as the Son of God is sufficient to lead its members to eternal life. They needed some theological foundation to stand on as they forged an identity apart from the Jewish institutions that had been the source of their understanding of God. Robert Kysar points out that the "exclusive claim for Christ" in John's Gospel "is due to the church's situation at the time. The church is playing defense, battling to defend its own goal line. It is struggling for survival against a formidable foe. Religious communities in this kind of situation state their cases in the most radical form."[7] John's community needed the comfort or security of knowing that, at the point of their expulsion from the synagogues, God loved them and, through Jesus, they belonged to God. Nothing could destroy this relationship; their embrace of and belief in Jesus Christ enabled the full experience of that love.

Several significant stories in the Gospel and Jesus' own words to his disciples and, by extension, the Johannine communities, shed light on the nature of God's mission in the world in the multicultural context that the church inhabits today. This new reality calls us to read certain passages in John's Gospel through a different interpretive lens. These texts include the Gospel's prologue, Jesus' conversations with Nicodemus and the Samaritan woman, Jesus' words to the church after the Last Supper, and the post-resurrection appearances of Jesus, including his appearance to Mary Magdalene, to the disciples in a locked house in Jerusalem, to Thomas, and to Peter in Galilee at the very end of the Gospel.

John 1:1-18—The Prologue

John's prologue is a sweeping and cosmic depiction of the Word who was with God from the beginning, who took on flesh and "lived among us," and who, by the end of the prologue, has been identified as Jesus Christ, God's only Son, who "has made [God] known" (1:1, 17-18). Despite its presence at the beginning of the Gospel, the prologue seems to be a later addition, perhaps even a hymn, as if someone, writing after most of the Gospel had been completed, decided to go back and ground the entire Gospel in a radically new perspective that provided a broad interpretive framework. Then, someone else edited the prologue again to add words about John the Baptist that provided concrete mooring for the cosmic portrayal of the Word or Logos of God. To put it another way, the prologue stands alone quite nicely without the inserted references to John the Baptist in verses 6-8 and 15. With these verses, the prologue offers both a macro and a micro perspective on the nature and identity of Jesus. Again, Segovia's perspective on the cosmic and earthly journeys of Jesus offers some clarity. Jesus is both the Word who was with God from the beginning and will always be with God and also Jesus Christ, the Son of God, to whom John bears witness and whose death and resurrection has implications for all of humanity.

Three movements occur across the prologue. In the first movement (1:1-5), John describes the relationship between the Word (Logos) and God and the role of the Word in creation. In the second movement (1:9-13), he describes the relationship between the Word and the world. Finally, in the third movement (1:14-18), he focuses on the "grace and truth," as opposed to the Law of Moses, that is given to humanity through the Word, now identified as Jesus Christ.[8] Every reader of the Gospel recognizes the first words of the prologue—"In the beginning was the Word" (1:1). The resounding words of the opening chapter of Genesis immediately come to mind. John carts us all the way back to the moment of creation, the first context, when "the earth was a formless void and darkness covered the face of the deep" (Gen 1:1-2). In the midst of that formless void, God and the Word began the creative work of bringing all things into being.

This is the very moment that God initiated God's mission in the universe. For this reason and in the light of its place here at the beginning of the Gospel, the passage is significant for a full understanding of the church's mission in the world. John has inserted into the story the preexistent Word, who stood with God at that moment and whom John identifies as God. John also introduces here the dichotomy between light and darkness that is present in the Genesis account. The Word is the source of the creation of all things and the light "that shines in the darkness, and the darkness did not overcome it" (1:5). Significantly, if "all things came into being through him, and without him not one thing came into being," (1:3) then the Word or Logos is the very source of the otherness and difference that exists in the creation, and that diversity and difference resides at the heart of God's intentions and purpose for the world.[9] John's Gospel thus squares quite powerfully with the primeval history of Genesis 1–11 in which God's constant insistence that humanity "be fruitful and multiply and fill the earth" was first ignored by human beings and then enforced by God at the point of the building of the Tower of Babel.

So what is this Word or Logos who created all things? Why would John seize upon it as a means of helping his church understand the mission of God in the world? How are we to understand it in our own context? The concept of the "logos" emerged from Hellenistic philosophy and obviously had some influence on the Gospel writer, who decided that it shed new light on the meaning of the life, death, and resurrection of Jesus Christ. Stoic philosophy, Gnostic literature, and the writings of Philo of Alexandria, a Jewish philosopher who sought to connect Jewish and Hellenistic philosophical thought, also spoke of the "logos." For Philo, the logos was the highest intermediary between God and the creation and was "the bond of everything, holding all things together and binding all the parts."[10]

Whether or not the Johannine School was familiar with Philo, it certainly understood the idea of logos in a similar way, though it viewed the *Logos* as both God and the intermediary between God and the creation. In this sense, the Logos could emerge from God and provide separation between the darkness of the creation and the light of God that emanated from the Logos. The Logos then was the source of life and of light in the midst of darkness. It allowed God to remain separate from the creation while at the same time remaining intimately connected to it through the Logos or Word. John's Gospel clarifies the relationship between God and the Son of God, describing the uniqueness of each while maintaining their essential oneness.

The second section of the prologue describes the relationship between the Logos and the world or, more specifically, humanity. Despite the role of the Logos in the creation, the Logos remained hidden from the world or rejected by the world—"the world did not know him" (1:10). He also came to "his own" or "to his own home" and "his own people did not accept him," an obvious reference to the Jewish people (1:11). Is it possible that this reference to the rejection of the Word by the Jewish people is about a rejection that occurred prior to that moment when "the Word became flesh and lived among us" (1:14)? Is John referring to the portion of Israel that rejected God's intention for it to "bless the families of the earth," or is John referring to Israel's rejection of Jesus as the Messiah of God? To put it differently, is there a pre-incarnational rejection of Jesus by certain members of the various families of the earth and, concomitantly, is there a pre-incarnational acceptance of Jesus by others?

Several scholars have interpreted the verses in this way, though the consensus has been that the reference is to the rejection of the Word *after* the incarnation of Jesus.[11] Nevertheless, suppose the reference is to the period prior to the incarnation? How might we then read the prologue? Is it possible that, prior to Jesus' incarnation, people could receive the Logos in some way that enabled them to become "children of God"? If this is the case, then what prevents people now from receiving the "Logos" apart from the person of Jesus Christ and thus becoming children of God? This would certainly fit the pattern in the Hebrew Bible in which a remnant of Israel responded to the call of the prophets toward repentance and engaged in acts of mercy and justice in the world. It would allow for the existence of the righteous strangers across the history of Israel who were obviously working alongside righteous Israelites to accomplish God's mission in the world. It would provide some foundation for partnership with righteous strangers of other religions and worldviews today who work as hard toward God's intentions for the world as do committed followers of Jesus Christ.

It would also fit well with the call of Abram in which God implied that the families of the earth would "bless themselves by Israel." Certainly, such blessing was not something that God intended to put off until the incarnation of Jesus. It was not something that a loving God would delay until Israel or the church finally figured out its divine calling and decided to follow it. Such action would elevate the place of Israel and the church above that of other families of the earth, something that a loving and gracious God who created human cultures and intended such diversity would never do. God's intention from the beginning was that human beings would live together as various families of the earth and that God would be present with each family no matter its location and unique cultural perspective. This book has argued that such geographical location and unique cultural perspective was an essential part of God's intention for humanity. Read differently and in the light of a diverse world, John's prologue lends support to such an interpretation.

The third movement of the prologue focuses on the Word or Logos as Jesus Christ, the source of grace and truth for all of humanity and the supreme revelation of God in the world. Christ embodies grace and truth to such an extent that, in him and through him, we see God more clearly than we have ever seen God before. John puts it this way: "from his fullness we have all received, grace upon grace" (1:16). Here John moves from impersonal pronouns to the very personal pronoun "we." We have all received this grace. It is available to all. This does not mean we have all accepted the grace offered to us; it does mean that "grace upon grace" extends to all of us.

So who is the "we" to whom John refers? Is it the church or is it all of humanity? To whom has such grace been given? This intimate language refers quite powerfully to the presence of Christ among and within all of humanity. Christ has pitched his tent in the world. Somehow, he has lived among all of us, including every family of the earth. This is the only kind of incarnation that makes sense given the diversity of families of the earth and our cultural and religious differences. R. Alan Culpepper points out that "John's Logos Christology allows Christians to affirm that adherents of other religious traditions may come to know God through the work of the Cosmic Christ."[12] In other words, in Christ, the Word has become flesh for all of us, and all have "seen his glory, the glory as of a father's only son, full of grace and truth." The Logos of God has made its way into every culture and tribe as the preexistent Word; most specifically, that Word has been embodied in Jesus of Nazareth, "the Lamb of God who takes away the sins of the world" (1:29).

John 3:1-21—Nicodemus and Jesus

The conversation between Jesus and Nicodemus in John 3 invites readers into its mysteries and ambiguities and toward deep contemplation about what it means to be born again and to "have eternal life" (3:16). John's community must certainly have understood Nicodemus as struggling with the same spiritual questions with which it struggled. What did it mean to be born again? Who was Jesus and why had God sent him into the world? How did one gain the eternal life that Jesus offered? Though Nicodemus came away from his conversation with Jesus rather perplexed by Jesus' answers to his questions, he will appear at least twice more in the Gospel, defending Jesus before the Pharisees in the Sanhedrin (7:50-52) and assisting Joseph of Arimathea in preparing the body of Jesus for burial (19:39-42).[13]

For this reason, Nicodemus models for John's community someone who has deep respect for Jesus and yet always stands just outside the circle of full embrace and belief in Jesus as the Son of God. His relationship to Jesus raises interesting questions about the nature of belief and belonging in John's Gospel and for the Johannine communities. First, he asks sincere questions about Jesus' identity and the nature of salvation. Then he defends Jesus with courageous words before his own peers, the Pharisees, reminding them of Jesus' right under the Jewish law to a hearing. Finally, he acts at the point of Jesus' death, bringing spices in which to wrap the body of Jesus when many of Jesus' followers (those who believed in him) have abandoned him. He belongs without ever believing.

Other characters in the Gospel also never fully embrace belief in Jesus or at least never fully enter into the community of the disciples. Among this number are Joseph of Arimathea, identified as a secret believer in John 19:38, and the Greeks who come to see Jesus in John 12:20-22. Acts 18 and 19 identify followers of John the Baptist who lived in Ephesus in Asia Minor, some of whom Paul baptized and who received the Holy Spirit.[14] Their presence in Asia Minor lends validity to the possibility that the Johannine School wrote the Gospel of John in part to convince others among them to follow Jesus instead of John. This conclusion is valid since, at the beginning of the Gospel, John the Baptist himself confesses that he is not the Messiah but rather the one preparing the way for the Messiah.[15]

In his conversation with Nicodemus, Jesus first uses the word *belief* to describe the action that is required of all who desire eternal life. The word seems at first to refer to intellectual assent to theological truth about Jesus. Is this, however, what the word means for John? How are we to understand the difference between *faith* and *belief* in John's Gospel when we are interpreting it through the lens of a modern world that placed significant focus on the intellect and not interpreting it in the context of the ancient world? What did the ancient world, and specifically the Johannine School, mean by *faith* and what did it mean by *belief*?

Despite the focus on *belief* in John's Gospel, Jesus implies in John 6 that God has *given* his followers to him (6:37, 39), that they must be "*drawn* by the Father" (6:44), and that there are *unbelievers among* the disciples (6:64), again raising questions about the boundaries of faith and belief for the Johannine community. Jesus says, "I have other sheep that do not belong to this fold. I must bring them also, and they will listen to my voice" (10:16). Later, in reference to his death, he says, "I, when I am lifted up, will draw *all people* to myself" (12:32). Alan Culpepper points out that, for many of these reasons, John's Gospel "undermines any confidence in faith as arising from human decision."[16] Belief and faith are not the same thing. Intellectual assent to theological truth, or *belief,* as the modern world understands it, is not the only basis of *faith* or belonging for the community. Some believe. God draws others, perhaps even some who may not yet "believe" in or "give intellectual assent" to propositional truth about Jesus. At the same time, there may be some counted among the disciples, and by extension within the Johannine community, who belong but do not believe.

What then does John mean by *pistevon eis auton* or "believes in him" in John 3:16? If faith is the work of God and not of humanity, then how should we understand the human action of belief, which seems to be what John demands as the first step toward eternal life? Again, Nicodemus makes no confession of belief in Jesus Christ at the point of his conversation with Jesus, and he disappears from the scene. John concludes with Jesus' words about belief. The word appears at least seven times in chapter 3. *Pistis* or "belief" seems grounded in the notion of conviction and of the trust that is born of faith and then joined with it. In other words, faith is God's work. Belief is humanity's work. God's work of faith, however, is and remains the first work. Humanity's work of belief follows it.

Add to this the reality that "God so loved the world" with all its diversity and complexity. God is the author of that diversity and multiculturalism as the Tower of Babel story makes clear. If this is the case, then the divine seed of faith must exist in families beyond the Jewish and Christian families. God did not put faith only into Abraham. God did not put faith only into the church. God put faith into all of humanity. We respond to this gift of faith with the determination to "come to the light, so that it may be clearly seen" that our "deeds have been done in God" (3:21).

John's affirmation that "God so loved the world" is a powerful affirmation of God's original purpose in the creation, and any current reading of John's Gospel through the lens of a diverse world must take that affirmation seriously. If God loves the world with all of its cultures, languages, and religions, then the Son and the believers represented in the disciples and John's church must love that world as much as God does. We who inhabit such a world now must embrace it with all of its otherness and difference. We must realize that the light that exists in the world is not restricted to those families of the earth who affirm certain doctrinal perspectives or theological propositions about Jesus Christ. The light and Word of God fills the earth. Acts of goodness and mercy carried out with pure intentions emerge from the same Word or Logos that has existed with God from the very beginning. This divine impulse exists in all of humanity and apart from any particular religious system. At the same time, the demonic impulse of evil and darkness exists in all of humanity and apart from any particular religious system as well. Good and evil are deeply embedded in all of us. The Word or Logos enters the world in order to expose the darkness and bring all things to the light.

For John then, Jesus was the source of light for the entire world. This light, represented in the cosmic Word or Logos of God, illuminated both the lovers of light and the lovers of darkness. It enabled those who possessed it to distinguish between Nicodemus, who stood on the side of goodness and light, and the Jews at the temple in Jerusalem later who "took up stones again to stone him" (10:31). John is particularly concerned to connect belief for his community specifically to the person of Jesus Christ because Jesus provided for them an identity apart from the synagogues. He wanted to reinforce that belief to such an extent that it would allow the community to stand strong in the face of adversity and persecution. Their belief and embrace of Jesus enabled them to distinguish their enemies from their friends.

How does this understanding of *pistis* or *belief* in John's Gospel influence our understanding of the mission of God in the world in the twenty-first century? Our belief in Jesus Christ signals our intention to live life out of our embrace of the way of Jesus and our confidence that in him we see and experience God. By following the path to which he calls us, we live our lives as God intended for us to live. Belief in Jesus is much more than intellectual assent to doctrine about Jesus; it is making the commitment to overcome the broken relationships that exist between others and ourselves. It is the intentional decision to express love for other families of the earth by deepening our relationships with them. In the process, our love for them deepens, as does their love for us. We begin to see from the perspective of the other. We understand the particular convictions that motivate them toward expressing love to us. We see and hear in them what we have never been able to see and hear before. They see and hear in us what they have never been able to see and hear before.

God then takes these mutual acts of love and does what God always does. God carries our deepening relationships of love in the direction that God desires. In some cases, this leads us to the verbal confession of our belief in Jesus Christ. We gladly share that the gift of grace that God has given us in Jesus Christ motivates us toward loving relationships. We bear witness to our primary motivation to love whenever the Spirit leads us to do so. We must also be open to the motivations that drive others to share love with us. God is as much concerned with our openness to them as God is concerned with their openness to us. The Word or Logos of God is at work in their lives as much as it is at work in our lives.

Years ago, prior to the terror attacks of September 11, 2001, I cultivated a close relationship with an imam of a mosque in a town in northwest Georgia. He and I worked together for a number of years in interfaith dialogue and collaboration. When the World Trade Center collapsed, the pastors of the town planned a prayer vigil for the community. My imam friend called me to ask if he could address the gathering. The pastors, uncomfortable with the idea and concerned about the response of the town, suggested that he come to the event together with others in the Muslim community but that he not address the group. Later, he and his community invited police officers, teachers, local government leaders, and others to share in an Iftar meal to break the Ramadan fast. Over the years, we shared many wonderful conversations about God, faith, global challenges, and our respective sacred texts.

One day, as he and I were sharing lunch with a mutual friend, the friend asked the imam if any Christians ever tried to encourage him to convert to Christianity.

He responded without hesitation. "I am constantly approached by people in the grocery stores and on Main Street downtown who know me and who immediately ask me if I know Jesus Christ as my personal Lord and Savior," he said. "They have good intentions. But they are not willing to listen to me and to my perspective on God and Jesus. They want to tell me what they believe, but they do not want to listen to what I believe."

He then added, "If I ever do decide to become a believer in Jesus as the Son of God, I will not do it because of them. They do not know me. If I become a believer in Jesus Christ, I will do so because of what I have learned about Jesus from the conversations that Rob and I have shared."

I was overwhelmed. Moreover, I must admit that if I ever become a Muslim, it will be because of the many conversations that Imam Muhammad and I shared. His perspective on God blessed me. Apparently, my perspective on God blessed him as well. I could never say that he did not possess faith or that, for some reason, Almighty God decided to put faith into me and not into him. He was the source of divine light to me, revealing to me my own evil and darkness and bringing my light and goodness to the surface. I was, in similar fashion, the source of divine light to him, revealing the same thing. This is what God has intended from the very beginning—the light shines in the darkness and the darkness cannot comprehend it. We engage in mutual sharing and love for each other in order to remove the darkness in us that cannot comprehend the light.

The idea that God has placed faith into the hearts of other people means that their faith illuminates our own faith. Their convictions and beliefs have emerged from the gift of faith with which God has blessed them. Their understanding of God is as limited as our own understanding. Because of the presence of faith within us, we can sense whether "their deeds have been done in God" (3:21). Because of the presence of faith within them, they can sense whether our deeds have been done in God. We bless them by sharing our perspectives and convictions with them. They bless us by sharing their perspectives and convictions with us. In the process, we engage in mutual blessing.

Our deepening relationships of love are not only about dialogue and the sharing of our convictions. They also lead us toward accomplishing the purposes of God in the world. God's intention from the beginning has been that all the families of the earth join God in God's mission in the world. Collaboration in this mission and purpose is essential. Mission is the work that we do now in order to bring about God's ultimate vision for the creation. For this reason, mission is not an exclusively Christian calling. Mission is the province of all creation, every human family who brings to the table its own particular cultural contributions motivated by the divine seed or Logos that gives light to all. At the same time, all families of the earth are called toward that light in order to distinguish between good and evil in the world and to work together on the side of goodness and light.

Again, I will use my relationship with my imam friend as an example. Because of the relationship of love, trust, and friendship that the two of us shared, an entire community of people began moving beyond the trauma of 9/11 by overcoming its prejudices against otherness and difference. Christians in the community moved beyond their fear of Islam when the Muslim community in the town hosted them at a series of Iftar meals to break the Ramadan fast. At the same time, Muslims in the community overcame their fears for their own safety because they met Christians in the community and learned to trust them. My relationship with the imam and the relationships of other Christians in the community to their Muslim siblings lead to a safer, stabler, and healthier city. This expression of mutual love emerged as the result of a concrete act of partnership together in God's mission in the world.

John 4:7-26—The Samaritan Woman at the Well

Like the story of Nicodemus, Jesus' conversation with the Samaritan woman at the well is unique to John's Gospel. The fact that the story takes place in Samaria right after Jesus has passed through the Judean countryside from Jerusalem makes for an interesting parallel between John and Acts—both move from Jerusalem to Judea to Samaria and ultimately to "the ends of the earth." While the events in John's Gospel never extend beyond Galilee, the Johannine community, located far from Jerusalem in Asia Minor, would certainly understand themselves to constitute another significant stage in the gospel's movement beyond Jerusalem, Judea, and Samaria.

In his conversation with the woman at the well, Jesus uses water as a powerful symbol for a deeper spiritual reality. Here the influence of Hellenistic philosophy on John's understanding of reality emerges again in the Gospel. Jesus points to himself as the Water of Life who quenches the deepest spiritual thirst. He does the same thing with the process of birth and rebirth in his conversation with Nicodemus and with bread after the feeding of the five thousand in chapter 6. He offers spiritual birth or birth "from above" through the Spirit that leads to eternal life, as opposed to birth of the flesh. He is the Bread of Heaven that gives life to the world as opposed to bread that simply alleviates physical hunger.

Here a dualistic perspective on reality sheds light on the nature and work of Jesus in the world. John's community receives insight on that work through divine light that comes to it from the wider culture. The earlier Synoptic Gospels do not contain this same kind of distinction between the Spirit and the flesh, heaven and earth, and lightness and darkness, or at least they do not emphasize it in the way that John's Gospel does. The other Gospels are provincial in this sense. Their interpretive grid remains grounded in the historical and philosophical context of Palestine. The Johannine School introduces perspectives on the nature of Jesus as the Logos of God that make it far more complex in its philosophical and theological foundations. Readers sense in it an "otherworldliness" that takes seriously certain worldviews and perspectives that the other Gospels could ignore or about which they were unaware. John's Gospel then provides a powerful example of the process by which Christian theology can embrace otherness and difference as having divine origins even if the source of those origins is outside the current and orthodox Judeo-Christian perspective.

To put it another way, John's Gospel offers a model that allows the church today to receive insight on the work of God in the world from beyond the boundaries of Christian theology and philosophy, perhaps even from the spiritual and philosophical truth contained in the doctrines and beliefs of other religions of the world and secular worldviews and perspectives. John's embrace of a philosophical perspective beyond purely Jewish and Christian theology signals his belief that other families of the earth bring truth and insight about God to the theological and experiential table. To read John is to step off into the deep end of the pool where we open ourselves up to spiritual insight from unexpected and unlikely sources.

To this end, Jesus' most significant exchange with the woman at the well comes at the point of their conversation about the worship of God. Samaritans, of course, believed that Mount Gerizim was God's holy mountain and that God should be worshiped there instead of in Jerusalem. Here Jesus effectively divorces worship from the temple in Jerusalem and makes the powerful claim that "the hour is coming, and is now here, when the true worshipers will worship the Father in spirit and truth, for the Father seeks such as these to worship him" (4:23). By divorcing true worship from the temple in Jerusalem and focusing it instead on "spirit and truth," John reminds his community that its worship has nothing to do with its location in Asia Minor or elsewhere and everything to do with the One to whom its worship is directed.

This text raises the question of the nature of true worship. Is it possible that those outside the bounds of either Judaism or Christianity who have the best intentions in their worship and who honestly and earnestly seek God in worship are worshiping "in spirit and in truth"? True worship emerges from the heart, Jesus says here, and not from the place or context where that worship occurs. This would explain why followers of Jesus might find themselves deeply moved by the sight of Muslims prostrating themselves in prayer at a mosque or by devout Hindu worshipers performing puja or the daily sacrifice in front of an image of the god Vishnu in a temple in India. The earnest desire to worship God in whatever form is a deep-seated human desire that emerges from the heart, and, while we might protest that such worship has nothing to do with the worship of the Triune God known to Christianity, we must affirm the impulse that is driving people to worship God in the first place.

Years ago, I took a group of students to visit a mosque in Atlanta for the Friday prayers. We were warmly welcomed and invited to sit at the back of the mosque as our Muslim friends prepared for the service. Some read from the Qur'an. Others went to the washroom to perform wudhu or the ritual washing of the hands, mouth, nose, arms, head, and feet that precede the daily prayers. Eventually all took their places and the imam lead the group through the prayer service. First, everyone stood, cupping their hands behind their ears to symbolize the removing of obstructions and an openness to God. Then they moved to their knees and prostrated themselves before God while reciting passages from the Qur'an. The sight of so many people on their knees before God in this powerful and global act of prayer performed toward the Kaaba in Mecca always moves me.

It moved my students as well. When we got back into the van to return to school, one very conservative Christian student, visibly shaken, leaned his big frame up toward me in the driver's seat.

"Dr. Nash," he said, "why don't we pray like that?"

"Some Christians do," I pointed out. I talked about the many revivals I had attended in northeast Georgia during my childhood when my grandfather would preach a sermon called "No Place to Run and No Place to Hide" about the tribulation period in Revelation, and almost every church member would come to the altar, get on their knees, and pray to be delivered from that period.

"That was a long time ago," he responded. "We don't do it in my church at all."

Then he said something that nearly made me lose control of the van.

"We ought to get together with these folks and learn something about prayer," he said.

I thought that was a great idea. I wonder if he ever made it to a mosque to inquire about some lessons.

Significantly, he experienced something quite powerful in that mosque. We all did. As strange and foreign as those prayers were to us, we felt the presence of God. The sheer power of community prayer focused toward God caused shivers to move up and down our spines. I know the Spirit when I sense it. I have felt it in church and I have experienced it in my own times of prayer. True worship is not restricted to a place or to a particular religion. Moreover, while I might protest and insist that my own worship of God is the highest form of worship, I must admit that my limited perspective on such worship does not bind God.

This is Jesus' point in his conversation with the woman at the well. Our limited perspectives on God do not bind God. My belief in the Christian perspective on truth does not bind God. God constantly breaks out of every limitation that I seek to place on God, including the limitation on where, when, and by whom God can be worshiped. For this reason, we who embrace Jesus Christ as the Son of God should be open to conversation and dialogue with people of other worldviews and religious perspectives. John's Gospel allows for the possibility that they can be the source of divine truth for us.

John 12:20-36—Cosmic and Earthly Implications of the Death of Jesus

In John 12, Jesus connects the cosmic implications of his death and resurrection with his earthly journey toward the cross. The text follows the story of the resurrection of Lazarus from the dead, Mary's anointment of Jesus' body for burial with costly perfume, and Jesus' triumphal entry into Jerusalem. It precedes the act of the washing of the feet of his disciples as an expression of servanthood and love. Most interestingly, the announcement that some Greeks or Gentiles want to see him precipitates his announcement of the cosmic implications of his death and resurrection. It is as if Jesus, upon receiving word of the arrival of Gentiles from outside the Jewish family, realizes that "the hour has come" (12:23). Their arrival is, obviously, a significant moment. Jesus immediately announces, "Unless a grain of wheat falls into the earth and dies, it remains a single grain; but if it dies, it bears much fruit" (12:24). He is now fully aware that the moment of his own death is at hand. The only possible conclusion here is that the arrival of other families of the earth at his door reminds him that God's mission in the world is a mission for all of humanity. Other families of the earth have now come to him.

For this reason, he prays, "Father, glorify your name."

A voice from heaven responds, "I have glorified it, and I will glorify it again."

The crowd interprets the voice as thunder. Some announce that an angel has spoken to him.

Jesus says, "This voice has come for your sake, not for mine. Now is the judgment of this world; now the ruler of this world will be driven out."

Then he adds, "And I, when I am lifted up from the earth, will draw *all people* to myself."

These words signal much about the cosmic journey of Jesus and the universal nature of the salvation he offers. His crucifixion on the earthly plane is a descent into insignificance and death, but on the cosmic plane it is an ascent toward his own glorification and accomplishment of God's purpose for him, a purpose that carries with it implications for every family of the earth. When Jesus "is lifted up" from the earth, he will draw "all people" to himself. The words of the hymn at the beginning of the Gospel come to mind—"The true light, *which enlightens everyone*, was coming into the world" (1:9). Jesus concludes this reflection on his death with a plea: "While you have the light, believe in the light, so that you may become children of the light" (12:36).

The Tower of Babel certainly comes to mind in these words of Jesus. At the tower, God drove human families away from each other, introducing barriers of language and culture that forced such dispersion. In the death and resurrection of Jesus, God draws humanity back toward God and toward the full expression of love and servanthood modeled by Jesus when he washes the feet of the disciples (13:1-20). Humanity tried to elevate itself at the Tower of Babel in order to make a name for itself; God lifts Jesus up at his crucifixion in order to reveal the humility, servanthood, and love that ought to characterize relationships among all families of the earth. Jesus then draws humanity to himself, imploring all families to "become children of the light."

John 14–17—Jesus' Word to the Church

Chapters 14–17 in John's Gospel are significant because here Jesus speaks powerfully and directly to John's community just prior to his death and about the interrelationships between Jesus, Jesus' followers represented in the disciples and John's community, and God. His words also get to the heart of the mission of the church in the world. Fred Craddock points out that in these chapters "the crowds are gone, the opponents are gone, and Jesus moves inside the church, sits down and speaks directly."[17] The theme of this section is the theme of presence: of Jesus' presence with God, of Jesus' presence with his followers, of the presence of the Holy Spirit with Jesus' followers in the wake of Jesus' ascension into heaven, and of the presence of Jesus' followers in the world.

This is the decisive moment for John's community. Here John's Jesus lays out for his church the most important and compelling truths of all, the very things that Jesus most wants that church to know and to do before he takes his leave of it. His words offer hope to the church. Jesus reminds it of God's care and love for it. Jesus assures it of God's provision despite the persecution and challenge that it will endure. He encourages it with powerful words of comfort and assurance: "Do not let your hearts be troubled. Believe in God, believe also in me. In my father's house, there are many dwelling places. If it were not so, would I have told you that I go to prepare a place for you?" (14:1-2).

This section of the Gospel is not only about Jesus' presence with the church. It is also about the presence of the church with Jesus. Here Jesus reminds the church of its calling to be present with him even as he is present with it. "I am the true vine," he says, "and my father is the vine grower." The source of life for the church is the Word or Logos of God incarnated in the person of Jesus Christ. This Word nourishes the church for its work in the world. It calls the church to the same expression of love, servanthood, and grace expressed in Jesus' life and ministry. In similar fashion, the Word or Christ offers the church a true picture of God's mission and purpose in the world. Jesus makes the powerful assertion that "whoever has seen me has seen the Father" and that, through him, "the Father who dwells in me does his works" (14:9-10). He then adds, "Abide in me as I abide in you. Just as the branch cannot bear fruit by itself unless it abides in the vine, neither can you unless you abide in me" (15:1-4). A little later he adds, "This is my commandment, that you love one another as I have loved you. No one has greater love than this, to lay down one's life for one's friends" (15:12).

John 14–17 invites the church today into the most intimate moment of Jesus' entire ministry. Nowhere else do we get the sense that we are in the room with Jesus and the other disciples and perhaps with Jesus' followers across space and time. Together, all of us who, for whatever reason, have determined that the way of Jesus will be our way and that we will live our lives as best we can by following in his steps and along his path toward a meaningful and purposeful existence listen to the voice of Jesus. We hear together Jesus' words about the intimate relationship that Jesus desires to have with us and for us to have with each other, with those beyond our community, and with God.

It is something akin to one of those rare moments in life when, suddenly, we come to grips with the way things are. I remember such a moment with my own father at the point of his death. In that moment, I realized that he was not going to be around much longer and that he wanted to prepare all of us for that reality. My dad was the kind of man who liked to make sure his car was in decent working order. He kept it clean. Kept the tires shiny. Kept the oil changed. Wrote down every mile he traveled and where he went so that he had a record for tax purposes.

I was standing by his hospital bed when it happened.

"Son," he said. "I want you to make sure that you check the tires on your mom's car and keep the oil changed. I am not going to be able to do that any longer. I need you to take care of it. Make sure she always has a good dependable car, too. Don't let her drive something she shouldn't be driving."

Translated into my father's way of speaking, all of this meant, "I've got to go away. Take care of your mom. She needs you." It cut through everything. It was not a weepy, sappy moment. It was a real moment. He was asking for my presence with my mother when he was not going to be able to be with her anymore. In his own way, he was telling me that I needed her as well. I needed to make sure she was safe and able to be present with me when he could not be.

This is Jesus' intention here in John 14–17. Here he says, "I'm going away. This is what I need you to do. I want to remind you that I have not left for good. I am going to prepare a place for you. Love one another. Abide in me and in each other. Take care of one another. Model your own ministry in the world after my ministry and be confident that the love, servanthood, and grace that I have told you to express to each other and to other people are the work of God."

Jesus also talks about the challenges that he and John's community will face. He informs them that "An hour is coming when those who kill you will think that by doing so they are offering worship to God" (16:2). The church will face persecution, and Jesus' followers will give up much because of their decision to follow Jesus. He then draws attention to the persecution and challenge that he is facing: "The hour is coming," he says, "when you will be scattered, each one to his home, and you will leave me alone. When that time comes, remember that I am not alone because the Father is with me. I have said this to you, so that in me you may have peace. In the world you face persecution. But take courage; I have conquered the world" (16:32-33).

Then, like any good preacher, at the end of this intimate conversation with his flock, Jesus closes with a prayer. He looks up to heaven and says, "Father, the hour has come . . . . I glorified you on earth by finishing the work that you gave me to do. So now, Father, glorify me in your own presence with the glory that I had in your presence before the world existed" (17:1-5). His words recall the first words in the Gospel of John: "In the beginning was the Word, and the Word was with God, and the Word was God" (1:1). His point now is that his followers have been with him from the beginning of his ministry and he has been with them. Because they have known him, they have known God as well. The way that they express their love for him is by keeping his commandments: "Those who love me will keep my word, and my Father will love them, and we will come to them and make our home with them" (14:23).

Jesus is calling the church to express in its own life and in its relationships to each other and with those beyond the church the love that God has put into it through Christ. This love is not an exclusive love that is available only to the church; in and through Christ as the true vine, the church expresses the love of God in the world. As the fruit of the vine, the church must "love one another as I have loved you" (15:12). It must also remember, "You did not choose me, but I chose you. And I appointed you to go and bear fruit, fruit that will last" (15:16). The church is the means by which God expresses God's love, through Christ, to other families of the earth. Its mission and calling is to remind the world to "love one another" and to "lay down one's life for one's friends" (15:13).

Jesus is about to do both. Immediately after he concludes this intimate conversation with his followers, Judas betrays him in a garden in the Kidron Valley. Throughout the story of his betrayal, arrest, and crucifixion, Jesus as the Word or Logos of God is in complete control of the events. John reports that he knew "all that was about to happen to him" (18:4). The trial and crucifixion proceed in similar fashion to the way that these same events unfold in the other three Gospels. In the end, Jesus expresses the love of God for the world by laying down his life for it. In doing so, he fulfills his promise that "I, when I am lifted up from the earth, will draw all people to myself" (12:32).

John 20:11–21:24—The Post-Resurrection Appearances of Jesus

Sandra M. Schneiders has pointed out that there are two sides to the death and resurrection of Jesus in John's Gospel: "Glorification is what happens to Jesus on the cross; resurrection is the communication to Jesus' disciples of his paschal glory through his return to them in the Spirit."[18] For her, the significance of the resurrection rests not so much in what happens to Jesus as in the powerful transformation that occurs in the lives of his followers. The crucifixion glorifies Christ. Jesus' post-resurrection appearances transform his community and provide it with powerful confirmation of its own calling and mission in the world.

Significantly, Jesus appears first to Mary Magdalene, who is overwhelmed with grief at being unable to locate his body and thus unable to recognize Jesus even when he speaks to her. She realizes who he is only when he speaks her name. Stunned, she responds in a surprising way: "Rabbouni!" she exclaims in Hebrew, referring to him as "Teacher." Her words represent an acknowledgment of her commitment to the way of grace and truth given through Jesus as the Logos or Word of God as opposed to the way of the Law given through Moses.[19] The implication is that God gave the Law of Moses to a single family of the earth. Jesus restores God's original purpose and intention to bless every family of the earth, Jew and Gentile alike. To this end, the Logos or Word of God "became flesh and lived among us," ensuring the means by which all families would receive God's blessing and through which they would bless each other. Mary's confession reminded John's community that, despite its expulsion from the synagogues, it would receive the "grace upon grace" that John had promised in his prologue.

She now makes the simple declaration to the other disciples that "I have seen the Lord" (John 20:18), and, with these words, she becomes the first witness to the resurrection of Jesus.

Jesus' resurrection appearance among the disciples occurs in the evening of that same day. The disciples have gathered behind locked doors out of fear that what happened to Jesus will happen to them. John simply reports, "Jesus came and stood among them and said, 'Peace be with you'" (20:19). These words apparently accomplish their intended purpose in John's Gospel. The disciples express no fear of him. Instead, he shows them his hands and his side, and "the disciples rejoiced when they saw the Lord" (20:20). By contrast, in Luke's Gospel, when Jesus appeared before the disciples and uttered the same words, "They were startled and terrified, and thought that they were seeing a ghost" (Luke 24:37). Jesus then asked them, "Why are you frightened and why do doubts arise in your hearts?" (Luke 24:38). John's account draws attention to the peace and wholeness that Jesus offers to the gathered community, both the one in Jerusalem and the one addressed by the Johannine School in Asia Minor.

Jesus then repeats the words, "Peace be with you," this time with the intention of connecting that peace to their participation in the mission of God in the world, a mission that he declares to be very much in line with his own: "As the Father has sent me, so I send you," he declares (20:21). This commission is far more general in John than it is in either Matthew 28:16-20 or Acts 1:8, with no reference at all to what they are to preach or what they are to do, except that they are immediately empowered with the Holy Spirit and with the capacity to forgive or retain the sins of others. It is also very much in keeping with the work of the Word or Logos of God as expressed in the prologue: "No one has ever seen God. It is God the only Son, who is close to the Father's heart, who has made him known" (1:18). In other words, as Jesus has made God known, so are Jesus' followers also to make God known in both their words and their actions.

John's readers are not privy to exactly what happened in that moment. We do know that Jesus showed the disciples his hands and his side as evidence of his identity. What we cannot know is how much Jesus connected his wounds to his words of commissioning. Did he point to his hands and his side when he said, "As the Father has sent me, so I send you?" If so, then the disciples would have recalled his earlier prayer in chapter 17 in which he pleaded with God to "protect them from the evil one" because "they do not belong to the world" (17:15-16). They would have understood the challenge of this simple commission. The way of Jesus in the world was a difficult and challenging way in which one must be willing to love without regard for the cost, giving up his life for his friends. The mission of Jesus' followers was to live out Jesus' words to Nicodemus by expressing in their words and actions God's love for every family of the earth. The challenge they faced rested in the fact that, as part of this process, they must address the sin in themselves and in others that precluded such love.

John's commission offers a powerful way forward for the church in a diverse world cohabited by various ethnicities, religions, cultures, and worldviews. Like Jesus, we must recognize the source of our own wounds and understand those wounds as the means by which we can offer a fuller expression of God's love in the world. All of us bear wounds. Other people have wounded us because they had the power to do so and perhaps because they themselves are wounded. We have done nothing at all to deserve our deepest wounds. Some of our wounds are self-inflicted. We who seek to follow Christ are a mixed lot of victimizers and victimized. In his commission in John's Gospel, Jesus calls us to journey through our own wounds and not around them so that we can emerge on the other side to work together with other families of the earth for the good of the world. In this way, our wounds become the wounds of Christ.

I never see myself more clearly than I do when I am in the company of people who are radically different from me. In the company of women, I see the ways in which I have taken advantage of my masculinity and have wounded the women in my life. In the company of my Black brothers and sisters, I see the ways in which I have taken advantage of my White privilege and wounded them through my racist attitudes and actions. In the company of people of same-sex orientation, I see the wounds that I have visited upon them as the result of my own homophobic attitudes. Such clarity only comes in the company of people who are radically different from me. I find myself exposed and vulnerable and open to what the Spirit is saying to me. I discover self-inflicted wounds that I did not know I carried. Jesus knows this. It is for this reason that Jesus calls us beyond our own kind and into the company of the stranger and the other. Jesus knows that his peace and wholeness comes alive in us only when we are able to move through our own wounds by virtue of the company of those whom we have wounded and by the growing realization of our self-inflicted wounds.

The last verse in this passage is a challenging verse to understand. How is it that we can forgive sins, or how is it that we can retain sins? We have the power to forgive because only we can forgive each other—until we do, we retain our sins against each other, and, once we do, our sins against each other are forgiven. Again, the path to forgiveness is only possible by moving through our wounds and not around them. Here Thomas becomes an example to us of the power of the wounds of Jesus and not simply a doubting disciple who has to see those wounds before he will believe. They are the source of his belief because they represent the love of God for him. Upon touching the wounds, Thomas declares, "My Lord and my God" (20:28). He experiences through the wounds of Christ the same peace and wholeness that the other disciples had experienced.

Jesus responds in an interesting way. "Have you believed because you have seen me?" he asks. "Blessed are those who have not seen and yet have come to believe" (20:29).

John then reminds his community of the purpose of his Gospel: "that you may come to believe that Jesus is the Messiah, the Son of God, and that through believing you may have life in his name" (20:31). The point here is not so much to believe in theological propositions about Jesus as it is to embrace the way of Jesus, a way by which the very wounds of Jesus give us the courage to move through our own wounds and toward loving relationship with others instead of away from them. Here, once again, I have to confess my own awe at the capacity for people who are other and different from me to love me despite the wounds that I, and by extension my gender and my ethnicity and my culture, have visited upon them. I am awed by the ways in which my Black brothers and sisters continue to embrace me and love me despite the unconscious discrimination that I have visited upon them. I am awed by the ways in which women continue to embrace me and love me despite the ways in which I have engaged in unconscious sexist behavior. To embrace those who have wounded you is to express the full depth of God's love for all families of the earth.

The final evidence of the challenge of Jesus' commission comes in Jesus' encounter with Peter at the end of the Gospel. John is drawing attention to Peter's denial of Jesus just prior to the crucifixion by having Jesus ask Peter three times if he loves him. Three times Peter responds that he does love Jesus, and Jesus' repetition of his question deeply hurts the disciple. The fact that this story comes at the end of the Gospel seems clear evidence that love is the full expression of belief in Jesus. By denying Jesus at the point of his death, Peter has raised questions in Jesus' mind about Peter's love for him. Jesus is far more concerned with Peter's love for him than with Peter's belief in him. This dialogue is not just a conversation to test Peter. Jesus wants to know that Peter abides in him as Jesus has asked. Once Peter has reassured Jesus of his love, Jesus declares that, when Peter grows old, someone will "fasten a belt around you and take you where you do not wish to go," signaling that, in the end, Peter will abide in Christ and glorify God. He will become an example to John's community of a wounded follower, one commissioned by Jesus, the wounded Word made flesh, to embrace otherness and difference rather than to avoid it.

In similar fashion, the church now, particularly in its Euro-tribal expression, must make a similar journey. It must "stretch out its hands" and allow other families of the earth "to take it where it does not wish to go" (paraphrase of 21:18). It must journey through the wounds that, to this point, it has not acknowledged: the wounds of racism, sexism, bigotry, homophobia, exclusivity, and the embrace of White superiority. These wounds have twisted and perverted the gospel that it has received. This path requires and even demands the company of the other families of the earth that it has wounded. Only by journeying through the pain and hurt of their wounds can Euro-tribal churches finally see our own wounds and find forgiveness and restoration.

To believe this is to believe the gospel of Jesus Christ and to embrace the way of Jesus to which John's Gospel called its community. Such belief carries us beyond the simple assertion of intellectual truths about Jesus and into a full embrace of the way of Jesus. Intellectual assent to a propositional faith among Euro-tribal churches has twisted and perverted the very gospel that it was intended to communicate. It has placed a bandage on a wound that is too deep for surface healing. The restoration of wholeness and peace is possible only in the company of others. God has known this from the beginning. This is why God dispersed humanity to the ends of the earth. It is why "God so loved the world" that God sent the Logos of God as God's reminder to humanity of God's vision for it. The embrace of the way of Jesus demands a constant process of conversion for the church of every tribe and nation, and especially for the Euro-tribal family that leans toward the assumption that it possesses the whole truth and must visit its own narrow perspective of God upon the rest of the earth.

The Gospels of Matthew, Mark, Luke, and John and the epistles of the Apostle Paul call us toward each other and not away from each other. In their own particular ways, each encourages an understanding of Christian mission that is marked far more by the embrace of otherness and difference than by the rejection of it. The Gospel of Matthew calls us to know our own culture and ourselves fully, acknowledging the weaknesses of our particular worldview and perspective as well as the contributions it can make to humanity's understanding of the divine. The Gospel of Mark encourages us beyond our own particular family of the earth and toward other cultures and people, an engagement that will be stormy and challenging but that is at the core of the teachings of Jesus. The Gospel of Luke and the Acts of the Apostles encourage us into the context of otherness and difference that surrounds us with marked humility and with the conviction that other peoples, cultures, and religions can enhance our understanding of the divine. Paul reminds us that the laws of God exist deep in the hearts of every family of the earth.

The Gospel of John calls us toward the embrace of concepts and ideas about God and truth from every human family, beckoning us toward the realization that God is much more than just the God of Christianity. God is the God of all the cosmos, the Creating Word who has established from the beginning that the only way to know God fully is to embrace the understanding of God that other families of the earth possess and that they offer to the rest of us as blessing.

Notes

1. Bill J. Leonard, *A Sense of the Heart: Christian Religious Experience in the United States* (Nashville, TN: Abingdon Press, 2014), 113.

2. Jörg Frey, *The Glory of the Crucified One: Christology and Theology in the Gospel of John* (Waco, TX: Baylor University Press, 2018), 61. Frey also addresses the tension between the Johannine School and communities in Asia Minor.

3. For the purposes of this chapter, I will refer to John as the Gospel's author with the understanding that this designation refers specifically to the Johannine School from which the Gospel emerged. I will also use the phrase "John's church" to refer to the Johannine communities to which that school wrote.

4. Fernando F. Segovia, "John 1:1-18 as Entrée into Johannine Reality," in *Word, Theology and Community in John*, ed. John Painter, R. Alan Culpepper, and Fernando F. Segovia (St. Louis, MO: Chalice Press, 2002), 34.

5. Frey, *The Glory of the Crucified One*, 63.

6. R. Alan Culpepper, *The Gospel and Letters of John* (Nashville, TN: Abingdon Press, 1998), 43.

7. Robert Kysar, *John: The Maverick Gospel* (Louisville, KY: Westminster/John Knox Press, 1976; 1993 edition), 56.

8. Fred B. Craddock, *John* (Atlanta, GA: John Knox Press, 1982), 10.

9. Miroslav Volf, "Johannine Dualism and Contemporary Pluralism," in *The Gospel of John and Christian Theology*, ed. Richard Bauckham and Carl Mosser (Grand Rapids, MI: Eerdmans, 2008), 30.

10. Philo, *De Profugis*, cited in Gerald Friedlander, *Hellenism and Christianity* (Sydney, Australia: Wentworth Press, 2019, reprint of 2012 edition), 114–15.

11. See Raymond E. Brown, *The Gospel According to John I–XII* (New York: Doubleday, 1966), 29.

12. R. Alan Culpepper, "The Gospel of John as a Document of Faith in a Pluralistic Culture," in *What Is John? Readers and Readings of the Fourth Gospel*, ed. Fernando F. Segovia (Atlanta, GA: Scholar's Press, 1996), 124.

13. Sandra M. Schneiders, *Written That You May Believe: Encountering Jesus in the Fourth Gospel* (New York: Crossroad Publishing, 1999), 118–19.

14. Culpepper, *The Gospel and Letters of John*, 45–46.

15. Culpepper, *The Gospel and Letters of John*, 45–46.

16. R. Alan Culpepper, "Inclusivism and Exclusivism in the Fourth Gospel," in *Word, Theology and Community in John*, 100.

17. Craddock, *John*, 100.

18. Schneiders, *Written That You May Believe*, 190.

19. Schneiders, *Written That You May Believe*, 197.

Chapter 8

Putting the Equator Down—The Church and Mission Now

The full confession of God's grace and glory can only take place through the assembled choirs of all human tongues and cultures.
—Darrell L. Guder, *The Continuing Conversion of the Church*

Let me restate my thesis. God's purpose and intention from the beginning has been a diverse world that shapes our understanding of God from multiple perspectives. For this reason, God commanded humanity at several points in the book of Genesis "to be fruitful and multiply and fill the earth." God forcibly dispersed the families of the earth into various languages, ethnicities, religions, and cultures at the Tower of Babel with the full realization and hope that, one day, human families would come together again as a New Humanity that understood God more fully because of these varied perspectives.

Humanity constantly frustrated this purpose as families, nations, and ethnicities forgot or ignored God's intention that the families of the earth should bless each other. In the Hebrew Bible and the New Testament, God reminded Israel and then the church that the path to the full knowledge of God is not a singular cultural or even religious path. No ethnicity, tribe, nation, or religion possesses the full truth about God. For this reason, the Hebrew prophets and Jesus pushed the boundaries of election beyond Israel to include the Gentile nations and families of the earth. In their Gospels, Matthew, Mark, Luke, and John left room for the embrace of new truths and interpretations of the life of Jesus that came from beyond the received tradition of the church and its particular interpretations of Scripture. Paul embraced otherness and difference both by his own example in the Acts of the Apostles and through his particular theology as expressed in his letters.

Now it is our turn. God is the author and creator of diversity. At the core and heart of every ethnicity, religion, and culture is the deep-seated desire to know God fully and to understand and make sense of human existence. Because God is the author and creator of diversity and difference, the church today must commit itself to the engagement of that otherness and difference in order to offer mutual blessing and to gain the deepest and fullest understanding of the nature of God and of God's mission in the world.

The mission of the church at this point in the twenty-first century emerges directly from this thesis. Remember that *mission* is our work in the world now to accomplish God's vision for the creation. That vision has always been for a world in which various families of the earth bless each other. God's grand design is a multicultural world where our various perspectives on God, the creation, and humanity are sufficient to fashion the community of peace and justice that God intends. Over the course of the previous era, Euro-tribal churches narrowed and restricted this grand vision for their own purposes, including the cultural and theological domination of other peoples and cultures. The tendency in the era was toward a single theological understanding of God supported across the entire Bible and legitimated by the internal evidence of Scripture as well as by its consistency with the discoveries and methods of science. This rut dictated the ways in which the Euro-tribal church read the Scriptures and the interpretations into which they immersed other families of the earth. Always, its reading supported a Euro-tribal worldview with its received theological traditions, merging that worldview with Enlightenment perspectives on the individual and the scientific method as the best way of proving that a thing was true.

The Great Commission in Matthew 28:16-20 served as the center and focus of the mission of the church in that previous era, grounding that mission in the authority extended to the church under the Lordship of Christ—a mission to teach, disciple, and baptize the rest of the world. This focus on the authority of a Euro-tribal church to accomplish this mission without sufficient regard for other biblical texts that stressed humility, a listening spirit, and openness to receive the blessings of other families of the earth resulted in a twisted gospel that is woefully unprepared for the present era. Its chief legacy is that it did enable Christianity to become a major living world religion even as it paid the high price of ignoring many of the most basic truths of its own Scriptures.

We are emerging from a context in the modern world in which the various major religions were in competition with each other. In the process of these encounters, a siege mentality developed within the church. We directed our energy toward the legitimation of our own understanding of God in order to win adherents to the Christian faith and thus make Christianity the dominant religion in the world. The language in the previous sentence exposes the weaknesses in such an approach. "Legitimation" and "domination" that leads to "winning" are characteristics directly opposed to the purposes and intentions of the life and teachings of Jesus. In the process, we allowed some of the lowest and most base values of a Western and predominately White cultural perspective to become the dominant values that dictated the way we participated in God's mission in the world.

This book has documented the possibility of an entirely different reading of Scripture, one that emerges not from the search for a single truth about God but rather from the acknowledgment of multitudes of perspectives on God, all of which contribute to our common human understanding of ultimate reality. Our journey through the Hebrew Bible, the Gospels, Acts, and some of the letters of the Apostle Paul, read in the light of this multitude of perspectives and the global realities of our own day, reveals a different sort of path, a path that is equally valid. This path can serve as a new way that lifts us up out of the "rut" of the previous era and charts a course toward the affirmation of otherness and difference rather than sameness and similarity. It represents the movement of the equator of our understanding of reality from one location to another. It is a movement that has never been possible before because humanity has never before lived in such a world: a world in which billions of people move across cultures, bringing with them worldviews and perspectives as sources of divine blessing upon the rest of humanity. Our context demands a fresh reading of the Bible no longer trapped by the limitations of the previous eras of church history and tradition and a renewed mission that emerges out of this fresh reading.

To this end, the mission of the church must change from what it has been in the modern missionary period of the church. While I am concerned about the mission of the global church in all of its various forms, my particular concern is for the Euro-tribal church, the one into which I was born and that has been the most influential and dominant repository of the Christian faith in the previous era. For this reason, its self-understanding of mission is particularly influential on the rest of the church. Its future mission or action alongside God in the world and in partnership with other peoples, tribes, and nations in this new day must embrace four dimensions or foci. First, it has a mission to the global church to confess the cultural domination of the faith that is its primary legacy. Second, it has a mission to demonstrate solidarity with marginalized and oppressed people in the world whose bondage it has perpetuated. Third, it has a mission to the other religions of the world and other worldviews and perspectives to be a good partner in creating healthy and holistic human communities. Finally, it has a mission to carry a different gospel to the world than it has carried in the past, one that champions the unconditional love of Christ even as it seeks to give meaning and purpose to human life.

In the rest of this chapter, I will weave these four dimensions into a vision for the Euro-tribal church that lifts it out of the rut of previous interpretations of its mission and encourages it toward the embrace of otherness and difference as the foundation for renewed mission in a diverse world. I do not speak only to this particular church, but I do recognize and affirm that my life is deeply embedded in it and that, by encouraging it toward the embrace of otherness and difference, I become a more whole and healthier follower of Christ. I will leave it to followers of Jesus from other families of the earth to determine what to take from these pages and what to leave behind.

These dimensions emerge from the embrace of otherness and difference that the Bible itself demands and that the Euro-tribal church has generally ignored as it focused its attention on imparting a single understanding of truth that it expected all cultures and peoples to acknowledge. Certainly, the equator of cultural and biblical interpretation must shift. For a time, the church must interpret its mission through the lens of culture, allowing the reality of diversity and multiculturalism to become the primary lens through which it reads Scripture. Only in this way can it recover truth that it has lost.

So how is a church that affirms a singular theological worldview and perspective supposed to open itself up to the full embrace of otherness and difference, especially when it comes to the conviction of many that Jesus Christ is the supreme revelation of God in whom all humanity should believe? The path to such openness is not easy or simple. As the church, I would suggest a pluralistic approach to our encounter with worldviews and perspectives that are different from our own. Pluralism is often misunderstood. It values the worldviews and perspectives that come from religions that are different from one's own without necessarily forcing the acceptance of those perspectives by anyone.

Peter L. Berger has defined pluralism as "a social situation in which people with different ethnicities, worldviews, and moralities live together peacefully and interact with one another amicably."[1] He argues that pluralism offers the best explanation for the continued proliferation of religions and spiritualities in a modern world of competing realities and that a paradigm of pluralism is a better way of interpreting our current reality than the model of secularization.[2] In other words, in Berger's estimation, pluralism is the best way of understanding the world that we now inhabit. I would also add that it is the best way of understanding the world as God intended for it to be.

Simply stated, pluralism offers the best possibility for the Christian family to receive blessings from other families of the earth. Pluralism does not insist that only one religion, Christianity, is the true religion (exclusivism). It does not insist that any single religion is truer than the others are (inclusivism). It also does not insist that all religions are true (universalism) or that no religion is true (naturalism or atheism). Rather, it affirms that no single religion or worldview is right in all of its assertions about ultimate reality, and so all religions and worldviews deserve a hearing in the marketplace of ideas.[3] Such a perspective meshes quite well with the Judeo-Christian perspective on God, at least when that tradition takes seriously its own assertions about truth.

Christian tradition has long insisted on the fact that God cannot be fully known, even from within the Christian faith itself. It affirms that human knowledge of God is finite and limited. At the same time, it has embraced certain convictions about God, insisting on the Triune nature of God, that Jesus Christ is the supreme revelation of God, and that belief in Jesus Christ is essential for salvation. Yet even as it makes these assertions, it has admitted that within the Christian understanding there is room for various interpretations of these doctrines. Its own theology insists that God is ultimately unknowable, and so no assertion is beyond reconsideration when exposed to the light of new insight or other religious perspectives.

Roger Williams, founder of the Rhode Island colony and early proponent of religious freedom and the separation of church and state in the American colonies, advocated for such freedom and separation based on the theological idea of the sovereignty of God. Williams argued that we violated God's sovereignty whenever we forced others to accept our particular understanding of God. Despite his religious extremism as a Puritan and strong Calvinist, Williams adopted a surprisingly progressive position on religious liberty and the separation of church and state. But he did not come to his position from the standpoint of enlightened thinking and the dignity of the individual person as did others like James Madison and Thomas Jefferson; rather he came at it from deep theological and sectarian roots that emerged out of his Puritan and Calvinist embrace of the ideas of the goodness and the sovereignty of God and, concomitantly, the total and utter depravity of humanity.

Roger Williams offers a way forward for us when it comes to fostering dialogue among all religions, not because he calls us toward tolerance for the sake of tolerance but rather because he calls us toward tolerance for the sake of our deepest convictions about our faith. It is possible to be so convinced of the rightness of one's own faith that it leads one to offer greater freedom to others rather than less. It was William's conviction that human beings ought to leave it all to God and embrace the conviction that "a false religion out of the church will not hurt the church, no more than weeds in the wilderness hurt the enclosed garden, or poison hurt the body when it is not touched or taken."[4] He also insisted that "a false religion and worship will not hurt the civil state in case the worshippers break no civil law."[5] His perspective was that God can choose to speak truth through any person, religion, or worldview, so people of all religions should be free. In this way, the church would not violate God's sovereign right to speak from whatever source God might elect to speak.

When I taught undergraduate religion courses early in my career, I began every freshman religion class with a single question: "What percentage of God do you believe you fully understand?" An immediate hush fell over the classroom whenever I asked the question. It was as if no one in the class had ever contemplated such a question.

I would then ask, "How many of you believe that you fully understand and grasp 100 percent of God?"

I am glad to report that no one ever raised his or her hand when I asked the second question. Generally, however, someone, usually an eighteen-year-old male, would jump in at about 70 percent.

Often my response was to slam my lecture book shut, announce that the class now had a new professor, and act as if I was about to exit the room and leave the eighteen-year-old in charge. It always brought a good laugh.

Fortunately, and, as the result of some good theology prior to their college experience, most students weighed in at less than 1 percent. They understood enough about God to admit to their own ignorance. Having gotten the attention of the class by reminding all of us how little any of us knew about God, I proceeded to share the syllabus for the class and move ahead.

The very definition of what it means to be a Christian is a simple one. Christians are people who devote themselves to Jesus Christ as the supreme revelation of God that offers meaning and purpose to human existence. Nothing in this definition prevents a person from entering into the marketplace of ideas about God and ultimate reality with conviction, deep faith, and an openness to other perspectives and understandings. Because a Christian has devoted herself to Jesus Christ, she must enter into relationship with others with the same kind of listening spirit and loving intention that Jesus exhibited in his relationship with others. She must be open to the possibility of her own transformation because of the encounter. Her own theological tradition dictates that she respond in this way because her tradition acknowledges that God is ultimately unknowable.

For this reason, every human being becomes a prospective teacher to her about who God is and about the truths about God that she might have missed. I love the teaching of the Chinese philosopher, Confucius, who says in the Analects, "When walking in a party of three, my teachers are always present. I can select the good qualities of the one and copy them, and the unsatisfactory qualities of the other and correct them in myself."[6] A powerful humility exists at the core of this teaching that should mark a follower of Jesus Christ who truly wants to know God and understand God's mission in the world.

The church or ecclesia then is composed of the *called-out ones* who have chosen for any number of reasons—their family of origin, the power of an encounter with the Risen Lord, the surrounding religious and cultural milieu that they inhabit, or their own need for community—to devote themselves to the way of Jesus. Jesus Christ is, for them, the ultimate revelation of God by which they understand God most fully. Their calling is to bear witness to the meaning and purpose that they have discovered in life because of their embrace of the way of Jesus and their conviction that Jesus Christ is the Son of God through whom they can live a full and abundant life. At the same time, the *called-out ones* who have embraced this way must also be open to the work of the Spirit that constantly breaks down the barriers that exist between them and the other families of the earth.

One of these is the barrier of religious superiority expressed in the desire for spiritual and global domination. The insistence on the truth of Christianity as the only means for the world's salvation even as we ourselves acknowledge the limitations of that truth is misplaced at best and duplicitous at worst. We cannot fully understand God. We cannot know beyond any doubt the boundaries of God's love. What we can know is that, in Christ, we have discovered a depth of love and grace that we want to share. Our love for Christ and Christ's love for us compel us into the lives of others in loving and gracious relationship. Our intention should be to know the other fully, to understand their motivations, to learn from their understanding of the divine, and to experience our own transformation because of the encounter.

Such encounters should begin not with a defensive attitude that insists on the superiority of our own limited understanding but rather with openness to what we might learn from the other person about God, the world, and ourselves. In the process, we acknowledge our mutual dependency, which God intended from the very beginning. When we enter into relationship with a person of another faith, culture, or ethnicity, we stand on holy ground because we are standing in the very place that God has intended for all humanity to stand. It is the reason God created us. Before we broke relationship with each other, in a single moment at the beginning of time God said to us, "Be fruitful and multiply and fill the earth." God intended that we should go our separate ways in order to come back together to share what we had learned. Our failure to do so was perhaps the greatest challenge to God's ultimate intentions for the world and, therefore, the ultimate disobedience.

The encounter with other cultures, religions, and ethnicities is a sacred encounter. At the most foundational level, even entering the home of a neighbor across the street is a holy action. In that act, we move across a boundary between our family and home and into a family and home that is other than our own. We cross the street. We move from our space and into their space. The act itself is a religious act. It gets back to the source of religion: the human need to create rituals that guide our encounters with otherness and difference beyond the boundaries of our own space.

My home is my space. However humble it might be, it belongs to me. It represents my family, my tribe, my ethnicity, my religion, and me. When I depart from my home, I take leave of those with whom I am most familiar and whom I love most deeply, those who are most like me. I enter into the lives of people who are different from me for the purpose of knowing them more fully and offering to them my friendship and partnership so that we can accomplish something together that benefits humanity. It may be the simple act of friendship between two neighbors. As neighbors, we deepen our knowledge of each other so that we get along in the world. It is a small contribution, but if every set of neighbors in the world makes a similar effort, then it is a powerful contribution.

I once lived in a neighborhood with a neighbor who was quite different from me. We both knew it. The bumper stickers on our cars made it clear. In election primaries, we saw each other standing in different lines to vote. We went to churches that were different in worship style and theology. I generally stayed inside my house when I saw him outside his house. I imagine he stayed in his house when he saw me outside mine.

Then, one Saturday, we accidentally bumped into each other.

I greeted him. He greeted me.

I asked him where he was headed so early on a Saturday morning.

"I'm going over to the high school," he said. "My insurance company pays for every student at the school to take the ACT and SAT preparatory exams if they want to do it. I always make a little speech before the exams to encourage them to do their best."

His words got my attention.

"I really like that," I said. "Why do you do it?"

"I believe it helps make our community a better community. It helps our kids go to better schools, and then, hopefully, they come back here and make a lifelong contribution to the area."

He then added, "Really, deep down, I do it because I think it is what Jesus would want me to do."

Suddenly, I saw my neighbor through new lenses. Our particular theological, political, and worldview differences faded into the background. As he pulled out of his driveway, I offered a simple goodbye wave. Religious meaning infused that wave. No longer simply "goodbye," it had become a blessing: "God be with you as you do this good work in the world." I now understood my neighbor, the one with whom I thought I had nothing in common, to be about the mission of God in the world.

The biblical witness bears testimony to this understanding, even as far back as the covenant with Abram. God called Abram into relationship or neighborliness with the other families of the earth. This calling was the purpose for which God entered into that covenant. God never intended that this covenant would narrow the boundaries of chosenness and election; God intended the opposite. God's desire was that Israel should be an example to other families of the earth, revealing the possibilities for every family contained within their specific histories, cultures, languages, and even religions. God's hope was that every family would eventually bring its blessings to the table of a New Humanity. By embracing its own Law as handed down by God, Israel reflected the kind of community that God desired for every family of the earth. It showed how a family ought to relate to itself and how a family ought to relate to other families of the earth.

In the church, Jesus called out a community of disciples to reflect the intentions of this original covenant. Humility and love marked the relationships within the community of disciples to the extent that, like Jesus, they were willing to "lay down their lives for their friends." That community treated people outside it as full human beings, affording dignity and respect to them. Jesus himself learned this lesson from a Canaanite woman who insisted that the blessings of God should be available to her. By example, he encouraged the disciples to be open to learning from those outside the community. The Hebrew Bible that served as the Scriptures of Jesus and the disciples modeled this pattern of openness to those outside the community. Melchizedek, Solomon in his dedication prayer at the temple, Naaman the Syrian, Rahab, the sailors and the Ninevites in the story of

Jonah, and Cyrus the Great modeled for Israel the dignity and respect that human families should afford to each other.

The challenge for the church today as it ministers in a diverse world is to enter into the myriad of families of the earth with a similar openness characterized by self-awareness, humility, a listening spirit, solidarity, and respect for the various cultural and religious worldviews of those families. The way of Jesus compels us toward such openness. We must know and understand ourselves first. We admitted our own fault in the broken relationships that exist in our lives when we acknowledged Jesus Christ as the supreme revelation of God. We are fully aware that we continue to break relationships with people both within the church and outside the church. Therefore, humility and respect for other individuals and families should be the foundation of our relationships with them.

Here is where the words and actions of Jesus in all four Gospels can be helpful to us when we interpret our mission calling in the world now. No single text should ever serve as the sole interpretive lens for our mission in the world lest we miss the challenges and implications of the full gospel. In the Gospel of Matthew (28:19) and the Acts of the Apostles (1:8), Jesus encouraged the disciples to carry the gospel into the world, moving from Jerusalem to Judea to Samaria and then to the ends of the earth. Jesus' intention was that the disciples would carry out this mission in the same way that Jesus had carried out his mission in the world. His words to the disciples in John's Gospel were specific: "As the Father has sent me, so I send you" (John 20:21). Their mission then was the same as the mission of Jesus: to bring good news to the poor, to proclaim release to the captives and recovery of sight to the blind, and to let the oppressed go free (Luke 4:18). They were to proclaim this message of repentance and the forgiveness of sins "to all the nations, beginning from Jerusalem" (Luke 24:47). They were to proclaim it with the full realization that their lives would be judged by their commitment to feeding the hungry, quenching thirst, visiting strangers, clothing the naked, caring for the sick, and visiting those in prison (Matt 25:31-40).

The calling of the disciples from Jerusalem to Judea to Samaria and to the rest of the world has been interpreted in the modern world as a calling to challenge those outside the church toward repentance and the forgiveness of sins through belief in Jesus Christ as the Son of God. Rarely have we focused attention on what is required of the church itself as we participate in this movement across cultures, at least not much beyond encouraging the church to bring other families and cultures to belief in Jesus Christ as the Son of God and the source of salvation.

The church must cultivate the sorts of attitudes and passions that mark the gospel, and it must do so at every stage of its encounter with the various cultures of the world. As the church moves from Jerusalem to Judea to Samaria and to the uttermost parts of the earth, it will be taking the gospel from a context with which it is familiar (Jerusalem) and toward a context with which it is unfamiliar (the uttermost parts of the earth). The church must be prepared to undergo its own transformation as it nurtures relationships with other families of the earth. It cannot transform others without being transformed by others; otherwise it makes people of other families and cultures into its own image instead of in the image of the God who encourages all families toward the embrace of otherness and difference.

The interpretation of this commission text in the modern missionary period was a geographical interpretation, much as it was in the first century. Local congregations worked in their own communities while sending financial and prayer support to missionaries who worked in other parts of the nation and around the world. Today a congregation can fulfill this commission in its own context without ever leaving the local community and region. The world now inhabits every community. For this reason, churches must be prepared to minister in Jerusalem, Judea, Samaria, and the uttermost parts of the earth without ever leaving home.

To put it another way, churches can engage globally because of the realities that they discover in their own backyards. Much has to happen to the church and in the church in this movement from the familiar to the unfamiliar within its own local community. Where the focus in the modern missionary period was on what happened in the hearts of those to whom the church was called, the focus in our current context must be on what happens within the church itself as it enters Jerusalem, Judea, Samaria, and the uttermost parts of the earth as a guest in its own community.

The disciples who served as Jesus' original followers had to overcome their fears of otherness and difference through personal and communal transformation. Jesus called them first to a simple walk across the street into the homes of their neighbors (Jerusalem), then to the engagement with other towns and cities around Jerusalem (Judea), then to a people whom they despised and against whom they held considerable prejudice (Samaria), and finally to a people whom they did not know at all (the Gentiles). They could not make their way to any of these places without experiencing their own "repentance and the forgiveness of sins."

Here is where the real shift of the equator happens. For some three centuries now, the church has focused its attention on changing those outside the church. We have taken the gospel to the world. Now we find ourselves inhabiting a context of diversity and difference in which the Spirit is speaking differently to us. We must open ourselves up to the possibility of our own transformation because of what Scripture says to us that we have missed in the previous era and because of what those outside the Christian faith can teach us about God.

Who must we become as we take the gospel to Jerusalem or to our own particular neighborhoods? How do we become good neighbors in our own cities and towns and among our own families and friends? How do we engage our own communities in ways that are helpful and not harmful? Such engagement is not as easy as it would first appear. We have lived for a long time with the conviction that we understood what was best for ourselves and for our communities. As a result, we have often stopped listening to what our friends and neighbors have been saying to us.

One of the most helpful and transformative approaches to mission in recent years has been one called assets-based community development (ABCD). ABCD makes a number of assumptions that are very much in line with the Jewish understanding of shalom or wholeness and with Jesus' teachings about the nature of the kingdom of God or the community of the faithful. Here are the principles that guide it as a methodology for community transformation:

1. Every community is unique.

2. The members of a community best understand the challenges and possibilities of that community.

3. Every community possesses within itself the possibility and potential for its own transformation.

4. By identifying the assets that it possesses, a community can meet its own challenges, determine the best partners to assist it toward transformation, and move itself along toward the full realization of its possibilities.[7]

ABCD is much more than a simple methodology for community transformation. It is also a way of understanding communities that is faithful to God's original intentions for the families of the earth. God intended for every human group, from tribes to ethnicities to nations, to develop ways of living in harmony with each other that were unique. Each family would then have its own contributions to make to the world, its own "assets" that it could bring to the common human table. It had to know and understand itself and nurture a way of ethical and moral living that made sense within its own context.

Early in human history, the various tribes and cultures of the world had little contact with each other, but with technological advancements in transportation and communication such contact became quite commonplace. This is the reason we must revisit our own perspectives on God and our understanding of the particular worldview or religion that we have embraced. The encounter with other families of the earth means that we can now integrate their experiences with ours and somehow absorb them into our community even as they absorb us into theirs. This integration is the only path toward full human community and transformation.

Several years ago, a congregation in north Georgia invited me to preach for two Sundays in a row while its pastor was on vacation. As I made my way into that town on the first Sunday morning, I passed a brick-ranch house on the city's edge. It appeared to be a normal brick home built in the 1960s when such homes were fashionable. What made this one different was the sign that stood in the front yard. It said simply, "Laotian Buddhist Temple." The sight of that temple in this north Georgia town stunned me to the extent that I nearly lost control of my car. Recovering quickly, I proceeded to the church and climbed into the pulpit to preach my sermon.

I started with a simple observation. "As I drove into town today, I noticed that you have new neighbors, some Laotian Buddhists who have opened a temple here. Have you all stopped by yet to welcome the Buddhists to town?"

Stunned silence greeted my question. The sanctuary was deathly quiet. People seemed to be considering why a Baptist church would ever welcome Buddhists to the neighborhood.

I plunged ahead.

"I see that you haven't visited yet. So let me tell you what I am going to do. This afternoon as I go home, I am going to stop by the temple and tell the Buddhists how excited you are that they are here and that you all want to visit them."

Again, stunned silence.

That afternoon I kept my promise. I pulled up in the driveway of that brick ranch temple and knocked on the door. The monks greeted me warmly, invited me inside, and offered me hospitality in the form of a Coca-Cola. They had learned how to entertain folks in the Deep South. I welcomed them to the community and asked them if the members of the First Baptist Church downtown could visit and welcome them to town.

The monks agreed.

So, on the following Sunday, I climbed into the pulpit again and shared with the congregation of the First Baptist Church that the monks of the Buddhist temple had invited them for a visit.

Again, stunned silence greeted my announcement.

To their credit and immediately after the service, several women of the church who belonged to the mission committee told me that they intended to do what I had suggested. They just wanted some guidance. I suggested that they do exactly what they would do for any new neighbors in the community. Bake a cake or some cookies, stop by the neighbor's house, knock on the door, and wait to see what happened.

I am glad to report that a small group from the First Baptist Church did make their way to that temple. They knocked on the door. They offered a gift. The monks reciprocated by inviting them in and thanking them profusely for taking the time to visit. Church members reported to me later that when they saw the monks on Main Street, they knew them as neighbors and no longer saw them as strangers.

Patterns of migration today have significantly increased the possibility of global encounters in the smallest towns and communities of the United States. The resulting cultural diversity dictates that congregations must become increasingly adept at crossing boundaries between families of the earth and somehow embracing each other with openness, love, and grace and not with hostility and suspicion. Such encounters are a divine gift. They hasten us along toward God's vision for all of humanity, that day when a New Humanity embraces otherness and difference by accepting each other because of our diversity and not in spite of it. We accomplish this most powerfully when we accept the gifts that the other gives to us out of their difference from us. By receiving and giving these gifts, we discover our common humanity. A new community emerges with greater assets than it possessed before because of its embrace of cultural difference.

My hope for every church is that it can apply the best practices of ABCD in order to understand its context, determine what God is calling it to do in that context, partner with others who are working alongside God to create a community of wholeness and shalom, and engage in the good work of nurturing it. Such an approach demands a different way of understanding both the church and the community, one that Paul Sparks, Tim Soerens, and Dwight J. Friesen focus on in their book, *The New Parish: How Neighborhood Churches Are Transforming Mission, Discipleship, and Community*. They advocate a return to a parish understanding of church, one that takes seriously the idea that the church as community should immerse itself in the full life of its neighborhood or in "all the dimensions of life for which everyone in your neighborhood shares a common concern."[8] This is exactly what my neighbor was doing in the example that I shared earlier in this chapter when he paid for all the students at the local high school to take the ACT and SAT preparatory exams. He had entered into the common space of his neighborhood as a follower of Jesus Christ in order to make our community a better community. It is also what that congregation in north Georgia was doing when it embraced its Buddhist neighbors.

Sparks, Soerens, and Friesen point to four realms in the common space of the community to which congregations should devote their full attention: economy, environment, civic space, and education. By *economy*, they mean the ways in which a community works together to ensure that everyone can have a flourishing life. By *environment*, they mean the ways in which everyone in the neighborhood can have clean air, good soil, and healthy spaces for play and for life together. By *civic space*, they mean the cultivation of local decision-making in which everyone has a voice and equal share. By *education*, they mean the ways in which a community teaches its children and develops the kind of wisdom for all community members that is essential for healthy relationships.[9]

Toward this end, churches should reflect on the following questions:

> Do we have a redemptive way of living out these dimensions of life together as a local body? And do we have a way of engaging faithfully together with the way things currently operate in our neighborhood? Or have we narrowed down the meaning of the church to something that excludes vast segments of life?[10]

The last question is the most significant question. Many congregations have lost the connection to the community, a connection that once existed as a dynamic and powerful relationship. The challenge now is to reenter the *new commons* by recognizing and affirming that God's ultimate concern is with the community to which the church is connected. God's mission in the world is not about the church; rather, the church is one means toward the end of God's mission in the world, a mission to create healthy and whole communities where people are able to live together in meaningful ways because of their unique gifts and potential and because of their love and concern for each other. We twist and pervert God's mission in the world when we assume that God's desire is for people to join churches. God's desire is for people to live holy and healthy lives in the context of meaningful community. God's ultimate concern is not for the church; rather, it is for the neighborhood in which God has placed the church.

To this end, the church must relocate the equator that has given meaning and purpose to its existence. God's calling is not for the church to convince the community to enter into the church; rather, the church's calling is to enter into the community in which God has placed it in order to help that community toward the wholeness and peace that should mark every human community. Such an approach demands far more of the church than was demanded when it focused its energies on inviting its neighborhood into the church. It compels the church to serve as a guest in the neighborhood and not as host in the church.

The role of guest demands that the church lay aside its need to be in control, its insistence that everyone should accept its beliefs, and its determination to enforce conformity to its own rules. Instead, it gives up its power in order to conform to the demands, beliefs, and rules of the parish or common space of which the church is just one small part. It joins others in shaping the community. It checks its own power and tendency toward self-aggrandizement and self-determination by its engagement with otherness and difference in the context of its own community. Other institutions such as civic and nonprofit organizations, schools, and businesses become partners together with the church in accomplishing far more together on behalf of the community than any single organization could accomplish on its own.

Such an approach dictates that we become open to the divine possibilities that God brings into our congregational orbits. My seminary professor, John Hendrix, has written a little book called *Nothing Never Happens.*[11] He drilled this mantra into my brain when I took his course on teaching, the only education course I took in my entire post-secondary education. Hendrix taught me to pay attention in the classroom by constantly asking the question, "What is happening here?" I have never forgotten this lesson. I think about it as students interact with each other in the classroom. What is stoking their passions? What might be causing their apathy? I have even learned to ask it of myself when a comment by a student causes me to become defensive or angry.

We would do well to ask it as churches when we are trying to determine God's intentions and purposes for our particular communities. Whom is God bringing into our orbits? How might a conversation at lunch with a member of the Rotary Club connect to a meeting of the church's mission committee last week? How might our chance encounter with the president of a nonprofit organization result in the merger of our particular assets and the assets of that nonprofit to bring about community transformation? Church leaders ought to be asking these sorts of questions every single day, confident in the realization that nothing never happens. God is always at work through the power of the Holy Spirit, moving us along toward the realization of God's vision for our particular community, our Jerusalem.

I once served as the interim pastor of a suburban Atlanta congregation and had one of those "Nothing Never Happens" conversations with a church member. I asked him how the previous week had gone for him.

"Well," he responded, "I'm an airline pilot. I spent the better part of last week in Mumbai, India, flying out, spending a couple of nights, and then flying back."

"Wow!" I exclaimed. "How cool is that?"

He did not think it was very cool.

"I never left the hotel," he said. "The airline doesn't like for us to risk our safety by walking the streets of a strange city."

Later, I reflected on his response and then asked myself a question: "Is it possible that God put that church member in Mumbai so that we as a church might participate through him in God's mission in the world?"

I started canvassing the church to see how many people left the country in the course of a month. As it turned out, about fifty members of that congregation spent at least some portion of every month outside the United States. I preached a sermon series based on the conviction that "nothing never happens," impressing upon the congregation that their world travel afforded the church the possibility of global engagement and mission. My prayer and hope were that they would pay attention to the possibilities that God was bringing into our orbit as they traveled the world.

Global possibilities also emerge out of our local community context. Churches sometimes pat themselves on the back for the fact that they take a mission trip once a year, rotating the location from their own state to somewhere else in the United States and then to somewhere outside the United States. Something about this approach has always disturbed me. Often churches fail to pay attention to the connection between their local communities and the national and international mission efforts that they undertake. Again, churches must learn to follow the serendipitous connections that God brings to them. Are teachers in the local elementary schools facing the challenge of diverse classrooms filled up with children from Central America? How might the church nurture a partnership in Guatemala or Honduras that would allow teachers to experience the context from which their students are coming? Does the church's city or town have a sister-city relationship with a city in another country? How might the church participate as a good partner in nurturing this relationship? Is there a church in that place with whom my church might collaborate?

Such an approach makes far more sense in our own context than simply leafing through a list of mission trip possibilities from a denomination or group that plans such experiences. The idea should be one of community partnership on a global level for the purpose of mutual transformation. Again, this gets back to the core values of assets-based community development. Healthy mission engagement should not just be about the transformation of the other. Healthy engagement should emerge from the conviction that our global connections as a congregation assist and enable the emergence of meaningful community in our own context as much as it encourages such community in the other context. We bless others even as we acknowledge our own need for blessing from others.

This concept of mutual benefit is challenging for churches that have long understood their mission calling to be that of imparting knowledge about God, the creation, salvation, and truth to others by convincing others to receive this knowledge. Mutual benefit and blessing demand that we understand our context differently and read Scripture through a new set of lenses. Like the Gospels of Matthew, Mark, Luke, and John and the Acts of the Apostles, we have to critique our own worldview (Matthew), reach out across cultural difference (Mark), embrace that otherness and difference by entering into the worldview of the other (Luke-Acts), and, ultimately, allow the worldview of the other to shape our own perspective on God and truth (John). Such a journey demands that we practice engagement with the other in loving and open ways that can lead to our own transformation.

This openness to the blessing of others demands some courage from us. My teaching philosophy emerges from the conviction that a good teacher makes the familiar unfamiliar and the unfamiliar familiar. The teacher makes strange the worldview that the student brings into the relationship, pointing out the assumptions of that worldview that demand questioning and noting where it is inadequate because of what it fails to take into account—an inadequacy that might be met by engagement with another worldview or perspective. At the same time, a good teacher helps a student to understand the worldviews of other cultures, ethnicities, and religions by pointing out commonalities and differences between those worldviews and the student's own. These commonalities are at first difficult to identify. Nevertheless, they are present. We are not nearly as different from the other as we would first assume. At the same time, the differences in perspective and worldview contribute to the student's own worldview and perspective in ways that could be helpful to that student.

Students have a choice. They can join the teacher on this journey or not. A good classroom is not the place for the weak-hearted. To participate demands courage. One of the ways I encourage the process is to require a class project in which seminary students identify a particular congregation of an ethnicity different from their own and with whom they have no connection. They must participate in at least two worship experiences with that church and provide the transcripts of ethnographic interviews with two of its members. Ethnographic interviews are interviews in which students ask open-ended questions intended to understand the worldview, perspective, and convictions of the interviewee rather than leading questions that expose the student's own biases and worldview. Put simply, it is what those sailors in the Mediterranean Sea were doing when they questioned Jonah. They truly wanted to know the nature of his relationship to his God. They wanted to understand the challenges that he faced. They hoped to learn something from him that would help them beyond the dire predicament of the storm on the sea. My hope is that my students will learn something in these worship services and interviews that assists them in bringing meaning, purpose, and hope into their own lives by virtue of their engagement with people who are other and different from them.

This project requires that students have the courage to put themselves in a context in which the other must respond to them. They become the guests in the community who are trying to learn something from the other rather than hosts in the church who want to teach the other. I am hoping to communicate at least two basic mission methodologies in this process. The first is that good missionaries put themselves out in the world in ways that force dependency on others. To this end, each student has to make an appointment with the pastor of the other congregation or with some church leader. They have to explain the assignment to that pastor or church leader. Sometimes the student is welcomed and warmly received. At other times, the church turns the student away, forcing them to seek another congregation for the project. This forced dependency on others requires courage and humility.

The second basic mission methodology emerges from the reality that the students are compelled to listen and not to respond. They receive from the other instead of giving to the other. A White student who visits a predominately Black congregation learns the significance and sacred nature of the altar in a Black congregation. A Black student who visits a predominately Central American congregation learns something about the fear of immigration control that might cause the church to be suspicious of strangers who want to visit the congregation and interview its pastor and members. An Ethiopian student who visits a predominately White congregation discovers the anxieties that exist in that church because of the increasing diversity of its neighborhood and the resulting lack of new members.

Somehow, congregations must learn the same lessons that my students learn. Church members must practice how to move across the lines that divide cultures. On some level, many church members already practice this skill every day at work. They are in multicultural work contexts in which they interact on a constant basis with people of other religions, ethnicities, and nationalities. They also practice crossing lines of ethnic, religious, and national divisions when they participate in national and international mission trips into other communities and global contexts. Despite these realities, most congregations divide along ethnic lines and seem challenged by the simplest daily cross-cultural relationships that emerge from their embrace of the way of Jesus. They work with others on the job because they must. They engage in international mission trips because of a deep desire to offer something to others. As churches, however, we have generally failed to teach ourselves to embrace otherness and difference *because it is good for us* and not simply because it is good for the other.

So how does a congregation practice such engagement? Simply put, we practice.

We cross the street, walk down the hall to the next apartment in our building, or park in our neighbor's driveway and knock on the door. As the church, we put ourselves out into the world in a way that forces our dependency on others. We do not know how the neighbor will respond to us until we take this step. The failure to nurture relationships with our own neighbors and to receive from them the blessing that they have to offer to us is the clearest evidence that we lack the courage, even in our own communities, to engage otherness and difference. Suppose a congregation determined that for the next year, it would encourage its members to enter into intentional relationships with their neighbors, the people next door, not for the purpose of growing the church or increasing its membership but rather in order to receive a blessing from their neighbors.

It is a simple commission and a powerful one. Get to know your neighbors. Receive the blessing that your neighbors, the people who live next door to you, want to give to you. Enter into relationship with them and see what happens. See what God will do with you and with them. Experience the transformation that happens when you put yourself out there as much to receive the blessing of others as to extend your own blessing to them.

In this way, we move the equator of our mission calling. Instead of asking, "How do we take the gospel to our communities?" we ask, "What blessing *are we missing* because we do not know our neighbors?" At first glance, this might seem to be a selfish motivation, but it is in line with God's intention from the very beginning. Yes, God intended that we should be a blessing to our neighbors. God, however, also intended that we should receive a blessing from our neighbors. It is up to our neighbors to determine whether to receive the blessing we offer and whether to offer a blessing to us. All we can do is put ourselves in the position to give the blessing and to receive the blessing. With courage, we knock and we wait to see which it will be.

For several years now, I have participated in Iftar meals in homes of Muslim families in the Atlanta area. Held each evening during the holy month of Ramadan when Muslim people fast during the daylight hours, Iftar meals are sacred moments for families when they are finally able to break the fast after sunset. Sponsored by the Atlantic Institute, an interfaith Muslim organization, these Iftar meals provide the opportunity for interfaith dialogue and conversation as Muslim families welcome strangers of other faith traditions into their homes. The institute provides me with an address. I follow my GPS and enter a neighborhood I have never visited before. I knock on the door with mixed feelings of fear and excitement. Always, the family welcomes me warmly even though we do not know each other at all. In my various conversations during these meals, I have learned about the challenges that Muslim families face in US communities. I have listened as they shared their hopes and dreams for their children. I have shared my own challenges with them and my own hopes and dreams for my children. I have also eaten some of the most delicious meals of my life.

Always I take a blessing away with me. That blessing emerges from my observation of that family's commitment to prayer and to God and from its willingness to open its door to a complete stranger and allow that stranger to join them in an intimate and spiritual meal. The experience demands far more from them than it demands from me. I am the guest. While it does require courage to be a guest, how much more courage does it require to welcome a complete stranger into your home? These meals have become symbols for me of the obligations that are upon me as a follower of Jesus Christ in the world to make space for the stranger in my midst. From my Muslim friends, I have learned the valuable lesson of hospitality to the stranger. Even as that lesson has blessed me, I have also learned to have enough courage to put myself out there in the world to receive the blessing that my Muslim friends want to give to me.

This mission calling of receiving and giving blessing is not without its challenges. Storms do arise whenever we move away from our own place, home, and church and into the lives of the neighbor and the stranger. For this reason, Jesus' commission in Acts emphasizes the significance of entering into Samaria, that region of Israel against which so many people in Jerusalem and Judea would have had considerable prejudice. Jewish bias against Samaritans existed for centuries and emerged from the conviction that the Jews of Samaria had deviated from the true worship of God by building a temple on Mount Gerizim and focusing on their own interpretation of the five books of Moses.

Jesus himself had traveled through Samaria and ministered to a woman at a well in the region (John 4), crossing a number of boundaries in the process, including geography, religion, and gender. Joy Jones-Carmack points out that this encounter with the Samaritan woman at the well went against Jesus' own directive to his disciples to "Go nowhere among the Gentiles and enter no town of the Samaritans, but go rather to the house of the lost sheep of Israel" (Matt 10:5-6).[12] Yet, ultimately, Jesus does make the intentional journey to Samaria and calls us to do the same.

In Jones-Carmack's estimation, "the cultural difference between Jews and Samaritans does not inhibit Jesus from including Samaritans in his mission. Jesus' journey into an unorthodox geographic location teaches leaders inside and outside the Church to offer equal privileges and opportunities for minority groups and dominant cultures."[13]

Obviously, the call to the Euro-tribal church to enter into Samaria[14] in our own day is a call to embrace minority groups in our communities against whom we hold both conscious and unconscious prejudices and to acknowledge in the mutual encounter our need for repentance, forgiveness, and solidarity in overcoming the systemic structures that support such objectification or racism. I have had the privilege of teaching for seven years now in a School of Theology that has a larger portion of Black students than White students. This experience has made me very aware of the unconscious racism that I carry into the encounter and of the White domination from which I have benefitted, often at their expense. I have as much learning as teaching to do. Every encounter with students and colleagues of color becomes a learning experience for me, and, generally, the picture of myself that I see reflected in them is a painful portrait that exposes realities about me and my White culture that I would rather ignore.

Perhaps this is why many predominately White congregations shrink from the challenge and often insist that they are free from such prejudices and that they should not have to seek forgiveness for sins they do not believe they have committed. Again, we inhabit a cultural reality that we cannot fully grasp and understand until we see it through the lenses of those whom it has harmed. Kelly Brown Douglas has documented the pernicious effects of Anglo-Saxon domination on the notion of American exceptionalism and its promotion of a stand-your-ground culture that has resulted in the deaths of so many innocent African Americans.[15] Grounded in the idea that Anglo-Saxon blood is the purest blood and Anglo-Saxon culture is the highest cultural expression of humanity, American exceptionalism seeped into White church life through English Puritanism with its myths of the American colonies as the New Israel with a divine errand to carry a White gospel to the ends of the earth.[16]

This evil assertion of the Anglo-Saxon worldview as the highest cultural expression of humanity has denied and denigrated the validities of the worldviews and perspectives of other ethnicities and groups and brought considerable harm to them in the form of oppressive injustice and bondage. In similar fashion, White people have harmed themselves by refusing to acknowledge or receive the cultural gifts and contributions of other families of the earth, thus causing their own cultural impoverishment and a twisted and inadequate perspective on God and on God's mission in the world.

We have witnessed the harmful and debilitating effects of unchecked racism in American political life over the last few years. The election of Barack Obama as president of the United States in 2008 seemed at first glance to represent a step forward for the nation as we elected our first Black president. More recently, however, we have witnessed a powerful resurgence of White nationalism and fear as political leaders parlayed these fears into political gain. Jeannine Hill Fletcher points out that "The history of the United States has been that of a White Christian nation in which the dominant racial project has been to create the category of White, sort some people into it, and assign material benefits on the basis of it to the exclusion of non-White others."[17] Chanequa Walker-Barnes puts it this way:

> Racial categories in the United States were constructed to "flatten" a person's identity so that the person fit easily into one box. Being White meant that you were free; being Black meant that you were enslaveable; and being Indigenous meant that you were extinguishable. Throughout US history, the task of every immigrant group has been to prove themselves "not Black," that is, not enslaveable. For western European immigrants, this has meant becoming inscribed into the racial category of whiteness. For other ethnic groups, it has meant reinforcing one's non-blackness.[18]

For these reasons, all people of White European descent, and not just those from Western Europe, are included under the White cultural umbrella. This happens at the expense of families from other parts of the world who are denied equal status with Whites and the opportunities for immigration that White immigrants received in earlier periods of US history.

My experience with my Black colleagues and students has convinced me that the only path forward toward reconciliation and healing is through the acknowledgment of the sins of Anglo-Saxon domination that have caused such harm. The protestation that "I am not a racist" rings hollow, especially when I am unwilling to admit that I have benefitted from White privilege and the oppressive structures put in place by my Anglo-Saxon forebears, even though I might have been unconscious until now of the reality of such racism. As a person of Anglo-Saxon ancestry, I must "cross over into Samaria" by intentionally entering into the space of those whom my culture and I have wronged, seek their forgiveness, hope for restoration and grace, and then work together with them in solidarity to dismantle the structures of White domination that perpetuate White authority and control.

My own congregation has just taken a small step in this direction. I serve as the part-time pastor of a small and predominately White church in northwest Georgia that recently began a relationship and partnership with a nearby Black congregation. We have now celebrated two church anniversaries with our sister church, and they have celebrated two church anniversaries with us. We have discovered in the process that the path toward reconciliation is not easy. Early in my pastoral tenure, I reached out to them to offer an invitation to our church anniversary. My efforts to contact the pastor by phone were unsuccessful, so one Sunday I walked into their sanctuary about 10 a.m. on Sunday morning, interrupting a men's Sunday school class that looked stunned to see a White man entering the sanctuary. I realized later that my visit occurred just shortly after the shooting of several Black worshipers by a White man at Emmanuel AME church in Charleston, South Carolina.

Despite the tensions generated by my clumsy entrance, the Sunday school class welcomed me and our relationship has deepened over the last two years. I recently preached a sermon at a joint worship service of the two congregations in which, on behalf of my congregation, I asked for their forgiveness for our conscious and unconscious racism. The sermon text was from John 20:19-23, the story of Jesus' appearance to the disciples in Jerusalem shortly after his resurrection. I confessed that, until we entered into our congregational relationship, I had difficulty understanding Jesus' words in John 20:23: "If you forgive the sins of any, they are forgiven them; if you retain the sins of any, they are retained." Here is how I put it in the sermon:

> I have always found the last verse in this passage to be a difficult verse. How is it that I can forgive sins or how is it that I can retain sins? As I struggled with this verse this time, the meaning suddenly became clear. The truth of the matter is that we do have the power to forgive because only we can forgive each other. Until we do, our sins against each other are retained. Once we do, our sins against each other are finally and forever forgiven.
>
> This is why I am glad we are here today with you at Hickory Log. By being with you, we see ourselves for who we really are. We see the wounds that we have visited upon you and we recognize that we have benefited from a system that has often oppressed you. For this reason, we confess our sins to you today. We do not just gather today for a joint worship service. We gather today because we who come from Heritage Fellowship are truly sorry and we seek your forgiveness. According to Jesus, you have the power to forgive our sins or to retain them. We will leave that up to you. We will confess that we need your forgiveness even though we do not deserve it.[19]

The Hickory Log Baptist Church received my sermon with grace and thanked me and my church members for our willingness to admit our sins and to seek their forgiveness. No one said, "You have no need to ask for our forgiveness." They knew as well as we did that the step of confession of sin and the seeking of forgiveness was an essential step forward in our covenant relationship with each other. Their response signaled their gift of grace, forgiveness, and mercy and their willingness to make the journey toward reconciliation with us.

Obviously, our actions in the future will be the best evidence of whether or not we meant what we said. Forgiveness is not absolution. It is only the first step toward reconciliation and restoration. The burden should not be on the Black church in the United States to extend forgiveness to the White church. The burden should be on the White church to demonstrate through the transformation of its actions and behavior its solidarity with the Black community and to prove that its petition for forgiveness is genuine. As Walker-Barnes points out, the goal of racial reconciliation is not about friendship; it is about solidarity: "In friendship, people run toward one another. In solidarity, people run together toward a greater objective."[20] Toward this end, our two congregations are now engaged in assessing the challenges faced by our community and working together toward its transformation. This is our opportunity to demonstrate solidarity in the wake of our admission of guilt by working to dismantle the structures of White domination that have been so harmful.

In similar fashion, Euro-tribal churches today must enter into Samaria in order to seek the forgiveness of the LGBTQ community for the alienation, objectification, and dehumanization that it has visited upon them and to demonstrate the integrity of that confession through solidarity and action. Christian ethicist David P. Gushee received considerable attention recently as he shared how his own mind changed about the matter of LGBTQ inclusion in the life of the church. He attributes this change in perspective to "the transformative encounters I have been blessed to have with gay, lesbian, bisexual and transgender Christians over the last decade."[21] His thoughtful analysis of biblical texts, historically interpreted as supporting such objectification and alienation, offers a path forward to the embrace of loving, committed LGBTQ people by congregations that have rejected such embrace in the past.

Once again, the transformation of the church is coming from outside the walls of the faith community rather than from inside it. Millennials are leaving the church in record numbers, with 31 percent of them citing their disappointment with the judgmental attitude of the church toward LGBTQ people as the reason for their departure.[22] The legalization of same-sex marriage in the United States and the general societal openness to LGBTQ people empower church members to acknowledge these individuals in their own extended families and to demand of the church a loving and holistic response to the issue.

The church has the opportunity to transform its own attitudes and perspectives in ways that bring hope and healing. Such transformation has happened throughout Christian history, as prejudice, hatred, and objectification grounded in gender, religious, ethnic, and cultural difference gave way to the gradual inclusion of people deemed "other" and alien. Jewish Christians extended to Gentile Christians freedom from the Law as the foundation for relationship with God. Christians who once used Scripture to justify the bondage of human beings and the denigration of other peoples and cultures confessed to their errors of interpretation. Congregations that once rejected the possibility of women serving in pastoral roles based on biblical passages that seemed to imply it now have women serving as pastors.

The church embraced these transitions because wider societal pressures forced the church to reexamine its own Scriptures. The inclusion of LGBTQ people in the life of the church is inevitable. Unfortunately, and once again, the church will be late to the table of that inclusion. The only path forward is for the church to seek forgiveness from LGBTQ people for their alienation and objectification and to welcome them into the church even as it embraces them outside the church, standing with them in solidarity against the oppression and injustice that they constantly experience.

The final dimension of Jesus' commission to the church is the challenge to take the gospel "to the uttermost parts of the earth." This book has already documented the ways in which technological advancements in transportation and communication have created diverse contexts in nearly every nation of the world. As a child in the Philippines, I daydreamed about the day when I would return to the United States and could make a pilgrimage to McDonald's and sink my teeth into a Big Mac. In the meantime, I had to content myself with the hamburgers at Jollibee, a local Filipino knock-off of McDonald's. I learned to love those Jollibee burgers, and upon my return to the US I started daydreaming about Jollibee burgers. Fortunately, Jollibee has now opened fast food restaurants here in the US. Globalization has made it possible for me to enjoy both a Big Mac and a Jollibee whenever the mood strikes.

While this hamburger example might seem a simplistic approach to the realities of globalization, it does remind us that otherness and difference exists just down the street or across town and that the church now can choose to embrace it and to open itself up to the transformation that can occur as the result of its embrace. At the same time, global tensions now take on local community implications. Recent shootings in synagogues, mosques, and churches demonstrate that global tensions between religions and ethnicities can lead to acts of hatred and violence in our own communities.

Interfaith and intrafaith dialogue by followers of the various religions of the world are effective paths toward alleviating such violence and hatred. I mention both forms of dialogue because I believe that both are essential for overcoming the objectification and demonization of the other. I have had the privilege for many years now of engaging in dialogue in both directions. Interfaith dialogue is dialogue with people of other faiths and religions. Much of my professional life has been spent nurturing interfaith relationships, participating in interfaith dialogue, and making every effort to engage in such dialogue as a reflection of my intentional decision to embrace and live out the way of Jesus.

The first step to a healthy perspective on other religions, however, begins with intrafaith dialogue: conversation within the church about the biblical and theological foundations for such interaction. Congregations who inhabit a diverse and multicultural context must prepare themselves for the encounter with otherness and difference. I have spent considerable time in local congregations leading workshops and seminars that introduce the basic beliefs, worldviews, and perspectives of the major world religions and that encourage attendees toward deeper relationship with brothers and sisters of other faiths. It is not enough to declare that we ought to love those who are different from us. Rather, the times demand a theology of religions from within the Christian faith that is adequate to the day. People of faith have far more in common with each other than they have with those who reject all forms of religion. We should deepen our relationships with people of other faiths whose motivations we trust so that we can be partners together with God in accomplishing God's mission in the world.

This book has already laid the foundations for such internal conversation and for a theology of religions grounded in the Bible. Diversity, even religious diversity, has been God's intention from the beginning. No single religious understanding of God, even the one emerging from historic Christian tradition and biblical interpretation, exhausts the mystery of God. For this reason, Christian people must cultivate an openness to the perspectives of other religions about God. At the same time, they are called to share their own perspective about God with others, always maintaining an open and listening spirit in the midst of the dialogue.

Take Islam, for example. Today the relationship between Christianity and Islam presents a significant challenge to helpful and hopeful global community. The truth is that Christianity has much to learn from Islam even though such an assertion may surprise many Christians. At its core,

Islam is a global religion. Despite its Arab roots, it has always understood itself to be a universal faith that offers space and a tolerant spirit toward people of other religious beliefs. Certainly its deep respect for Judaism and Christianity reflects this openness. The Qur'an refers to Jews and Christians as "people of the Book." It accords high honor to both Moses and Jesus as the prophets who received the books of the Law and the Gospel respectively, both of which advocated belief in the one true God and a call to live holy and moral lives.

Islamic empires across history have been far more open and tolerant than the Christian empires against which they often found themselves in conflict. Many Christian groups who found themselves in the minority in terms of fidelity to Christian orthodoxy preferred to live under a tolerant Muslim ruler than an intolerant Christian ruler. They received better treatment from an Islamic community that at least respected their Christian faith than they did from a Christian community that branded them as heretics. This tolerance certainly had its limits, and I do not want to imply that Muslim armies did not engage in acts of violence against people of other faiths even as did Christian armies. Certainly, in our own day, a radical form of Islam has encouraged violence against Christians, Jews, Buddhists, and many other religions even as mass shooters in the United States have been motivated by a virulent form of Christianity. These radical forms are a departure from the kind of openness that has generally characterized Islamic and Christian communities across their histories.

Again, Christians must practice both interfaith and intrafaith dialogue. Within our own Christian community, we must soften the hard edges of our theology of otherness and difference, recognizing that diversity is God's intention and that the only path toward a full understanding of God is in intentional dialogue with our Buddhist, Muslim, Jewish, and Hindu neighbors. We must understand the call of Jesus as much more than a call to simply take our limited perspective on God to the world and, instead, acknowledge that the way of Jesus demands humility and a listening spirit in the midst of the journey from Jerusalem to Judea to Samaria and to the ends of the earth. Our journey to embrace the other demands that we listen at least as much as we speak and that we acknowledge our own need for transformation even as we seek to transform the lives of others.

None of this is possible without deep sensitivity to the leadership of the Holy Spirit in the life of the church. Here the role of the Holy Spirit in the book of Acts is helpful to us. The Spirit encouraged the disciples across the boundaries of Jerusalem, Judea, and Samaria and into the rest of the world. Sensitivity to the Spirit's leadership caused God's people to reassess the boundaries that they thought God had placed upon them by encouraging them to see that "what God has made clean, you must not call profane" (Acts 10:15). The Spirit impressed upon the church in Jerusalem that the gospel was for Gentiles as well as Jews, freeing Gentiles from the obligations of the Jewish law. The Spirit prohibited Paul and Silas from preaching the gospel in Asia and pressed them to go over into Macedonia and Europe (Acts 16:6-10) where Paul would proclaim the gospel in the Areopagus, albeit in a much different form than he preached that same gospel in Asia (Acts 17:22-31).

In a diverse and multicultural world, this same Spirit encourages the church beyond the boundaries of exclusivity that the church of our day has now placed on the gospel. Wes Howard-Brook argues that "Jesus' and Paul's vision of a living network of wildly inclusive, vulnerable communities, grounded in the fullness of love and embodied truth, has been replaced with institutional fortresses dedicated to keeping out dissenters and all sorts of 'outsiders' with fear-based threats from a judgmental God."[23] God is calling us beyond our institutional fortresses and toward vulnerability, inclusivity, and open hearts that are willing to receive from other families of the earth the blessings that God intends for us through them. Such vulnerability is the only way forward to meaningful participation together with the other families of the earth in God's mission and purpose for the world.

The intentional act of taking the gospel "to the uttermost parts of the earth" is often misunderstood as an act of taking the God that we have come to know through Jesus Christ to places where that God has never been before. Nothing could be further from the truth. This perspective exposes a theological inadequacy that has embedded itself deeply in the consciousness of the Western church. Diane Butler Bass points out that "God is *with us, within* creation, culture and the cosmos. If anything, recent decades have revealed not a dreadful, distant God, but have slowly illuminated that an intimate presence of mystery abides with the world, a spirit of compassion that breathes hope and healing."[24] When we take our perspective on God "to the uttermost parts of the earth," we only take our particular perspective, one limited by our language, culture, and religion. We take that worldview into the safe space of the world, a space that the divine mystery of God already inhabits. We are opening ourselves up to that mystery as much as we are hoping to share the limited perspective on it that we do possess.

In light of this reality, what should the church become in the future? This is the critical question for our time. We live in this powerful moment in which God is bringing the families of the earth together for mutual blessing. As followers of Jesus Christ, we bring to the table a particular understanding of God that is rooted in the way of Jesus, a path of suffering and vulnerable love that embraces otherness and difference. We should enter into the world with the determination and courage to share that love with every family of the earth, making no apology for our own conviction that Jesus Christ can transform human lives and create a new heaven and a new earth where justice and mercy reign. We should enter into dialogue with every family of the earth in order to share all that we have learned about God through Christ. We should undertake this mission and calling in every corner of the earth and especially in the particular community in which God has placed us. We should offer the good news of God in that space, doing all we can do to partner with others in creating a community of justice and mercy.

We should never assume that we alone bear the whole truth of God's interaction with humanity. We are but one family among all the families of the earth. God never intended to accomplish God's mission in the world just through a single family, even the Christian family. Douglas Jacobsen has pointed out that "Christianity is now incarnated in the beliefs and behaviors of people from all cultures of the world, and the result is an astonishingly varied palette of Christian experience."[25] While we celebrate such diversity within the Christian faith, we must also remember that no single faith or culture possesses a full understanding of God and that every religion and culture can be the source of such understanding.

To enter into dialogue with others based on the conviction that the truth we proclaim is the sole truth about God is a violation of Jesus' way of humility and vulnerability in our relationships with other people. This way of humility and vulnerability does not represent a compromise of the truth that we believe we have received through Christ; it is an affirmation of that truth and a powerful witness to the confidence we have in it. If I am convinced that the way of Jesus brings meaning and purpose to my life and that Jesus is the Savior of the world, then I should proclaim that message with conviction. Any other approach would mean that I do not possess the love and hope for all the families of the earth that I claim Jesus has given to me for them.

But I must also enter into my relationship with the other families of the earth with humility and vulnerability, recognizing that they have a blessing to give to me that could bring even deeper meaning and transformation to my life and to that of the Christian family of the earth to which I belong. This vulnerability requires and even demands a wholly different approach to the engagement of otherness and difference than has been the approach of the church throughout the modern missionary period.

I once took a group of Christian students to visit a Jewish synagogue where we observed a Shabbat or Sabbath service of worship and enjoyed a meal with synagogue members. After the meal, the rabbi invited us to ask him questions about the Jewish faith.

One of my students asked if the rabbi ever tried to encourage Gentiles to become Jewish.

The rabbi smiled. Then he offered the traditional rabbinic response to such a question.

"If a Gentile wants to become Jewish, I look at him and say, 'Are you crazy? Why would you want to be Jewish?'"

He continued, "Sometimes the Gentile will come back to me later and say, 'No, Rabbi, I really do want to be Jewish.' Once again, I will tell him that he really doesn't want to be Jewish and to go think about such a decision very carefully. I remind him about the Holocaust and all the persecution that has been visited upon Jews."

The rabbi added, however, "If the Gentile comes back to me a third time and wants to be Jewish, then we begin the process of conversion that will make him Jewish."

The rabbi's words reminded me of the process of conversion, honed in the modern missionary period and by a Euro-tribal church that wanted people to embrace its particular understanding of faith in Jesus Christ. Such conversion was based on beliefs about Jesus much more than it was based on a decision to follow in the way of Jesus. It was far more about intellectual assent to truth rather than the embrace of the way of life to which Jesus called his followers.

The time has come to embrace the way of Jesus and, in the process, to acknowledge the reality that the equator has moved. The church's insistence on the truth of Christianity as an intellectual system of belief rather than an embrace of Jesus' way resulted in the perpetuation of an arrogant faith diametrically opposed to the teachings of Jesus. It led to "institutional fortresses" that separated people from the love and mercy of Christ rather than the "wildly inclusive, vulnerable communities" that it must become in a diverse world of otherness and difference that so badly wants to bless it.

I mentioned four steps at the beginning of this chapter that I believe to be essential steps as the church, particularly in its Euro-tribal expression, rediscovers its mission and purpose for a new era. Two of these steps involve a process of forgiveness and restoration that acknowledges the domination of its particular perspective on God at the expense of the perspectives and contributions of other families of the earth and that confesses and laments its oppression of marginalized groups such as women, African Americans, and LGBTQ people. The third involves the intentional embrace of healthy and holistic partnership with people of other religious traditions, worldviews, and perspectives and a movement away from competition with and objectification of people who embrace these worldviews. Deeply embedded in all three of these particular forms of mission is the intentional embrace of otherness and difference as a primary calling of the church and as the vision of God for all humanity.

The church will be able to enter into the final stage of its mission and calling to carry a different gospel to the world only after it has taken these steps. This new mission must champion the unconditional love of Christ even as it seeks to give meaning and purpose to human life and to cele-brate the diverse world that God created. This mission is different from the mission that the Euro-tribal church embraced in the past, one that focused on a singular perspective on God that emerged out of its own particular cultural tradition. To fulfill it, Christian people do not have to sacrifice anything of their own convictions about God, truth, and the belief that Jesus Christ is the ultimate revelation of God who brings the good news of salvation to the world. These are the beliefs that make us a unique religious family of the earth. They are the beliefs and convictions that give meaning and purpose to our lives. We know beyond doubt that the truth about God is a single truth.

That truth, however, is ultimately a truth that we cannot fully know or understand until God chooses to reveal it to us. Until then, God has left us only one path: the path of the embrace of otherness and difference legiti-mated in Scripture and modeled for us in Jesus Christ, who called us out into the deep water beyond our own cultures, families, languages, and reli-gions, toward as full a comprehension of the mystery of God as is humanly possible. The church must now make its way to the new Areopagus by putting the equator down in a different place, one that allows it to share the blessings it has received in Jesus Christ with others and to receive blessing from others as they share their particular perspectives on reality and truth. The church's mission then becomes partnership and solidarity with people of other cultures, religions, worldviews, and perspectives in loving dialogue and action that lead to personal and global transformation, sharing with each other our deepest convictions about God and truth, knowing that such mutual sharing has been God's intention from the beginning and the only means by which the full knowledge of God will ever be possible.

Notes

1. Peter L. Berger, *The Many Altars of Modernity: Toward a Paradigm for Religion in a Pluralist Age* (Boston, MA: Walter de Gruyter, Inc., 2014), 1.

2. Berger, *The Many Altars of Modernity*, x–xi.

3. Perry Schmidt-Leukel, *Religious Pluralism and Interreligious Theology: The Gifford Lectures—An Extended Edition* (Maryknoll, NY: Orbis Books, 2017), 3.

4. Roger Williams, *The Bloudy Tenent of Persecution for Cause of Conscience discussed in A Conference between Truth and Peace. Who, In all tender Affection, present to the high Court of Parliament, (as the result of their Discourse) these, (among other passages) of highest consideration*, ed. Richard Groves (London: 1644; repr., Macon, GA: Mercer University Press, 2001), 120.

5. Williams, *The Bloudy Tenent*, 120.

6. Confucius, *The Analects* (New York: Dover Publications, 1995), chapter XXI, 36.

7. See Donald W. Littrell and Doris Littrell, *Practicing Community Development* (Columbia, MO: University of Missouri Extension, 2006), 25–52 for a more extensive introduction to the principles and values of assets-based community development.

8. Paul Sparks, Tim Soerens, and Dwight Friesen, *The New Parish: How Neighborhood Churches Are Transforming Mission, Discipleship, and Community* (Downers Grove, IL: InterVarsity Press, 2014), 95.

9. Sparks, Soerens, and Friesen, *The New Parish*, 96.

10. Sparks, Soerens, and Friesen, *The New Parish*, 97.

11. See John Hendrix, *Nothing Never Happens: Experiential Learning and the Church* (Macon, GA: Smyth and Helwys Publishing, 2004).

12. Joy Jones-Carmack, "Relational Demography in John 4: Jesus Crossing Cultural Boundaries as Praxis for Christian Leadership," *Feminist Theology* 25/1 (2016): 45.

13. Jones-Carmack, Relational Demography in John 4," 45.

14. I use the term "Samaria" with considerable caution and only in the sense that every family of the earth must guard against prejudice that elevates itself at the expense of other families. Samaritans were objectified and devalued by many Jewish people in Jesus' day. Each family of the earth must determine for itself who its "Samaritans" might be and work to overcome its own tendency toward their objectification and devaluation.

15. Kelly Brown Douglas, *Stand Your Ground: Black Bodies and the Justice of God* (Maryknoll, NY: Orbis Books, 2015), 6.

16. See Robert N. Nash, Jr. *The Influence of American Mythology on Southern Baptist Foreign Missions: 1845–1945*, unpublished PhD dissertation, The Southern Baptist Theological Seminary, Louisville, KY, 1989.

17. Jeannine Hill Fletcher, *The Sin of White Supremacy: Christianity, Racism, and Religious Diversity in America* (Maryknoll, NY: Orbis Books, 2017), 3.

18. Chanequa Walker-Barnes, *I Bring the Voices of My People: A Womanist Vision for Racial Reconciliation* (Grand Rapids, MI: Eerdmans, 2019), 31.

19. Robert N. Nash, Jr. "A New Commission," sermon preached at Hickory Log Baptist Church, Canton, GA, May 5, 2019.

20. Walker-Barnes, *I Bring the Voices of My People*, 216.

21. David P. Gushee, *Changing Our Mind* (Canton, MI: Read The Spirit Books, Inc., 2017), 5.

22. Gushee, *Changing Our Mind*, 3.

23. Wes Howard-Brook, *Empire Baptized: How the Church Embraced What Jesus Rejected (2nd–5th Centuries)* (Maryknoll, NY: Orbis Books, 2016), 296.

24. Diane Butler Bass, *Grounded: Finding God in the World, A Spiritual Revolution* (New York: HarperOne, 2015), 15.

25. Douglas Jacobsen, *Global Gospel: An Introduction to Christianity on Five Continents* (Grand Rapids, MI: Baker Academic, 2015), xvi.

Bibliography

Augustine, Saint. *City of God: An Abridged Version.* Translated by Gerald G. Walsh, Demetrius B. Zema, Grace Monahan, and Daniel J. Honan. New York, NY: Bantam Doubleday Dell Publishing, 1958.

Berger, Peter L. *The Many Altars of Modernity: Toward a Paradigm for Religion in a Pluralist Age.* Boston, MA: Walter de Gruyter, Inc., 2014.

Bevans, Stephen. "From Edinburgh to Edinburgh: Toward a Missiology for a World Church," in *Mission after Christendom: Emergent Themes in Contemporary Mission.* Edited by Ogbu U. Kalu, Peter Vethanay-agamony, and Edmund Kee-Fook Chia. Louisville, KY: Westminster John Knox Press, 2010.

Bianchi, Enzo. "The Centrality of the Word of God" Dei Verbum, Sec. 8 or p. 8, in *The Reception of Vatican II.* Edited by Giuseppe Alberigo, Jean-Pierre Jossua, and Joseph A. Komonchak. Translated by Matthew J. O'Connell. Washington, DC: The Catholic University of America Press, 1988.

Boas, Franz. "Language," in *General Anthropology* (Madison, WI: United States Armed Forces Institute, 1938.

Boda, Mark J. "'Declare His Glory among the Nations': The Psalter as Missional Collection." In *Christian Mission: Old Testament Foundations and New Testament Development.* Edited by Stanley E. Porter and Cynthia Long Westfall. Eugene, OR: Wipf and Stock, 2011.

Borg, Marcus J. *Reading the Bible Again for the First Time.* San Francisco, CA: HarperSanFrancisco, 2001.

Borgman, Paul. *The Way According to Luke: Hearing the Whole Story of Luke-Acts.* Grand Rapids, MI: Eerdmans, 2006.

Bosch, David. *Transforming Mission: Paradigm Shifts in Theology of Mission.* Maryknoll, NY: Orbis Books, 1991.

Brown Douglas, Kelly. *Stand Your Ground: Black Bodies and the Justice of God.* Maryknoll, NY: Orbis Books, 2015.

Brown, Raymond E. *The Gospel According to John I-XII.* New York, NY: Doubleday, 1966.

Brueggemann, Walter. *The Land: Place as Gift, Promise, and Challenge in Biblical Faith.* Philadelphia, PA: Fortress Press, 1977.

Butler Bass, Diana. *Grounded: Finding God in the World, A Spiritual Revolution.* New York, NY: HarperOne, 2015.

Cahill, Thomas. *The Gift of the Jews: How a Tribe of Desert Nomads Changed the Way Everyone Thinks and Feels.* New York, NY: Anchor Books, 1999.

Carey, William. *An Enquiry into the Obligations of Christians to Use Means for the Conversion of the Heathen.* Leicester, England: Ann Ireland, 1792.

Cherry, Conrad. *God's New Israel: Religious Interpretations of America's Destiny.* Englewood Cliffs, NJ: Prentice-Hall, 1971.

Clines, David J. A. *The Theme of the Pentateuch.* 2nd edition. Journal for the Study of the Old Testament Supplement Series. Edited by David J. A. Clines and Philip R. Davies, no. 10. Sheffield: Sheffield Academic Press, 1997.

Confucius. *The Analects.* New York, NY: Dover Publications, 1995.

Craddock, Fred B. *John.* Atlanta, GA: John Knox Press, 1982.

Culpepper, R. Alan. "Inclusivism and Exclusivism in the Fourth Gospel." In *Word, Theology and Community in John.* Edited by John Painter, R. Alan Culpepper, and Fernando F. Segovia. St. Louis, MO: Chalice Press, 2002.

————. "The Gospel of John as a Document of Faith in a Pluralistic Culture." In *What is John? Readers and Readings of the Fourth Gospel*. Edited by Fernando F. Segovia. Atlanta, GA: Scholar's Press, 1996.

————. *The Gospel and Letters of John*. Nashville, TN: Abingdon Press, 1998.

————. "The Knowledge of God: Prophetic Vision and Johannine Theme." In *"A Temple Not Made with Hands": Essays in Honor of Naymond H. Keathley*. Edited by Mikeal C. Parsons and Richard Walsh. Eugene, OR: Pickwick Publishers, 2018.

Daly, Robert J. *Origen, Spirit and Fire: A Thematic Anthology of His Writings*. Edited by Hans Urs von Balthasar. Washington, DC: Catholic University of America Press, 1984.

Davis, Ellen. *Scripture, Culture and Agriculture: An Agrarian Reading of the Bible*. New York, NY: Cambridge University Press, 2009.

deClaisse-Walford, Nancy L. "God Came Down and God Scattered: Acts of Punishment or Acts of Grace?" *Review and Expositor* 103 (Spring 2006): 403–16.

————. *Introduction to the Psalms: A Song from Ancient Israel*. St. Louis, MO: Chalice Press, 2004.

Ditchfield, G. M. *The Evangelical Revival*. London, UK: UCL Press, 1998.

Douglas, Kelly Brown. *Stand Your Ground: Black Bodies and the Justice of God*. Maryknoll, NY: Orbis Books, 2015.

Dunn, James D. G. *The New Perspective on Paul*. Grand Rapids, MI: Eerdmans, 2005.

Escobar, Samuel. *The New Global Mission: The Gospel from Everywhere to Everyone*. Downers Grove, IL: InterVarsity Press, 2003.

Fletcher, Jeannine Hill. *The Sin of White Supremacy: Christianity, Racism, and Religious Diversity in America*. Maryknoll, NY: Orbis Books, 2017.

Foote, Robert T. "Twentieth Century Shifts in the North American Protestant Missionary Community," *International Bulletin of Missionary Research* 22/4 (October 1998): 152–53.

Frey, Jörg. *The Glory of the Crucified One: Christology and Theology in the Gospel of John.* Waco, TX: Baylor University Press, 2018.

George, Timothy. *Theology of the Reformers.* Nashville, TN: Broadman Press, 1988.

Goldsworthy, Graeme. "Biblical Theology and the Shape of Paul's Mission." In *The Gospel to the Nations: Perspectives on Paul's Mission.* Edited by Peter Bolt and Mark Thompson. Downers Grove, IL: InterVarsity Press, 2000.

Green, J. B. "Proclaiming Repentance and Forgiveness of Sins to All Nations: A Biblical Perspective on the Church's Mission." In A. G. Padgett, editor, *The Mission of the Church in Methodist Perspective: The World is My Parish.* Lewiston, NY: Edwin Mellen Press, 1992.

Guder, Darrell. *The Continuing Conversion of the Church.* Grand Rapids, MI: Eerdmans Publishing, 2000.

Gushee, David P. *Changing Our Mind.* Canton, MI: Read The Spirit Books, Inc., 2017.

Hauerwas, Stanley, and William H. Willimon. *Resident Aliens: Life in the Christian Colony.* Nashville, TN: Abingdon Press, 2014 edition.

Hendrix, John. *Nothing Never Happens: Experiential Learning and the Church.* Macon, GA: Smyth and Helwys Publishing, 2004.

Hetter, Katia. "The Golden Days of Air Travel: How Glorious Were They?" *CNN Travel.* http://www.cnn.com/2012/05/25/travel/nostalgia-travel/ (accessed July 29, 2019).

Hinson, E. Glenn. *The Evangelization of the Roman Empire: Identity and Adaptability.* Macon, GA: Mercer University Press, 1981.

Howard-Brook, Wes. *Empire Baptized: How the Church Embraced What Jesus Rejected (2nd–5th Centuries).* Maryknoll, NY: Orbis Books, 2016.

Hutchinson, William R. *Errand to the World: American Protestant Thought and Foreign Missions.* Chicago, IL: University of Chicago Press, 1987.

Iverson, Kelly R. *Gentiles in the Gospel of Mark: "Even the Dogs Under the Table Eat the Children's Crumbs."* New York, NY: T&T Clark, 2007.

Jenkins, Philip. *The Next Christendom: The Coming of Global Christianity.* New York, NY: Oxford University Press, 2011.

Jones-Carmack, Joy. "Relational Demography in John 4: Jesus Crossing Cultural Boundaries as Praxis for Christian Leadership." *Feminist Theology* 25/1 (2016): 41–52.

Jordan, Clarence. *Sermon on the Mount.* Valley Forge, PA: Judson Press, 1952, 1970 edition.

Kelber, Werner H. *The Kingdom in Mark: A New Place and a New Time.* Philadelphia, PA: Fortress Press, 1974.

———. *Mark's Story of Jesus.* Philadelphia, PA: Fortress Press, 1979.

Kinnaman, David. *You Lost Me: Why Young Christians Are Leaving Church and Rethinking Faith.* Grand Rapids, MI: Baker Books, 2011.

Knowles, Michael P. "Mark, Matthew, and Mission: Faith, Failure, and the Fidelity of Jesus." In *Christian Mission: Old Testament Foundations and New Testament Developments.* Edited by Stanley E. Porter and Cynthia Long Westfall. Eugene, OR: Wipf and Stock, 2011.

Kostenberger, Andreas J., and Peter T. O'Brien. *Salvation to the Ends of the Earth: A Biblical Theology of Mission.* Downers Grove, IL: InterVarsity Press, 2001.

Kysar, Robert. *John: The Maverick Gospel.* Louisville, KY: Westminster/ John Knox Press, 1976, 1993 edition.

LaGrand, James. *The Earliest Christian Mission to "All Nations" in the Light of Matthew's Gospel.* Grand Rapids, MI: Eerdmans, 1999.

Lambert, Frank. *Inventing the "Great Awakening."* Princeton, NJ: Princeton University Press, 1999.

LaSor, William Sanford, et al. *Old Testament Survey: The Message, Form and Background of the Old Testament.* Revised edition. Grand Rapids, MI: Eerdmans, 1996.

LaVerdiere, Eugene. *Luke.* Wilmington, DE: Michael Glazier, 1986.

Lee, Chee-Chiew, "Once Again: the Niphal and the Hithpael of ברך in the Abrahamic Blessing for the Nations," *Journal for the Study of the Old Testament* 36/3 (2012): 279–96.

Leonard, Bill J. *A Sense of the Heart: Christian Religious Experience in the United States.* Nashville, TN: Abingdon Press, 2014.

Littrell, Donald W., and Doris Littrell. *Practicing Community Development.* Columbia, MO: University of Missouri Extension, 2006.

Malbon, E. S. *Narrative Space and Mythic Meaning in Mark.* San Francisco, CA: Harper and Row, 1986.

Marsden, George M. *Fundamentalism and American Culture: The Shaping of Twentieth Century Evangelicalism, 1870–1925.* New York, NY: Oxford University Press, 1980.

McLaren, Brian D. *Everything Must Change: Jesus, Global Crises, and a Revolution of Hope.* Nashville, TN: Thomas Nelson Publishing, 2007.

Meier, John P. *Matthew.* Wilmington, DE: Michael Glazier, Inc., 1980.

Miller, Donald. *Blue Like Jazz: Nonreligious Thoughts on Christian Spirituality.* Nashville, TN: Thomas Nelson, 2003.

Mitchell, Joan L. *Beyond Fear and Silence: A Feminist-literary Reading of Mark.* New York, NY: Continuum Publishing, 2001.

Mounce, Robert H. *Matthew.* San Francisco, CA: Harper and Row, 1985.

Nash, Jr., Robert N. "A New Commission." Sermon preached at Hickory Log Baptist Church, Canton, GA, May 5, 2019.

———. "Anglo-Americans." In *Many Nations Under God: Ministering to Culture Groups in America.* Edited by Ele Clay. Birmingham, AL: New Hope Publishing, 1997.

———. *An 8-Track Church in a CD World: The Modern Church in the Postmodern World.* Macon, GA: Smyth and Helwys Publishing, 1997.

———. *The Influence of American Mythology on Southern Baptist Foreign Missions: 1845–1945.* Unpublished PhD dissertation. The Southern Baptist Theological Seminary, Louisville, KY, 1989.

Noll, Mark A. *The Scandal of the Evangelical Mind.* Grand Rapids, MI: Eerdmans Publishing, 1984.

Okoye, James Chukwuma. *Israel and the Nations: A Mission Theology of the Old Testament.* Maryknoll, NY: Orbis Books, 2006.

Parratt, John, editor. *An Introduction to Third World Theologies.* Cambridge, UK: Cambridge University Press, 2004.

Penney, John Michael. *The Missionary Emphasis of Lukan Pneumatology.* Sheffield, England: Sheffield Academic Press, 1997.

Philo. *De Profugis.* Cited in Gerald Friedlander, *Hellenism and Christianity.* Sydney, Australia: Wentworth Press, 2019. Reprint of 2012 edition.

Polhill, John B. *Paul and His Letters.* Nashville, TN: Broadman and Holman, 1999.

Rauschenbusch, Walter. "A Conquering Idea." *The Examiner,* July 31, 1892. Reprinted in Winthrop Hudson, *Selected Writings of Walter Rauschenbusch.* Mahwah, NJ: Paulist Press, 1984.

———. "The New Evangelism." *The Independent,* 1904. Reprinted in William H. Brackney, ed., *Walter Rauschenbusch: Published Works and Selected Writings, Vol. 1, Christianity and the Social Crisis and Other Writings.* Macon, GA: Mercer University Press, 2018.

Richardson, Don. *Eternity in Their Hearts.* Ventura, CA: Regal Books, 1984.

Rolfe, John. "A Relation of the State of Virginia" (1616). In *The Virginia Historical Register and Literary Advertiser* I (1848), 11–12. Quoted in Perry Miller, *Errand to the Wilderness.* Cambridge, MA: Harvard University Press, 1956.

Ronson, Jon. "How One Stupid Tweet Blew Up Justine Sacco's Life." *New York Times Magazine,* February 12, 2015.

Roxburgh, Alan J. *Missional: Joining God in the Neighborhood.* Grand Rapids, MI: Baker Books, 2011.

———. *Structured for Mission: Renewing the Culture of the Church.* Downers Grove, IL: InterVarsity Press Books, 2015.

Russell, Jeffrey Burton. *A History of Medieval Christianity: Prophecy and Order.* Arlington Heights, IL: AHM Publishing, 1968.

Schmidt-Leukel, Perry. *Religious Pluralism and Interreligious Theology: The Gifford Lectures—An Extended Edition.* Maryknoll, NY: Orbis Books, 2017.

Schneiders, Sandra M. *Written That You May Believe: Encountering Jesus in the Fourth Gospel.* New York, NY: Crossroad Publishing, 1999.

Segovia, Fernando E. "John 1:1-18 as Entrée into Johannine Reality." In *Word, Theology and Community in John.* Edited by John Painter, R. Alan Culpepper, and Fernando F. Segovia. St. Louis, MO: Chalice Press, 2002.

Segundo, Juan Luis. *The Liberation of Theology.* Maryknoll, NY: Orbis Books, 1976.

Senior, Donald, and Carroll Stuhlmueller. *The Biblical Foundations for Mission.* Maryknoll, NY: Orbis, 1983.

Shah, Anup. "Poverty Facts and Stats." *Global Issues: Social, Political, Economic and Environmental Issues that Affect Us All.* http://www.globalissues.org/article/26/poverty-facts-and-stats (accessed July 29, 2019).

Sparks, Paul, Tim Soerens, and Dwight Friesen. *The New Parish: How Neighborhood Churches Are Transforming Mission, Discipleship and Community.* Downers Grove, IL: InterVarsity Press, 2014.

Stott, John R. *Christian Mission in the Modern World.* Downers Grove, IL: InterVarsity Press, 2008.

Surk, Barbara, and John Hellprin. "UN: 50M Displaced Worldwide." *The Atlanta Journal-Constitution,* June 21, 2014.

Tannehill, R. C. *The Narrative Unity of Luke-Acts: A Literary Interpretation, 1.* Philadelphia, PA: Fortress Press, 1986.

Tatum, Beverly Daniel. *"Why Are All the Black Kids Sitting Together in the Cafeteria?" And Other Conversations about Race.* New York, NY: Basic Books, 1997, 2017 edition.

Taylor, Barbara Brown. *Holy Envy: Finding God in the Faith of Others.* New York, NY: HarperOne, 2019.

Tertullian. *Prescription Against Heretics.* http://www.newadvent.org/fathers/0311.htm, Chapter 7 (accessed October 2, 2019).

Tew, W. Mark. *Luke: Gospel to the Nameless and Faceless.* Eugene, OR: Wipf and Stock, 2012.

Tickle, Phyllis. *The Great Emergence: How Christianity is Changing and Why.* Grand Rapids, MI: Baker Books, 2008.

Tippett, Krista. "The Adventure of Civility." Presentation at the Cooperative Baptist Fellowship General Assembly, Birmingham, AL, June 21, 2019.

Ver Beek, Kurt Alan. "The Impact of Short-term Missions." In *Missiology: An International Review* 34/4 (October 2006): 478.

Volf, Miroslav. *Exclusion and Embrace: A Theological Exploration of Identity, Otherness, and Reconciliation.* Nashville, TN: Abingdon Press, 1996.

———. "Johannine Dualism and Contemporary Pluralism." In *The Gospel of John and Christian Theology.* Edited by Richard Bauckham and Carl Mosser. Grand Rapids, MI: Eerdmans, 2008.

von Rad, Gerhard. *Old Testament Theology.* Volume 1, translated by D. M. G. Stalker. New York, NY: Harper and Row, Publishers, 1962.

Walker-Barnes, Chanequa. *I Bring the Voices of My People: A Womanist Vision for Racial Reconciliation.* Grand Rapids, MI: Eerdmans, 2019.

Walls, Andrew F. *The Missionary Movement in Christian History: Studies in the Transmission of Faith.* Maryknoll, NY: Orbis Books, 1996.

Westfall, Cynthia Long. "The Hebrew Mission: Voices from the Margin." In Stanley E. Porter and Cynthia Long Westfall, editors. *Christian Mission: Old Testament Foundations and New Testament Developments.* Eugene, OR: Wipf and Stock, 2011.

Whorf, Benjamin L. "The Relation of Habitual Thought and Behavior to Language." In *Language, Thought, and Reality: Selected Writings of Benjamin Lee Whorf.* Edited by John B. Carroll. Cambridge, MA: Massachusetts Institute of Technology Press, 1956, 1974 edition.

Williams, Roger. *The Bloudy Tenent of Persecution for Cause of Conscience discussed in A Conference between Truth and Peace. Who, In all tender Affection, present to the high Court of Parliament, (as the result of their Discourse) these, (among other passages) of highest consideration.* Reprint, edited by Richard Groves. Macon, GA: Mercer University Press, 2001. Originally published in London, 1644.

Woodberry, Robert. "The Missionary Roots of Liberal Democracy." *American Political Science Review* 106/2 (May 2012): 244–74.

Wright, Christopher. *The Mission of God: Unlocking the Bible's Grand Narrative.* Downers Grove, IL: InterVarsity Press, 2006.

Wright, N. T. *Surprised by Hope: Rethinking Heaven, the Resurrection, and the Mission of the Church.* New York, NY: HarperCollins, 2008.